Meg Jump s

WHERE TO STAY
IN FRANCE

A Parasol Publication

To David & Jo

hoping this book will help
you enjoy your retirement

Meg

Entrevaux
Feb 1993

A Parasol Publication

Published by Nicholas Publishing Ltd
212 Broad Street
Birmingham B15 1AY
UK

Printed in Great Britain

Cover photograph: Château d'Ayres
(Languedoc-Roussillon)

ISBN 1 897612 04 4

Contents

For Jack and Hilda

*F*RANCE IS A GLORIOUS COUNTRY *whose many charms have long been appreciated by the world's travelling public. For centuries Paris has been recognised as one of the most delightful of capital cities; the Alpine mountains are famous for their breath-taking scenery and bracing fresh air; the fantastic fairytale castles strung along the valley of the River Loire are without equal; the exotic Riviera has an unsurpassed reputation for sophisticated holiday-making and the Mediterranean south generally, and Provence in particular, has won wide acclaim. Add to this the French flair for wines, their wizardry with food, their inimitable mode de vie and the fascination of France is easy to understand.*

It is hardly surprising then that some francophiles became a little jaded by their favourite country's ever-increasing popularity and felt the urge to delve deeper, to search out lesser-known areas untouched by mass tourism, to discover … or rediscover … 'the real France'. They were captivated by what they found and today a new generation of discriminating travellers dream of branching out themselves to look for their own hidden France.

The visitor to France is therefore faced with so many tempting options. There is much ground to be covered in terms of sights and experiences as well as mileage. The old haunts are as enticing as ever: Paris will never lose its charisma. The magic of Versailles will never change. Chenonceaux, Carcassonne, Mont St Michel, the cathedral at Chartres, Monet's garden at Giverny, the Palace of the Popes in Avignon, Roman remains at Arles and Nîmes … In July the lavender fields of Haute Provence are magnificent, the flower-filled villages of Alsace are a joy to behold. Wine lovers will head straight for the great Champagne houses of Epernay. Food lovers have distractions at every turn.

Yet the secret France beckons too. Unspoilt villages nestling deep in tranquil countryside, market day in unheard of towns, summer fêtes and local festivals, traditional cooking in rustic restaurants, a comfortable bed and fresh-baked breakfast in a welcoming home.

But for the independent traveller intent on planning his or her own itinerary, the language barrier can present a daunting prospect. It is a fact that very few English-speaking visitors feel confident speaking and understanding French. Any idea of straying too far from the well-beaten tourist track, let alone attempting to penetrate truly rural areas, can so easily appear to be impractical … but this is not so. My book — which is not a travel guide but a source of information on places to stay — will, with English-speaking hosts, make it surprisingly easy.

In compiling this book, I began with a firm belief that accommodation forms the backdrop to a successful holiday. Whatever else may happen, if you and your travelling companions consistently fail to get a good night's sleep in pleasant surroundings, it will eventually spoil everyone's enjoyment. Conversely, attractive accommodation and genial hosts will help to compensate for any number of unforeseen setbacks and irritating minor problems.

Variety ... as we all know ... is the spice of life and that certainly applies to satisfying holidays. I have therefore selected a carefully considered range of accommodation to appeal to different tastes, budgets and travelling circumstances — reliable hotels to be booked in advance in main centres of interest; charming country inns and friendly chambres d'hôtes in off-the-track places; romantic castles and splendid manor houses offering old-fashioned luxury. Then perhaps a week in a self-catering cottage, a cosy apartment or a nicely restored village house. A short walking or cycling holiday might give quite a new perspective on France. A painting or cookery course could be great fun.

If interesting and varied accommodation is an essential component of a well-planned holiday, sympathetic hosts and friendly staff also have a vital role to play. They can create much more than a convivial atmosphere. They possess the invaluable knowledge that enables guests to find their way around the locality in a way that no guide book — however well-researched — can ever do. When they speak English too , as do many of the hosts featured here, communication is so much easier.

The entries in this book therefore have been selected not only for the diversity and quality of accommodation, but because the owners and staff know their region well and are prepared to take time and trouble in sharing that knowledge. In addition, I believe that they all personally take great pride in the genuine warmth of welcome that they extend to their guests. For travellers in a strange and foreign land, that counts for a lot.

Bon Voyage!

Meg Jump
Entrevaux,
September 1992

ABOUT THIS BOOK

This accommodation guide cannot, and does not, seek to fulfil the requirements of all visitors to France. It has been compiled specifically to help the discerning, independent, English-speaking traveller wherever in the world his homeland may be. Prices range from quite inexpensive to rather expensive. Ultra-low-budget hostels, very basic lodgings and campsites have not been included. The grandest of grand hotels have also been omitted although some of the establishments are really magnificent and undeniably up-market.

You will find in the following pages a diverse choice of interesting rural and urban accommodation — hotels big and small; country auberges *or inns;* chambres d'hôtes *or Bed & Breakfast offered in family homes that range from pretty farmhouses to splendid mansions; self-catering cottages and apartments; activity holidays and special interest courses with*

accommodation provided (and instruction in English, of course); plus a few unexpected surprises. The majority of buildings are full of character, reflecting the cultural and architectural heritage of their particular region. Where restoration has been carried out, this has been done sympathetically and with taste. Most of the hosts speak at least some English; many are fluent.

The selection has been entirely my own personal choice. There is no charge for entry and owners have not been able to buy their way into this guide.

I have made no attempt to grade properties or to rate one against another. No confusing symbols have been used to describe facilities and where hotels have been awarded stars, this is the classification of the appropriate French authorities. Some properties have no stars but this in no way implies that they are substandard or inferior: they are simply outside the system.

Where prices are concerned, I have opted for giving actual figures rather than indicating a broad price band. Prices were correct at the time of printing but they could change and inevitably they are more likely to go up than down. Please be prepared for this. All rates are quoted in French francs but some owners may be prepared to accept other currencies.

THE REGIONS OF FRANCE

The accommodation is presented by region, each of which is a collection of départements *or counties.*

For administrative purposes, France is divided into 96 départements *including the inner Paris area and two* départements *in Corsica. The* départements *are grouped into regions. The regions in this book generally correspond with the official groupings but occasionally I have attached a* département *to another neighbouring region if it seems to me to be more logical from the visitor's point of view.*

Each département *is identified by two digits (eg. Vaucluse is 84; Aude is 11) forming the first two numbers of the five-digit postal code which is attached to every address. Thus any address can be roughly located on the map of France by its postal code.*

The regional sections in this book are listed alphabetically starting with Aquitaine in the extreme south-west. Within each section, a small map shows the position of the region in relation to the rest of France. A second more detailed map of the regions shows département *boundaries and the location of individual addresses. Addresses are grouped by* département*. In the case of Aquitaine, these are Dordogne (24), Lot-et-Garonne (47), Gironde (33), Landes (40) and Pyrénées-Atlantique (64).*

Where a region is generally known by different names in French and English — eg. Bourgogne and Burgundy, Bretagne and Brittany — both names are given.

A WORD ABOUT FRENCH HOTELS

Hotel-keeping is an honourable profession in France at whatever level. Small family-run hotels form the backbone of the hospitality business and many of them have been in the same family for generations, with duties in the kitchen passing from father to son while the wife and daughters look after the restaurant and bedrooms. There is always work to be undertaken by active grandparents and children start their informal apprenticeship at an early age.

With outside staff kept to a minimum, family workers need some time off. It is therefore normal for the hotel restaurant ... and sometimes the bedrooms too ... to close for at least one day per week. Sunday evening and all day Monday are popular closing days but it is very variable. In areas that depend heavily on holiday trade, hotels may close completely during the winter months. Information on closures is included with each entry.

Départements of France

01 Ain
02 Aisne
03 Allier
04 Alpes-de-
Haute-
Provence
05 Hautes
Alpes
06 Alpes-
Maritimes
07 Ardèche
08 Ardennes
09 Ariège
10 Aube
11 Aude
12 Aveyron
13 Bouches-du-
Rhône
14 Calvados
15 Cantal
16 Charente
17 Charente-
Maritime
18 Cher
19 Corrèze
20 Corsica
21 Côte-d'Or
22 Côtes-du-
Nord
23 Creuse
24 Dordogne
25 Doubs
26 Drôme
27 Eure
28 Eure-et-Loir
29 Finistère
30 Gard
31 Haute-
Garonne
32 Gers
33 Gironde
34 Hérault
35 Ille-et-
Vilaine
36 Indre
37 Indre-et-
Loire
38 Isère
39 Jura
40 Landes
41 Loir-et-Cher
42 Loire
43 Haute-Loire
44 Loire-
Atlantique
45 Loiret
46 Lot

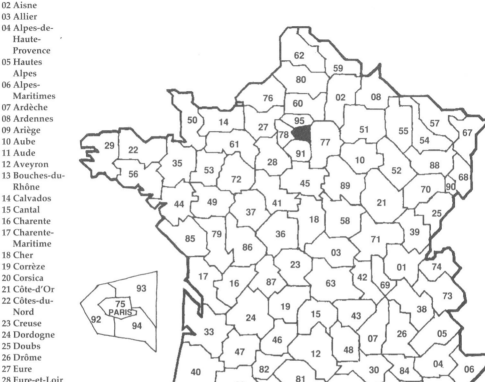

47 Lot-et-
Garonne
48 Lozère
49 Maine-et-
Loire
50 Manche
51 Marne
52 Haute-
Marne
53 Mayenne
54 Meurthe-et-
Moselle
55 Meuse
56 Morbihan

57 Moselle
58 Nièvre
59 Nord
60 Oise
61 Orne
62 Pas-de-
Calais
63 Puy-de-
Dôme
64 Pyrénées-
Atlantiques
65 Hautes-
Pyrénées
66 Pyrénées-

Orientales
67 Bas-Rhin
68 Haut-Rhin
69 Rhône
70 Haute-Saône
71 Saône-et-
Loire
72 Sarthe
73 Savoie
74 Haute-
Savoie
75 Paris
76 Seine-
Maritime

77 Seine-et-
Marne
78 Yvelines
79 Deux-Sèvres
80 Somme
81 Tarn
82 Tarn-et-
Garonne
83 Var
84 Vaucluse
85 Vendée
86 Vienne
87 Haute-
Vienne

88 Vosges
89 Yonne
90 Terriroire de
Belfort
91 Essonne
92 Hauts-de-
Seine
93 Seine-St-
Denis
94 Val-de-
Marne
95 Val-d'Oise

Introduction

Some older traditional French hotels are renowned for the idiosyncrasies of their plumbing arrangements. The majority of hotels featured here however have conventional private shower or bathrooms with very adequate facilities.

In some countries tea and coffee-making equipment is standard in almost every hotel room. This is not the case in France and it is unusual to find such facilities although beverages will probably be available from the bar or room service.

It is not normal either for an iron or ironing board to be at the disposition of guests. An in-house laundering service is usually only provided in larger hotels and international chains. As public laundrettes are not commonly found in French towns, laundry can be a problem. I advise readers to pack their suitcases accordingly!

Unless otherwise stated, the nightly rate for rooms does not include breakfast. Some hotels offer a demi-pension or half board rate to cover bed, breakfast and one main meal which may be lunch or dinner. This special rate may only apply to a minimum stay of three days and sometimes the meal served is cheaper (and not so nice perhaps) than the table d'hôte options on the set menu. It is wise to enquire which menu is included in any demi-pension tariff. Some hotels also insist that overnight guests dine in the hotel restaurant. Conversely in some hotels with a popular restaurant, overnight guests may find there is no table available unless reserved in advance ... especially at weekends.

The prices quoted are for a single or double room. Often it is possible to have an extra bed put in a room and some hotels have rooms that will accommodate up to four people. Suites too are frequently available. Ask for accommodation and prices to suit your travelling group.

Chambres d'hôtes/Bed & Breakfast

Chambres d'hôtes have existed for many years in rural France. Their main function has been to allow city dwellers the opportunity to enjoy country life in simple, cheap accommodation. Traditionally much of the accommodation has been very basic indeed (some still is) but in recent years owners of gracious country houses have also been opening their homes to more discriminating paying guests. Sometimes these are properties that have been in the family for generations; others have been bought recently and renovated specifically to receive paying guests. A few are run by English-speaking francophiles who have been attracted to French rural living and find offering hospitality to house guests a pleasant way of augmenting their incomes.

For the traveller, they provide an alternative to hotels and offer the opportunity of being received into a French home. Many hosts invite their guests to join the family for an evening meal; this is a rare chance to sample French home-cooking at its best. Some chambres d'hôtes are attached to working farms or vineyards, giving guests the additional pleasure of tasting products fresh from the home farm.

The accommodation I have chosen is all of a very adequate standard, some is luxurious, and most hosts speak some English. Generally speaking, chambres d'hôtes will be markedly cheaper than a hotel room of a similar standard and represent excellent value for money. One or two of the addresses I have included are nonetheless at the top of the price range. This is because the hosts offer exceptional hospitality in unique surroundings.

As a paying guest, the normal courtesies that you would naturally expect to show during any visit into a private home should also apply when staying in chambres d'hôtes. Do not arrive without booking, or at least telephoning, in advance and let your hostess know if you have to cancel or will be arriving late. If she is preparing a meal for you, advise her beforehand of any foods you do not eat.

Self-catering accommodation

The self-catering accommodation in this book varies from units that are suitable for a large group of up to 10 or 12 people to studio apartments ideal for a couple. Most are situated in open countryside or small villages. Lettings are usually weekly from Saturday to Saturday (occasionally change-over day is Wednesday) but some owners will accept more flexible bookings. The facilities that are included in the rental

15

price are clearly listed. Some owners do not normally supply bed linen and towels but, in the interests of overseas visitors who will be travelling to France by air, I have only chosen properties where linen will be supplied automatically or on request. In some cases this might involve an additional charge so please check when booking.

Most owners ask for a security payment on arrival. Generally this is approximately FF500 and will be returned on departure or soon after, minus any costs to cover breakages or cleaning.

The properties included here all have the owner or the owner's representative on site or nearby. There should therefore be no problems concerning collecting the key and sorting out difficulties that may arise.

Reservations and Bookings

It is an intrepid traveller indeed who will venture into France without any advance bookings at all. Most visitors will want the security of some pre-booked accommodation along the way; many will feel happier if the majority of their itinerary bas been planned ... and paid for ... well in advance.

The prime aims of this book are first of all to help you get information on a variety of accommodation IN ENGLISH so you can decide upon main stop-over points during your French holiday, and secondly to help make actual booking easier. In the additional information for each entry, it is stated if brochures will be sent on request. Smaller establishments may have very little available, but most hotels and property owners have excellent publicity material, much of which is written at least in part in English. They give an accurate idea of the accommodation available and will be sent anywhere in the world. A clearly-written request in English for further information is all that is needed. In addition, general tourist information on the area may be enclosed as well.

Having decided on an address that you wish to book in advance, the next hurdle is to make contact from your home base. Without doubt, the quickest and surest way to ascertain if the accommodation is free when you want it is by telephoning. Where hosts are native English-speakers or speak good English, this should present no problems but may be expensive if you are calling from the other side of the world. Where only a little English is spoken, you may feel that writing is a more sensible approach. Due to the time taken for correspondence however, many hosts find it impractical to reserve dates for the length of time necessary to obtain confirmation and to receive deposits. Where fax communication is possible, this is probably the most satisfactory all-round way to book in advance. All establishments in this book have owners or staff who know sufficient English to handle enquiries in written English.

It is worth mentioning that dates are expressed differently around the world. Thus 9.6.1993 may be interpreted as either June 9th or September 6th. In order to avoid any confusion, it is always better to write dates in full.

If you choose to telephone or fax France from overseas, the country code for France is 33, followed by an eight-digit number, except for Paris numbers which are prefixed by (1). Please note that the first two figures do NOT correspond with the département code. For calls within France, simply dial the eight-digit number EXCEPT when calling from Paris (région Parisienne) to the provinces when you should dial 16, wait for the tone to change and then dial the eight-digit number; or when calling to Paris from the rest of France when you should dial 16, wait for the tone to change and dial 1 followed by the eight-digit number.

Many public phones in France today will not accept cash. It is necessary to use a telephone card which is on sale in all Post Offices.

If you reserve a hotel room, a deposit may be required (see below). If the booking is at short notice and/or no deposit has been paid, hotels will normally honour a reservation up until 1800 hours. If you know you are unlikely to arrive by then, explain this when booking. If you find that you are falling behind schedule during the day, it is a wise precaution to call and explain. If not, your room may be given to someone else.

On the subject of schedules, overseas visitors do sometimes tend to underestimate travelling times when driving on French roads. It is possible to make good progress on France's excellent autoroutes but itineraries that pass through major towns can involve tiresome delays. Long distances on roads where there is no alternative autoroute can also be time-consuming.

Deposits

Attitudes toward the payment of a deposit or arrhe *(pronounced as for the letter 'R') vary greatly. For self-catering accommodation, it will almost invariably be necessary to submit a 25 per cent deposit in order to secure a reservation, with the balance being paid within two months of the arrival date. Some owners may accept payment of the balance on arrival, but this does mean when the key is collected, not a day or two later. Travellers' cheques may not be acceptable so, if cash is required, do ensure that you have enough.*

Many hotels require a deposit too for advance bookings, particularly for stays of more than one night. The actual amount will depend upon individual hotels. Where credit cards are accepted, this is the easiest form of payment from overseas. If not, it is necessary to arrange a bank draft in French francs. Most owners will not accept cheques in foreign currencies.

Deposits for Bed & Breakfast accommodation are entirely at the discretion of the owners.

Organisers of special interest holidays will always require a substantial deposit with payment in full well before the starting date.

Electricity

The voltage all over mainland France is 220 (similar to Britain and Australia but double that of North America). If you intend to use any electrical appliances, you may need an adaptor which is compatible with French two and/or three-pin sockets. These may be difficult to buy in France and should be purchased at home

Maps

Many of the properties in this book are situated on minor roads. If you are driving, a really detailed road map of France is indispensable.

Restaurants

*One of the joys of visiting France is wining and dining, and many of the hotels featured here have excellent restaurants. The restaurants, like the accommodation, vary ranging from those serving regional home-cooking (*cuisine familiale*) to the ultimate in contemporary gastronomy. Every restaurant offers at least one* table d'hôte *or set menu in addition to* à la carte. *These are*

very good value for money, especially in smaller restaurants, but the cheaper menu may not always be the most interesting. Sometimes the higher-priced set menus offered do not only include more expensive basic ingredients but consist of extra courses. Diners with limited appetites could find five or six courses overwhelming.

The French take food very seriously and expect a proper meal to run to a minimum of three courses in the traditional manner. The current fashion of opting for two smaller starter courses in preference to the usual starter followed by a main course, does not generally attract them although some top restaurants do offer a menu dégustation (a series of smaller taster servings that allow the chef to demonstrate his creativity and skill).

French restaurateurs are notorious for the mark-up on wines served in a restaurant. This can be 300 per cent or more. If a house wine is available, it is well worth trying, especially in a wine-producing area. This may be served bottled or in a pichet (jug) or carafe.

French attitudes to meal times are conservative and fairly rigid. Lunch is still the main meal of the day (especially on Sunday when, for popular restaurants, it is advisable to book). In country areas, many restaurants that are not attached to hotels do not open in the evening except in mid-summer. Lunch is eaten fairly early from mid-day. Except in large towns and cities, hungry clients arriving after 1.30pm may be turned away. The same applies to dinner in rural areas where the evening meal is served from about 7 - 9.30pm.

On the other hand, sandwiches and hot or cold snacks are widely available at any time of the day or night in tea shops (salon de thé) and bars.

Bon Appétit!

Limoges

Angoulême

LES POULOULEIX

ST-JORY ART
SCHOOL

MOULIN DU ROC

LA BOUTEILLE OUVERTE

MOULIN DE LA CROUZILLE

Perigueux

Brive

LA PETITE RENAVDIE

24
DORDOGNE

LE MANOIR D'HAUTEGENTE

CHATEAU DE FOULON

AUBERGE DU NOYER

Bergerac

LE VIEUX LOGIS

LA PRADERIE

33
GIRONDE

Bordeaux

VIRCOULON HOLIDAY GITES

CHATEAU DE
COMMARQUE

CHATEAU DE
SCANDAILLAC

LORMERAIE

LE MOULIN DE ST-AVIT

Montflanquin

47
LOT-ET-GARONNE

Cahors

THE GRANGE

Agen

40
LANDES

LA BERGERIE

Biarritz
LE CHATEAU DU CLAIR DE LUNE

Toulouse

LA PATOULA

Pau

64
**PYRENEES-
ATLANTIQUES**

AQUITAINE

S P A I N

*Aquitaine comprises the
following départements:*
  Dordogne (24)
  Lot-et-Garonne (47)
  Gironde (33)
  Landes (40)
  Pyrénées-Atlantiques (64)

*A*QUITAINE IS A VAST STRETCH OF LAND *extending down France's Atlantic coast from Bordeaux to the Pyrénées and the Spanish border. The inland* départements *of Dordogne and Lot-et-Garonne have long been favourites with overseas visitors, for this is an area of unmatched pastoral landscapes rich in prehistoric sites, mediæval villages and magnificent castles. The Gironde too is well-known, for it contains the world's largest and most prestigious vineyards where Bordeaux wines are produced. The southern region remains relatively unknown. The Landes offers endless sandy beaches, great pine forests and tranquil lakes; and in the southernmost corner of Aquitaine is Pyrénées-Atlantiques. Sheltered by the mighty Pyrénéan range, this is a land of warm plains and valleys, of good walking, excellent trout fishing and superb cooking. This too is Basque country with a language and culture closely akin to that of north-west Spain, quite unlike that of the rest of France.*

Auberge du Noyer

Le Reclaud-de-Bounty-Bas, 24260 Le Bugue
Tel: 53 07 11 73, Fax 53 54 57 44

Country hotel** with restaurant

When Paul and Jenny Dyer left England in 1978 and bought a dilapidated 18th century Périgordienne farmhouse, they were committing themselves to five years of restoration. During that time, winters were devoted to rebuilding and summers were spent working in nearby hotels and restaurants. The sheer determination and hard labour has paid off, for today the Dyers have their Auberge du Noyer (walnut tree) – a totally charming small hotel with 10 delightful bedrooms, each attractively furnished and full of character. Jenny looks after the pretty rustic restaurant and Paul is in the kitchen where the emphasis is on a simple yet sophisticated cuisine using seasonal ingredients. Seating in the restaurant is limited … and much in demand. The *auberge* has its own swimming pool and is surrounded by 3 hectares/7 acres of peaceful meadows and woodland. Set in the heart of the Périgord Noir, chez-Dyer is well-placed for exploring this very popular area.

Situated 35 km/21 miles east of Bergerac and 45km/28 miles south of Périgeux. Nearest international airport: Bordeaux at 120km/75 miles. Nearest national airport: Bergerac. Nearest station: Périgeux.

Additional information:

Open mid-March to end of October. 10 bedrooms all with private bath/WC. Price FF340-FF390 per person half board. Dinner Ff150. Swimming pool. Mastercard and Visa. Colour brochure in French and additional information in English sent on request.

La Praderie
Le Suquet-Haut, 24220 Le Coux-et-Bigarouque
Tel 53 31 69 58

Chambres d'Hôtes/Bed & Breakfast

La Praderie is a typical Dordogne farmhouse set in its own gardens and flanked by two impressive old chestnut trees. Its English owners, Joan and Ed Tyson, have five guest bedrooms and Joan – an enthusiastic cook – is happy to provide evening meals of local specialities. Thursday night is devoted to dinner Perigord-style with Garlic Soup, Gezier salad, *magret de canard* and usually a walnut gâteau (the largest walnut grove in France is not far away). Joan's French home cooking is much appreciated by her guests but there is also a good selection of reasonably priced restaurants nearby. La Praderie is in the southern Dordogne, in the area known as the Périgord Noir which is rich in mediæval towns and châteaux. It is close to the famous caves of Les Eyzies and Lascaux and to the wine-growing areas of Cahors and Bergerac.

Situated 45km/28 miles east of Bergerac, 67km/41 miles north-west of Cahors and 2km/1 miles from the village of Siorac-en-Périgord. Nearest international airports: Bordeaux at 100km/62 miles or Toulouse at 130km/80 miles. Nearest station: Siorac-en-Périgord.

Additional information:

Open all year. 3 bedrooms all with private shower/WC and 2 bedrooms with shared bath/WC. Price FF180-FF250 single or double. Half board FF200 per person (sharing). Breakfast FF25. Dinner FF80 (including wine). Brochure in English and photo sent on request. Suitable for visitors without a car.

Le Manoir d'Hautegente
Coly, 24120 Terrasson
Tel 53 51 68 03, Fax 53 50 38 52

Hotel*** with restaurant

This superb Perigord manor house was originally the mill and blacksmith's forge attached to an ancient monastery. Romantically located beside a meandering mill stream with ducks and geese, the walls of the manor are clad in rambling ivy. The property has belonged to the Hamelin family for three centuries and it is Monsieur and Madame Hamelin who welcome their guests today. Set in a garden of flowers and surrounded by private woods, the hotel offers extremely comfortable and

The caves of Périgord and Quercy

Numerous underground caverns, lakes and rivers in the Dordogne region can be visited, but perhaps the most interesting are the prehistoric decorated caves of the Vézère Valley. Cave art flourished in the area between 15,000 and 8,000 BC; the paintings in the Lascaux caves near Montignac are regarded as the most important examples in existence.. These were discovered by schoolboys in 1940

and contain hundreds of superlative animal paintings. Sadly the caves had to be closed some years ago due to deterioration, but a realistic facsimile – Lascaux 2 – has been created near the original site and should not be missed. Other cave paintings can be seen around the region and there is also a museum of pre-history at Les Eyzies-de-Tayac which provides both invaluable background information and details of all sites worth visiting.

well-appointed bedrooms furnished with antiques. On chilly evenings, a fire is lit in the charming and cosy dining room but in summer meals are served outside. Many of the house specialities served in the restaurant are home-produced and are for sale in a small gourmet boutique in the reception area. Hamper-lunches are also available. Keen fishermen are invited to try their luck in the river which passes by the hotel, offering first-class fishing. Le Manoir d'Hautegent is central to the many attractions contained within this area and your English-speaking hosts will happily discuss with their guests how best to explore the region.

Situated 63km/38 miles east of Périgeux and 30km/18 miles west of Brive-la-Gaillarde. Coly is 6km/2 miles south of Le Lardin on D62. Nearest international airport: Bordeaux at 170km/105 miles. Nearest national airport: Périgeux. Nearest station: Brive-la-Gaillarde (TGV).

Additional information:

Open mid-March to end October. 10 bedrooms all with private bath/WC. Price FF500-FF800 single or double. Half board FF490-FF670 per person. Breakfast FF50. Dinner FF230 or a la carte. Carte Bleue, Mastercard and Visa. Further information sent on request.

Moulin de la Crouzille
Tourtoirac, 24390 Hautefort
Tel 53 51 11 94

Chambres d'Hôtes/Bed & Breakfast
Courses in painted furniture

Diana and John Armitage bought this attractive riverside mill house in 1989 and have since restored it to provide guest accommodation and to allow Diana to run courses on painted furniture. These sessions are for up to six students who have the opportunity to learn various techniques and to practice a variety of designs. The courses are offered on a daily basis (and Diana says that much can be learned in just one day) or they may be extended for up to five days. Course participants are invited to stay at Crouzille or accommodation can be arranged nearby. Non-course guests are also very welcome and they will be offered one of the distinctive bedrooms that are furnished with some of Diana's painted furniture. In the evening, house guests have the choice between a light supper or alternatively dinner is served *en famille*.

Situated 180km/110 miles north-east of Bordeaux, 56km/37 miles north-west of Brive-la-Gaillarde and 2km from the village of Tourtoirac. Nearest international airport: Bordeaux. Nearest national airport: Périgeux at 33km/20 miles. Nearest station: Brive-la-Gaillarde.

Additional information:

Open all year except Christmas. 2 bedrooms with private shower or bath/WC. Price FF250 per person including breakfast. Super FF100. Dinner FF150. Painted furniture courses FF700 per day including materials and lunch. No credit cards accepted. Further information in English on request.

Saint-Jory Art School
Auberge Saint-Georges, Saint-Jory-de-Chalais,
24800 Thiviers
Tel 53 52 06 34, Fax 53 55 29 19

Painting courses with auberge accommodation

Two-week courses at Saint-Jory provide an ideal opportunity for experienced painters or beginners to improve their skills in a relaxing holiday environment, to visit places of interest in one of the most beautiful areas of France, to enjoy musical evenings and lively instructive lectures in the company of fellow enthusiasts. The school is in the northern part of Dordogne – the Périgord Vert – in a landscape of rolling hills, oak and chestnut woods, lakes, rivers, historic castles, picturesque villages and towns that provide real inspiration for painters. Expert professional advice is offered on perspective, composition, design and the use of colour. There is practical tuition in oil/acrylic, watercolour and pastel. Whenever possible, sessions are held out of doors with a course tutor to accompany the painting group, advising and guiding each student during the day. In the evening, the day's work is displayed in the school's studio for group discussion. The courses are conducted by experienced English-speaking tutors who have taught in several well-known art schools and have exhibited internationally.

Accommodation is provided in Auberge Saint-Georges, situated in the small village of Saint-Jory. The bar and restaurant are open to the public but the charming patio garden and studio are for painters only. There is also an art materials shop and art library. Alternative accommodation is available either at another *auberge* in the village or *chambres d'hôtes*. Non-painting partners are welcome and can be provided with an alternative programme of interesting cultural activities.

Accommodation in the *auberge* is also available to non-painters.

Situated 160km/100 miles north-east of Bordeaux, 60km/36 miles south of Limoges and 13km/8 miles north of Thiviers. Nearest international airport: Bordeaux. Nearest national airport: Périgeux at 34km/20 miles. Nearest station: Thiviers or Angoulême (TGV) at 75km/46 miles.

Additional information:

Open all year. Painting courses April to October. 7 bedrooms all with private shower and shared WC. Price FF6,000 per person for a two-week course. Price includes bedroom, breakfast, evening meal with wine, tuition and outings. Not included – lunches, transport to the school and painting materials. Prices on request for non-painting partners depending on programme. Room rates FF180 double. Breakfast FF25. Carte Bleue, Mastercard and Visa. Full colour brochure in English sent on request. Suitable for visitors without a car.

Les Poulouleix
Saint-Jory-de-Chalais, 24800 Thiviers
Tel 53 52 06 34, Fax 53 55 29 19

Self-catering studio and chambres d'hôtes

This restored farmhouse 2km/1 miles outside the village is the home of Jasper and Susi Jacob, English owners of Saint-Jory Art School. A wing of the main building contains a self-contained apartment comprising double bedroom, a large studio room with a convertible bed, bath/WC, kitchenette and outside terrace. The house is set in 3 hectares/7 acres of garden and guests have use of the family swimming pool. The Jacobs also have three chambres d'hôtes – two double and one single – with a shared bathroom.

See Saint-Jory Art School (above) for location details.

Additional information:

Open all year. Apartment sleeps 2/4. Price FF1,500 per week including gas, electricity, bed linen and towels. Chambres d'hôtes prices FF150 double. Breakfast FF30.

La Petite Renaudie
24600 Villetoureix
Tel 53 90 25 43

Self-catering cottage

La Petite Renaudie is a small hamlet of six or seven houses in a secluded position surrounded by the lovely Dordogne countryside, yet it is only 5km/2 miles from the bustling market town of Riberac. A single-track lane leads to the hamlet. As this is not a through road, there is very little traffic. Main shopping is in Riberac, but there is a small village shop within walking distance at Villetoureix. The English owner, Hester Gordon, also lives in the hamlet, so is on hand to sort out any problems and to generally ensure that guests have an enjoyable stay. Accommodation is for up to six people and offers two double-bedded rooms, one single-bedded room, bathroom, large open plan living/dining/kitchen with french windows that open onto a large private garden. La Renaudie has been successfully rented out for many years and is very popular.

Situated 37km/23 miles west of Périgeux and 51km/31 miles north of Bergerac. Nearest international airport: Bordeaux at 100km/62 miles. Nearest station: Angoulême (TGV) at 45km/27 miles or Périgeux.

Additional information:

Open March to October. 3 double bedrooms. Sleeps 6 people. Price FF1,800-FF3,000 per week depending on season. Price includes electricity, water and gas. Logs for the open fire extra. Bed linen and towels can be supplied extra on request. Information in English and photo available from Hester Gordon at the above address.

Le Vieux Logis
24510 Trémolat
Tel 53 22 80 65, Fax 53 22 84 89

Hotel*** with restaurant

This lovely old house has belonged to the same family for over 400 years. It became a hotel 35 years ago and it is the son of the original hoteliers who is in charge of operations today. Le Vieux Logis is in the attractive village of Trémolat which overlooks the famous Cingle de Trémolat – the great U-bend in the Dordogne River overshadowed by high wooded cliffs. Set among beautifully-kept gardens, the hotel accommodation is divided between the ivy-clad main house and numerous out-buildings that were originally drying and storage areas for tobacco (this is still the main tobacco-growing region of France),

Bastide towns and villages

Bastides *are one of the outstanding features of the area known as Périgord and Quercy in the* départements *of Dordogne and Lot-et-Garonne. Built by both the French and English during the 13th and 14th centuries, they were invariably designed on a regular plan of a central square with covered arcades on all four sides from which a regular grid of streets extended. During the Hundred Years' War, many* bastides *were fortified by adding outer protective walls with towers, gateways and moats, and by the construction of churches with a dual function as impenetrable keeps. The strategic positions chosen for* bastides – *on rivers or hilltops – were as picturesque as they were practical. Many of them have remained more or less intact with the result that they provide a fascinating insight into life as it was in mediæval France.*

the gardener's cottage, farm workers' lodgings. Each bedroom therefore has its own individual personality and there is a splendid dining room with a magnificent upper gallery that has been created from what was once a hayloft. The cooking does justice to such grand surroundings and has been awarded a Michelin rosette. Full information is available for outings in the vicinity either on foot, bicycle, horseback or car and picnic hampers can be provided for *al fresco* lunches. Service is courteous and attentive; and everything possible is done to ensure that guests enjoy their stay … there is even a heliport on the property for the convenience of visitors. English spoken.

Situated 33km/20 miles east of Bergerac and 45km/28 miles south of Périgeux. Nearest international airport: Bordeaux at 120km/75 miles. Nearest national airport: Bergerac. Nearest station: Périgeux.

Additional information:

Open all year except January and early February. 22 bedrooms all with private bath/WC; telephone; TV; minibar. Price FF650-FF1,090. Breakfast FF65. Lunch and dinner FF210-FF300 or a la carte (closed Tuesday and Wednesday lunch except June-September). Swimming pool All major credit cards accepted. Brochure in French and English sent on request.

Moulin du Roc
24530 Champagnac-de-Belair
Tel 53 54 80 36, Fax 53 54 21 31

Hotel**** with restaurant

In the heart of Périgord Vert on the banks of the River Dronne, Moulin du Roc was originally a mill for producing walnut oil. The river flows through the picturesque property and superb gardens on either side are connected by a small bridge. Bedrooms are very prettily decorated with colourful floral prints and some have canopied four-poster beds. The hotel's main claim to fame however is its restaurant which has been awarded a Michelin rosette. Madame Solange Gardillou – one of France's best-known lady chefs – is now assisted in the kitchen by her son Alain in the tradition of so many French family-run hotels. Meals are served in a most luxurious dining room or outside on a flower-filled riverside terrace. English is spoken.

Situated 120km/74 miles north-west of Bordeaux, 27km/17 miles north of Périgeux and 6km/3.5 miles north-east of Brantôme. Nearest international airport: Bordeaux. Nearest national airport: Périgeux. Nearest station: Périgeux or Angoulême (TGV) at 60km/36 miles.

Additional information:

Open all year except mid-November to mid-December. 14 bedrooms all with private bath/WC; telephone; TV; minibar. Price FF380-FF680 double. Half board FF1,020-FF1,350 for two people. Breakfast FF55. Lunch and dinner FF200-FF350 or a la carte (closed Tuesday and Wednesday lunch). Swimming pool and tennis court. All major credit cards accepted. Full brochure in French and English sent on request.

La Bouteille Ouverte

Bouteilles-St-Sébastien, 24320 Verteillac
Tel 53 91 51 98 / 53 91 51 40

Village auberge with restaurant and self-catering cottage

The tiny village of Bouteilles-St-Sébastien nestles peacefully among the rolling hills of Périgord, clustered around an 11th century fortified church. Right next to the church is the auberge, owned and run by a Scottish couple, Tom and Pat Carruthers. Pat does the cooking which, like the wines served, has a local flavour. A full five-course dinner is served in the evening, there is a *plat du jour* at lunchtime and snacks are available throughout the day. The four bedrooms are simply furnished in French country style with a shared bathroom but at the edge of the village the Carruthers have a second property offering two more luxurious rooms with private shower/WC. This 250-year-old farmhouse is set in 1 hectare/2 acres of orchard with walnut and fruit trees and also contains an independent self-catering cottage which has been beautifully restored with a double bedroom, shower/WC, lounge with TV, kitchenette with washing machine. The cottage and guestrooms all have separate entrances and terraces. The auberge is only 12km/7 miles from the bustling market town of Ribérac and convenient for all the places of regional interest which your friendly hosts will be very happy to explain.

Romany caravans and independent horseback journeys in Dordogne

For anyone looking for a holiday away from the motorised masses, the romance and adventure of a Romany caravan may well appeal. The holidays are run by an English woman, Iris Winn, from her home in Monflanquin, one of the famous bastide villages. Iris provides her holidaymakers with an authentic hand-painted Romany caravan fully-equipped with a kitchenette and sleeping accommodation for up to four people, plus a gentle cart horse. The carefully planned route along quiet country lanes passes through a pastoral landscape of plum orchards, vineyards, fields of brilliant sunflowers, meadows and woodland. There is the opportunity to stop in quaint mediæval villages, to buy provisions in colourful street markets and to enjoy a cooling drink in friendly open-air cafés. Every night is spent at a different venue – perhaps a farm or village auberge – offering pasturage for the horse and shower facilities for his passengers. An optional evening meal is usually available too or dinner may be prepared in the caravan and served beside a flickering camp fire. Holidays can be for five, seven, 10 or 14 days and although previous experience with horses is helpful, it is not essential. A love of animals and a practical attitude are more important.

Some riding experience is however preferable for the independent horseback journeys. France is one of the few countries in the world with a network of well-marked tracks and bridlepaths that allows for regular overnight stops. For these holidays Iris uses locally-bred horses that have been chosen for their good temperament and surefootedness. Parties consist of two to four people and may or may not be accompanied by a guide. Distances of up to 25km/15 miles per day are covered with overnight stops at farmhouses or country inns that offer stabling for the horses. Riders are accommodated in ferme-auberges or country inns and are served an evening meal. Luggage is transported independently during the day.

Additional information:

Caravan and horseback holidays are operating from late April to the end of October. Duration of holidays is flexible. Horse-drawn Romany

caravans: Price FF1,000-FF1,300 per person per week based on 4 people sharing. This includes a fully-equipped caravan with horse, tuition and back-up service, all overnight fees. Meals are not included. Insurance is FF120 per person extra. Fixed caravans are also available at FF400 per person per week based on 4 people sharing. This price includes a fully-equipped Romany caravan and site fees. Independent holiday on horseback: Price FF4,000 per person for 5 nights. This includes fully-equipped horse, back-up service, shared twin bedrooms (with private bath/WC wherever possible), breakfast and dinner. Lunches are not provided. Insurance is FF120 per person extra.
Further information and colour brochure in English available (November-April) from Iris Winn, Aldby Park, Buttercrambe, York YO4 1AU, United Kingdom, Tel: (0)759 71398, Fax: (0)759 71628 or (April-October) from Iris Winn, Dantou, 47150 Monflanquin, France, Tel: 53 36 48 95.

Situated 100km/62 miles north-east of Bordeaux, 50km/31 miles north-west of Périgeux and 5km/3 miles west of Verteillac. Nearest international airport: Bordeaux. Nearest national airport: Angoulême at 47km/30 miles. Nearest station: Montmoreaux (with connections for TGV at Angoulême) at 12km/7 miles.

Additional information:

Open all year except November. 6 bedrooms – 4 with shared bath/WC, 2 with private shower/WC; all with tea and coffee-making facilities. Price FF190 and FF250. Reduced weekly rates available. Breakfast FF25. Lunch FF50. Dinner. FF110. No credit cards accepted. Brochure in English sent on request. Suitable for visitors without a car as collection can be arranged but there is no public transport passing through the village. Bikes can be hired and there are excellent walks in the area.

Cottage: Sleeps 2/4. Price FF2,250-FF2,500 per week. Daily rates can also be negotiated.

Le Moulin de St Avit
Gavaudun, 47150 Monflanquin
Tel 53 40 86 60

Country hotel**

Ideally placed on the *'bastide* circuit' between the picturesque *bastide* towns of Monflaquin and Monpazier, this friendly hotel was once a watermill – one of 12 along the lovely Gavaudin valley. The building was completely renovated three years ago by its English owners, Anne and Christopher Winchurch. The mill is surrounded by 5 hectares/11 acres of private woodland and guests are invited to fish in the mill stream. On summer evenings, Anne and Chris host informal barbecues beside the river. There is also a floodlit swimming pool. Bedrooms are simply furnished in pine and one has been adapted for use by handicapped guests in a wheelchair. There are two sitting rooms filled with old furniture brought from the owners' cottage in England, and a small dining room. The bar is in the old kitchen with its monumental fireplace. At the moment dinner is not served at the hotel but there are two good restaurants within 2km/1 mile serving regional specialities. Light snacks are available at mid-day. Le Moulin de St Avit offers comfortable accommodation at very reasonable prices and guests can be sure of a warm welcome.

Situated 60km/37 miles north-west of Cahors on D150, 4km/2.5 miles north of Gavaudun. Nearest international airports: Toulouse and Bordeaux both at 150km/93 miles. Nearest national airport: Bergerac and Agen both at 60km/37 miles. Nearest station: Fumel/Monsempron-Libos at 10km/6 miles.

Additional information:

Open all year. 8 bedrooms all with private shower/WC. Price FF170-FF250. Discounted prices for low season and weekly bookings. Breakfast FF25. Mastercard and Visa. Information in English sent on request.

The Grange

Au Bourg, Saint-Maurin, 47270 Puymirol
Tel 53 95 34 42

Self-catering country cottage and apartments

Some years ago, a young English couple, Nigel and Priscilla Lowe, bought a semi-derelict farmhouse on the edge of a village in south-western France with the idea of converting it into a home for themselves. They intended to grow their own vegetables, keep a few chickens and goats and to create self-catering accommodation in the out-buildings of their property. After nearly three years of hard work with Nigel, an ex-boat builder, undertaking much of the renovation personally, the result today is a charming complex of the Lowe's own home, a detached stone cottage and two apartments all sharing a communal swimming pool. All the holiday letting units have two bedrooms, bathroom, kitchen and living area. Each will

Bordeaux wines

Bordeaux is the greatest vineyard in the world both in terms of prestige and the area under vine cultivation – 100,000 hectares/225,000 acres all across the Gironde département. On average 500 million bottles of wine are produced here every year, including some of the finest and most expensive in the world. Thousands of producers – mighty châteaux-estates and more modest vignerons alike – welcome potential buyers and interested amateurs into their cellars to taste their wines …and to purchase. In every town, every village, every hotel, information is readily available on how, when and where visitors may take part in wine-tastings. But … many establishments require an appointment in advance; some do not speak English; others charge for tastings and/or expect purchases to be made. For the serious wine-lover, this will be within his expectations, but for the casual enthusiast a visit to Château Prieuré-Lichine may be the most satisfactory option. Despite (or perhaps because) it is among the most respected of châteaux in the Médoc region, it is the most organised and welcoming for visitors. Knowledgeable tri-lingual hostesses conduct guided tours of the chais or cellars and explain the various processes in detail. Wine tastings are optional and a charge is made. Wines, books and accessories are on sale in the château shop.

Château Prieuré-Lichine, Cantenac, 33460 Margaux, Tel: 56 88 36 26. Open every day of the year from 9am-7pm.

accommodate from two to six people. Saint-Maurin is only a short walk away and has all the usual shopping amenities. Bicycles can be hired on site and there are facilities for horse-riding, windsurfing, sailing, fishing and tennis nearby.

Situated 20km/12 miles east of Agen. Nearest international airports: Toulouse at 100km/62 miles and Bordeaux at 150km/93 miles. Nearest national airport: Agen at 26km/16 miles. Nearest station: Agen.

Additional information:

Open all year. Weekly booking Saturday to Saturday.During July and August a minimum of two weeks only accepted.Units sleep 2/6 people. Price FF1,000-FF3,500 per week including electricity, gas, bed linen, BBQ and garden furniture. Maid service available on request. Information in English and photo sent on request. Suitable for visitors without a car and collection is possible from Agen.

Château de Scandaillac
St-Eutrop-de-Born, 47210 Villereal
Tel 53 36 65 40

Chambres d'Hôtes/Bed & Breakfast

Château de Scandaillac is a small recently-restored castle in the heart of the *'bastide* district' of southwestern France, amidst the rolling hills that lie between the Rivers Dordogne and Lot. This is home to Peter and Dorothy England who bought the property in 1985 and spent a year restoring the main house – which dates from the 12th century with later Renaissance additions – to provide very comfortable guest accommodation. Their aim is to create an intimate house-party atmosphere at Scandaillac where every evening at 7.30pm house guests assemble for cocktails before moving to the Long Gallery where dinner is served. Here everyone dines together at one long table, sampling up to six different dishes all freshly prepared from local seasonal produce. Lunches are not provided but guests are welcome to borrow plates and cutlery for a do-it-yourself meal by the swimming pool or for a picnic in the gardens which, under Dorothy's expert care and attention, have won first prize in the local gardening competition for two years running. For the more energetic visitors, there are two golf courses within a 10km/6 mile radius, and facilities for tennis, horse-riding and wind-surfing nearby.

Situated 150km/90 miles east of Bordeaux, 38km/24 miles south-east of Bergerac and 10km/6 miles north-east of Cancon on D153. Nearest international airport: Bordeaux. Nearest national airport: Bergerac. Nearest station: Bergerac or Bordeaux (TGV).

Additional information:

Open March-October. 8 bedrooms all with private bath/WC. Price FF250 single or double. Half board (2 or more nights) FF405 double. Breakfast FF30. Dinner FF170 including aperitifs, wines, liqueurs and coffee. (No dinner is served on Wednesdays but there are restaurants nearby.) No credit cards accepted. Brochure in English sent on request.

L'Ormeraie
47150 Paulhiac
Tel 53 36 45 96

Chambres d'Hôtes/Bed & Breakfast

L'Ormeraie is a lovely old country house built of mellow stone in the Périgord style with a steep triangular roof and ornamental *pigeonnier* or dovecote. It is set in its own peaceful gardens with extensive views over wooded countryside. The bedrooms are extremely comfortable, each furnished with family antique furniture and oriental carpets. Care and attention are obvious everywhere – fresh flowers, a sewing kit, parlour games in the *salon* and lots of information on the many local attractions. Dinner is served in the family dining room and your host, Michel de l'Ormeraie, invites his house guests to browse through his library of more than 3,000 books. Comfort, calm, luxury, refinement and good home cooking are the hallmark of l'Ormeraie. Only a little English is spoken but visitors can be assured of a very cordial welcome.

Situated 140km/86 miles east of Bordeaux, 50km/31 miles south-east of Bergerac and 9km/5.5 miles north-east of Monflanquin. From Monflanquin take D272 to Laussou and turn right at the church towards Bonnenouvelle. L'Ormeraie is 1.5km/1 miles on the right. Nearest international airport: Bordeaux. Nearest national airport: Bergerac. Nearest station: Monsempron-Libos at 15km.

Additional information:

Open March-November. 4 bedrooms all with private shower or bath/WC. Price FF260-FF480 double including breakfast. Dinner FF130. Swimming pool. No credit cards accepted. Colour brochure in French and English sent on request.

Château de Commarque
Sauternes, 33210 Langon
Tel 56 76 65 94/56 76 68 08, Fax 56 76 64 30

Château hotel with restaurant and producing Sauternes vineyard

This interesting hotel-cum-vineyard is owned and run by an English couple, Nigel and Georgea Reay-Jones, who acquired the property in 1986. At that time both the hotel and the vines were in a somewhat neglected state; today they are thriving and a stay at the château is sure to be

fascinating for wine-lovers. Placed close to the centre of the tiny yet prestigious village of Sauternes, famous for its sweet white wine, accommodation is provided in self-contained, centrally-heated suites that open onto the château courtyard. Each suite consists of a small sitting room (with sofa bed), bedroom and shower room. There is a high quality restaurant specialising – naturally – in cuisine *au Sauternes*. Georgea is in charge of the cooking which includes a selection of regional dishes such as *foie gras au Sauternes, magret de canard au Sauternes,* and *veau braisées aux champignons sauvages.* The house Sauternes is of course also a speciality. Wine tour holidays can easily be arranged either quite informally (Nigel knows many of the local vineyard owners personally and will organise introductions) or alternatively, comprehensive itineraries may be prepared and visits arranged in advance. A modest fee is charged for this service and transport can be provided in the château minibus. In addition all-inclusive wine tour holidays are available with programmes for a weekend, five days or longer. More detailed information will be sent on request.

Situated 48km/30 miles south-east of Bordeaux and 10km/6 miles south-west of Langon in the village of Sauternes. Nearest international airport: Bordeaux. Nearest station: Langon or Bordeaux (TGV).

Additional information:

Open all year except February. 7 bedroom/suites all with private shower or bath/WC. Price FF180-FF375 single or double. Breakfast FF30. Lunch or dinner FF75-FF175 or a la carte. Swimming pool. All major credit cards accepted. Full colour brochure in English sent on request. Suitable for visitors without a car if participating in a minibus tour.

Vircoulin Holiday Gîtes
St-Avit-de-Soulége, 33220 Ste-Foy-la-Grande
Tel 57 41 08 24

Self-catering cottages

Vircoulin consists of two self-catering cottages set amongst vineyards in just over a hectare/3 acres of private garden and only five minutes from the lovely Dordogne River. The area will be of particular interest to wine-lovers being within easy reach of all the major Bordeaux wine-growing villages. Although in the *département* of Gironde, Vircoulin is on the borders of Dordogne and thus convenient for the many attractions it has to offer – *bastide* towns, prehistoric caves and delightful pastoral countryside. The Studio is a pretty cottage at one end of the main farmhouse with exposed beams and tiled floors. Downstairs is an open-plan living/dining/kitchen, bedroom and bathroom. There is also a first-floor gallery bedroom. The Cottage is larger with an open-plan living/dining/kitchen and wood-burning stove, bedroom and bathroom downstairs and two further bedrooms upstairs. The

English owners, Mike and Jackie Andrew, are in residence for part of the year. In their absence, English friends living permanently nearby look after the properties and are always on hand to welcome guests and help in any way they can.

Situated 60km/36 miles east of Bordeaux, 80km/48 miles south-west of Périgeux and 8km/5 miles south-west of Ste-Foy-la-Grande. Nearest international airport: Bordeaux. Nearest station: Ste-Foy-la-Grande.

Additional information:

Open all year. Studio sleeps 4/5. Cottage sleeps 6/8. Price FF1,000-FF2,200 for the Studio, FF1,200-FF2,700 for the Cottage depending on season. All bookings weekly Friday to Friday. Price includes electricity and gas. Bed linen and towels can be supplied on request.Further information and photos sent on request. Please contact owners Mike and Jackie Andrew at the Vircoulon address or at Manor Cottage, Mavelstone Road, Bickley, Kent BR1 2PB, United Kingdom. Tel (0)81 464 1333 or (0)323 762381. Suitable for visitors without a car if you join one of the Andrews' escorted 'house party' holidays. More details sent on request.

Château du Foulon

33480 Castelnau-de-Médoc
Tel 56 58 20 18, Fax 56 58 23 43

Chambres d'Hôtes/Bed & Breakfast

Château du Foulon is the home of Vicomte and Vicomtesse Jean de Baritault du Carpia. The house was built in 1840 and is set in 50 hectares/125 acres of private park and woodlands. All bedrooms are very comfortable and beautifully decorated, with views over the park. In the centre of the Médoc vineyards, this makes the perfect base for wine-lovers and there are also two golf courses nearby. The Vicomte and Vicomtesse speak a little English.

Situated 28km/17 miles north-west of Bordeaux just outside the village of Castelnau-de-Médoc. Nearest international airport and station: Bordeaux.

Additional information:

Open all year. 3 bedrooms, a suite for 4 and an apartment for 6, all with private bath/WC. Price Ff350-FF600 double including breakfast. No credit cards accepted. Further information sent on request.

La Bergerie

Avenue du Lac, 40140 Soustons
Tel 58 41 11 43

Private hotel** with restaurant

The *département* of Landes occupies the southwestern corner of France on the Atlantic coast with

wide sandy beaches that stretch as far as the eye can see. Just inland on the shores of a large salt water lake is the small town of Soustans, in the heart of Basque country. La Bergerie is a typical long, low *maison bourgeoise* dating from the turn of the century. Rooms are attractively furnished in traditional *Basquais* style. The dining room is only open to residents and the evening fixed menu is displayed every morning. The cooking includes regional specialities using fresh local produce. Although close to the town centre, La Bergerie is surrounded by a large well-kept garden. Madame Clavier speaks only a little English but guests can be sure of a warm welcome.

Situated 47km/29 miles north-east of Biarritz. Nearest international airport: Bordeaux at 150km/98 miles. Nearest national airport: Biarritz. Nearest station: Dax at 26km/15 miles.

Additional information:

Open March-November. 12 bedrooms all with private bath/WC; telephone; TV. Price FF240-FF300 single or double. Breakfast FF30. Dinner FF150-FF180. Parking. Carte Bleue and Visa. Information in French and a photo sent on request.

Le Château du Clair de Lune
48 avenue Alan-Seeger, 64200 Biarritz
Tel 59 23 45 96

Town hotel***

On the southern Atlantic coast of France very close to the Spanish border, Biarritz was – until the First World War – one of the most fashionable European seaside resorts. It can no longer claim to be the favourite holiday spot for kings and

queens, the rich and famous but time has not changed its romantic headland setting, its secret rocky coves, its magnificent sandy beaches nor its enviable climate. There are still some very grand hotels on Avenue Impératrice and two gambling casinos. Other distractions include horse racing, the *Basquais* version of bull-fighting (where the bull always survives) and assorted sea sports. Perhaps one of the nicest places to

35

stay in Biarritz is the Clair de Lune which is located 2km/1 miles from the centre, surrounded by delightful gardens which were planted in 1902 when the house was built, and are now in their prime – a horticultural wonderland of mimosas, camelias, magnolias, rhododendrons and roses. Bedrooms are divided between the main house – more a comfortable manor house than a real château – and a villa in the grounds. This *pavillion de chasse* is in a semi-colonial style and each room opens onto a charming terrace. Bedrooms bear the name of a herb or perfumed plant – Marjolaine, Lavande, Vanille etc – and are very prettily furnished. Madame Beyière speaks only a little English but is very charming.

Situated 190km/118 miles south of Bordeaux and 2km/1 mile from the centre of Biarritz. Nearest international airport: Bordeaux. Nearest national airport and station: Biarritz.

Additional information:

Open all year.15 bedrooms all with private bath/WC; telephone; TV; some with minibar. Price FF380-FF600 single or double. Breakfast FF50. Parking. Amex, Diners and Visa. Full colour brochure in French sent on request. Suitable for visitors without a car but there is a walk of 800 metres/yards to the bus stop.

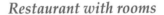

La Patoula
64480 Ustaritz
Tel 59 93 00 56, Fax 59 93 16 54

Restaurant with rooms

A delightful riverside gourmet stopover, La Patoula has the reputation of being one of the *bonnes tables* of the region. The attractive dining room has traditional Basque furnishings and a cosy log fire in winter. In summer meals are served on an outside terrace with views over the River Nive. Specialities on the menu change with the seasons: There are plenty of fish dishes and delicious deserts. Rooms are light, airy and spacious, opening onto the garden. For golf enthusiasts, there are four courses within a 15km/9 miles radius. A little English is spoken.

Situated 15km/9 miles south-east of Biarritz in the centre of Ustaritz opposite the church. Nearest international airport: Bordeaux at 200km/125 miles. Nearest national airport: Biarritz. Nearest station: Ustaritz.

Additional information:

Open all year except mid-January to mid-February. 9 bedrooms all with private shower or bath/WC; telephone. Price FF300-FF430 double. Half board FF325-FF390 per person. Breakfast FF55. Lunch and dinner FF130-FF240 or a la carte (closed Sunday evening and Monday except high season). Visa. Colour brochure in French and English sent on request. Suitable for visitors without a car. Train and bus service from Biarritz and Bayonne.

*T*HE *AUVERGNE LIES AT THE VERY HEART OF FRANCE in the wild uplands of the* Massif Central *– a countryside of splendid scenery with sleeping volcanoes, dramatic mountains, lush green valleys and tranquil tree-lined lakes., Famed for its healthy bracing climate, it is a paradise for nature lovers and sportsmen alike. The region is also steeped in history and rich in ancient monuments and buildings.*

Hôtel des Sources
15580 Saint-Jacques-des-Blats
Tel 71 47 05 33

Country hotel with restaurant

Saint-Jacques-des-Blats is quietly situated in the valley of the River Cère among the grandiose scenery of Haute Auvergne. Just outside the village is Hôtel des Sources owned and run by an English couple, Ian and Pauline Smith. Their simple, friendly accommodation is ideal for visitors seeking an inexpensive base from which to explore the many rural attractions of this little-known and totally unspoilt region which offers superb walking, riding and driving through stunning mountain landscapes. Bedrooms are comfortably furnished but do not have *en suite* facilities. The hotel's restaurant offers two very reasonably priced menus of Pauline's good wholesome home-cooking including local specialities (and a steak and kidney pie which is fast gaining a reputation with the local French clients!) Bar snacks and packed lunches are also available.

Situated 130km/80 miles south-west of Clermont-Ferrand and 32km/19 miles north-east of Aurillac. Nearest international airport: Toulouse, Bordeaux or Lyon all at 250km/160 miles. Nearest national airport: Aurillac. Nearest station: Saint-Jacques-des-Blats.

Additional information:

Open all year. 13 bedrooms all with wash basin. Showers/WC on each floor. Price FF135 double including breakfast. Half board FF150 per person, dinner FF70 and FF90. Carte blanche, Eurocard and Visa. Colour brochure in English sent on request. Suitable for visitors without a car.

03
ALLIER

Auvergne comprises the
following département
   Allier (03)
   Cantal (15)
   Haute-Loire (43)
   Puy-de-D ome (63)

Clermont-Ferrand

63
PUY-DE-DOME

St-Etienne

BELVEZIN
LE BURON DE MOUTISSOUS

CHATEAU DE
TRANCIS

Allanche

43
HAUTE-LOIRE

HOTEL DES SOURCES

Le Puy

15
CANTAL

LE PRE BOSSU

Aurillac

AUBERGE DE
LA TOMETTE

AUVERGNE

Auberge de la Tomette
Vitrac, 15220 St-Mamet
Tel 71 64 70 94, Fax 71 64 77 11

Village hotel** with restaurant

Vitrac is an attractive friendly village in La Chataigneraie – an area of great natural beauty in southern Cantal. The pretty stone auberge is located near the church but has an annex just across the road containing extra rooms, a swimming pool and large gardens. Bedrooms are simply but pleasantly furnished and the restaurant specialises in traditional regional country cooking. Prices are very reasonable and the owners, Monsieur and Madame Chauzi, speak English.

Situated 190km/117 miles south-west of Clermont-Ferrand, 70km/43 miles north of Rodez and 25km/15 miles south-west of Aurillac. Nearest international airport: Toulouse at 250km/155 miles. Nearest national airport and station: Aurillac.

Additional information:

Open all year except January to mid-March. 14 bedrooms all with shower. Price FF220-FF280 single or double. Half board Ff200-FF250 per person. Breakfast FF26. Lunch or dinner FF60-FF150. Swimming pool. Eurocard and Visa. Colour brochure in French and English sent on request. Suitable for visitors without a car as the hotel can arrange collection from Autillac. There is no transport in the village but the location is ideal for walkers.

Rambling holidays in Haute Auvergne

Seven-day walking holidays based at Hôtel des Sources are available during May, June, July, September and October. The weekly programme includes a total of four and a half days of walks,some of which will be full day itineraries, others will cover shorter half-day routes, all with an experienced local guide. One full day coach outing is also offered. Groups will normally consist of a maximum of 10 participants. The price per person is FF1,500 to include room, breakfast, a packed lunch and dinner. Holidays are Saturday to Saturday.
Further information in English from Ian and Pauline Smith at Hôtel des Sources.

Belvézin
Landeyrat, 15160 Allanche
Tel 71 20 48 39, Fax 71 20 48 65

Chambres d'Hôtes/Bed & Breakfast

Belvézin is a typical old Auvergnate farmhouse in an area known as Cézallier – a vast plateau at 1,300 metres/4,000 feet above sea level – which is slashed by spectacular deep valleys carrying fast-flowing streams that feed such mighty rivers as the Dordogne and the Loire. This is home to English country-lovers Rex and Helen Barr, who have carefully restored the house using traditional materials to provide modern

comforts. Guest accommodation is on the first floor where there is also a sitting room with television, music facilities, books, maps etc. An evening meal is prepared by Helen and served *en famille* in the large farmhouse kitchen with its original fireplace. This magnificent unspoilt region will appeal to walkers and nature-lovers but has, in addition, a fascinating history and offers a wealth of architectural treasures. The Barrs know the area extremely well and are enthusiastic in sharing their knowledge with house guests. For trips over rugged terrain a 4x4 vehicle is at the disposal of visitors depending on availability.

Situated 120km/74 miles south of Clermont-Ferrand and 10km/6 miles north-west of Allanche via D679. Nearest international airport: Lyon at 300km/180 miles. Nearest national airport: Clermont-Ferrand. Nearest station: Neussargues at 22km/12 miles with a bus connection to Landeyrat.

Additional information:

Open all year. 3 bedrooms all with wash basin and shaver point. Shared bath/WC and shower/WC. Price FF130 single, FF180 double including breakfast. Dinner FF90 including wine. No credit cards accepted. Further information in English sent on request. Suitable for visitors without a car.

Le Buron de Moutissous

c/o Belvézin, Landeyrat, 15160 Allanche
Tel:71 20 48 39, Fax: 71 20 48 65

Self-catering mountain cottage

Buron is the local Auvergne word for a summer farm. There were many of these in the High Auvergne dating back 100 to 160 years when farmers from the

The architectural heritage of Auvergne

One of the numerous pilgrim routes from Rome to Santiago de Compostella in northern Spain traversed this region and was much used during the 10th, 11th and 12th centuries by pilgrims wishing to give thanks for France's release from Moorish occupation. Thus many Romanesque churches with their perfect semi-circular arches, magnificent west portals and heavy solid walls are to be found here.. They range from simple village churches such as Lavaudieu and Chauriat, to the very grand and ornate at La Bourboule, St-Nectaire and Issoire. Perhaps the most perfect lies in the old town of Clermont-Ferrand; the most spectacular is perched on top of a bizarre volcanic rock needle at Le Puy – St-Michael-l'Aiguille.. The cathedral in Le Puy itself was one of the great pilgrimage churches of France during the Middle Ages.

Also of interest in this area are ancient stone crosses which were used to mark the route for later travellers, and the remains of buildings and castles used by the Knights Templars whose task it was to protect the routes used by pilgrims.

The many imposing Auvergnate castles bear witness to the 40 years of occupation during the Hundred Years' War. Even after the English had left there existed an enormous problem caused by brigands and former mercenary soldiers who terrorised the countryside, holding entire villages to ransom for food and money. As a result communities were given permission to construct protective ramparts around their villages. There are several of these fortified villages in Haute Auvergne:.The most picturesque is at Salers which took its name from a local breed of cattle (and which, incidentally, is the breed from which the basic prairie cattle in the USA have been developed).

Auvergne cheese

The Auvergne with its lush green upland meadows has long been famed for cheese-making. Many areas have the right to label their cheeses Appellation d'Origine contrôlée (AOC) as do wine producers, eg. Cantal (named after the département – an uncooked pressed cheese rather like Cheddar), Saint-Nectaire (a creamy cheese with a delicate nutty flavour), Bleu d'Auvergne and Fourme d'Ambert (both blue cheeses). Cheese-making methods are demonstrated at La Maison des Fromages d'Auvergne, Egliseneuve d'Entraigues in the Département of Puy-de-Dôme (63) which is situated west of Bort-les-Orgues on D978. Cheeses are also on sale together with local Auvergne wines. Open every day from June 15 to September 30. Tel: 73 71 93 69.

lowland valleys used to bring their milking cows up to the mountains for the rich summer grazing. The family stayed with their dairy herd for four months, using the milk to produce the traditional large Cantal cheeses. These were allowed to mature in the *buron* and were ready for sale when the family returned to their home base in the autumn. With modern farming methods, the summer farms are no longer required and, sadly, many are falling into disrepair. This particular *buron*, however, now belongs to an English family who have lovingly restored it as a holiday home.

Constructed of local basalt rock with walls a metre thick, it is built into natural rock at the summit of a low hill. It has ash trees along the windward side and is open to the south to take advantage of the summer sun. The very simple accommodation is on two levels: the upper contains a large bed/sitting room and shower/WC. Internal steps lead down to the lower level which is a spacious sitting room/dining/kitchen with an open fireplace. The *buron* is reached via a rough track across two fields and for most of the year is negotiable by cars with care. Services in the house include mains water which comes directly from a mountain stream and is not chlorinated or treated in any way but is regularly tested for purity; bottled gas for water heating and cooking. There is no electricity and lighting is provided by gas lamps and candles. The buron offers a rare opportunity to those seeking the simple (but comfortable) life among stunning scenery in this totally unspoilt area of France. The owners use their holiday home only a few weeks each year and in their absence it is looked after by Rex and Helen Barr (see Belvézin) who live nearby and are on hand to welcome visitors and assist with any problems.

Situated120km/74 miles south of Clermont-Ferrand and 10km./6 miles north-west of Allanche. Nearest international airport: Lyon at 300km/180 miles. Nearest national airport: Clermont-Ferrand. Nearest station: Neussargues.

Additional information:

Open May-October. Sleeps 2 to 4 people. Price FF1,000-FF1,300 which includes gas for cooking, water heating and lighting, candles and firewood. Bed linen and towels can be provided on request. All booking arrangements and further information are handled by the Barrs at Belvézin.

Château de Trancis

15210 Ydes
Tel: 71 40 60 40, Fax: 71 40 62 13

Château Chambres d'Hôtes/Bed & Breakfast

Château de Trancis is the epitome of a fairytale castle. Built in the graceful and elegant Renaissance style, it stands majestically in beautiful secluded gardens and parkland at the 'gateway' to the Regional Volcanic Park and close to the spectacular gorges of the River Dordogne. The castle is owned by Innes and Fiona Fennel, English travel writers with a wide knowledge of France and a particular interest in this region. Since taking over the property in 1989, they have carried out a total renovation and now offer sophisticated

accommodation of a very high standard. Bedrooms have been tastefully restored and decorated to provide comfort and luxury. In addition there are three *salons* for the use of house guests. The main reception rooms open onto a spacious balustraded terrace from which a stunning curved stone staircase leads down to the swimming pool with extensive views over the surrounding countryside. In the evening guests are invited to enjoy the gastronomic delights prepared for them by their hosts and served

Auvergne Regional Volcanic Park

The Parc des Volcans stretches 120km/74 miles from north to south and covers 393,000 hectares/900,000 acres of two départements – Cantal (15) and Puy-de-Dôme (63). It encompasses two extinct volcanic areas – Monts du Cantal and Monts Dore – plus the basaltic plateau of the Cézallier in between and is part of France's high central plateau known as the Massif Central. It is the most important volcanic site in Europe but happily has been inactive for 5,000 years. The most southerly area, the Monts du Cantal, was formed by a massive crater 8km/5 miles in diameter with 50 'chimneys' all pumping explosive lava. There were 26 lava flows which, after glacial activity, formed 26 valleys which radiate from the centre. Today the highest point is around 1,860 metres/5,500 feet. Just to the north of the Monts du Cantal lies the plateau of Cézallier, also originally volcanic but formed by an emission of 'oozing treacle' leaving 300 metre/900 feet deep finger-like valleys on the edge of the plateau. Further north again the Monts Dore were formed by a much younger volcanic eruption and here are found perfect crater lakes and the shells of unexploded cones.

The entire area is magnificent for walking, offering a wide range from easy rambles to demanding climbs and is also rich in flora and fauna. Tourist information is widely available on site. Main centres of information are at Aydat (63) Tel: 73 65 67 19 and Aurillac (15) Tel: 71 48 68 68.

in the gracious dining room. Château de Trancis is conveniently placed for discovering the many fascinating castles and churches of the region. There are golf and riding facilities nearby and the Fennels can also arrange excellent fishing for their guests.

Situated 90km/54 miles south of Clermont-Ferrand, 80km/48 miles north of Aurillac and 1.5km/1/2 mile west of the village of Saignes. Nearest international airport: Lyon at 250km/155 miles. Nearest national airport: Clermont-Ferrand. Nearest station: Saignes.

Additional information:

Open April to September. 7 bedrooms all with private bath/WC; telephone; TV; hairdryer; minibar; tea and coffee making facilities. Price FF500-FF700 double including breakfast. Dinner FF200. Swimming pool. Eurocard and Visa. Colour brochure in English sent on request. Suitable for visitors without a car.

Le Pré Bossu
43150 Moudeyres
Tel: 71 05 10 70, Fax: 71 05 10 21
Restaurant with rooms

Moudeyres is a tiny remote village of great charm set high in the unspoilt peaks of the Massif Central. The cluster of solid stone cottages and farm buildings have been well-maintained and are either thatched or tiled in natural slate. Le Pré Bossu is one such restored farmhouse retaining all its authentic rustic simplicity... but with one important difference. The cooking

of its Flemish owner has earned the restaurant a Michelin rosette. Add to Monsieur Grootaert's culinary skills Madame's immaculate house-keeping and friendly welcome, and Le Pré Bossu is an unusual hotel that is well worth a detour. Country lovers will be captivated by the spectacular wild surroundings and Madame Grootaert has full details of local walks, excellent trout fishing and pony trekking. Mountain bikes are also available and packed lunches can be provided. The Grootaerts speak English.

Situated 160km/100 miles south-west of Lyon and 25km/.15 miles south-east of Le Puy-en-Velay. From Le Puy take D15 and D36 to Moudeyres. Nearest international airport: Lyon. Nearest national airport: St-Etienne at 90km/56 miles. Nearest station: Le Put-en-Velay.

Additional information:

Open March to early November. 10 bedrooms all with private shower or bath/WC; telephone. Price Ff310-FF380 single or double. Half board FF430-FF570 depending on menu. Breakfast FF50. Lunch and dinner FF165-FF360 or a la carte (closed for lunch on weekdays). Amex, Diners, Eurocard and Visa. Further information in English sent on request.

BOURGOGNE
BURGUNDY

*Bourgogne/Burgundy
comprises the following
départements:
    Côte-d'Or (21)
    Saône-et Loire (71)
    Yonne (89)
    Nièvre (58)*

O Tonnerre
*LA FONTAINE
AUX MUSES*

**89
YONNE**

Auxerre

LES
ORTIES
Tonnerre

*HOSTELLERIE
DES CLOS*

LE CASTEL
Mailly-le-Chateau

Avallon

Vézelay

**21
CÔTE-D'OR**

O Cosne-sur-Loire

LA RÊVERIE
Pouilly-sur-Loire

**58
NIÈVRE**

HOSTELLERIE DU VIEUX MOULIN

HÔTEL LE MANASSÈS

Dijon

*LA VIEILLE
AUBERGE*

Nuits–St. Georges

Cosne-sur-Loire

Beaune
*HOTEL
LE PARC*

Chagny
HÔTELLERIE DU VAL D'OR

Le Cruesot

Chalon-sur-
Saone

HÔTEL DE LA HALLE

Montceau
-les-Mines
**71
SAÔNE-ET-LOIRE**

Buxy
*LE CHÂTEAU
A SASSANGY*

LA ROSERAIE

Mâcon

LES RÉCOLLETS
Marcigny

*B*URGUNDY IS A WONDERFULLY RICH REGION *in many senses. As one of the great historic power bases of both France and Europe, the Dukes of Burgundy were renowned for their dazzling wealth and liking for ostentatious display. The lush rolling Burgundian countryside is among the most fertile in France, producing a plentitude of fine food and some of the world's most sought-after wines. The region is also a treasure-house of architectural and artistic gems — monasteries, castles, splendid cities, unspoilt villages and delightful bustling towns. The area possesses a remarkable network of navigable waterways extending over hundreds of kilometres and, in contrast, toward the east the densely-wooded mountains of the Jura — a land of upland lakes and rushing ricers — has a very different sort of appeal. The traditional hospitality of the local people is well-known, as is their deep love and appreciation of great food and wine. For the gourmet traveller therefore, Burgundy will prove to be a seductive culinary wonderland.*

Hôtel Le Manassés

Curtil-Vergy, 21220 Gevrey-Chambertin
Tel 80 61 43 81,
Fax 80 61 42 79

Private hotel

Your host at Hôtel Le Manassés is Monsieur Chaley, a *vigneron* who continues to produce fine Burgundy wines although the family have recently converted their farmhouse into a small and very comfortable hotel. Placed in the centre of the *Côtes de Nuits* and equidistant from the famous Burgundy wine villages of Gevrey-Chambertin and Nuits-St-Georges, Le Manassés is a wine-lover's dream come true. Guests are invited to sample the best of the wines from Monsieur Chaley's cellars and to visit his small wine museum. There is no restaurant at the hotel but a wide selection of dining venues are close by, offering the finest Burgundian cooking. The Chaley family speak English.

Situated 22km/13 miles south-west of Dijon and 7km/4 miles north-west of Nuits-St-Georges via D25 and D35. Nearest international airport: Geneva and Lyon at 200km/120 miles. Nearest national airport: Dijon. Nearest station: Nuits-St-Georges.

Additional information:

Open all year. 7 bedrooms all with private bath/WC; telephone; TV; minibar. Price Ff350 single or double. Breakfast FF50. All major credit cards accepted except Amex. Brochure in French and English sent on request.

La Vieille Auberge
Epernay-sur-Gevrey,
21220 Gevrey-Chambertin
Tel and fax 80 36 61 76

Chambres d'Hôtes/Bed & Breakfast

Ideally placed for wine-lovers at the heart of the famed Burgundy vineyards, this old *auberge* is about 300 years old. It had however been unused since the early 1960s until it was bought in 1989 by a young English couple, Jules and Jane Plimmer. They have totally renovated the building to provide five bedrooms including a family room, a billiards room and a large south-facing dining room which opens onto a pleasant garden. Both Jules and Jane used to work on French hotel barges before embarking on this new venture. Jules continues as a barge captain during the summer months. Jane, who was head chef for a large barge company, now looks after the *auberge* and provides evening meals for her guests. Understandably the standard of cooking is very good indeed with a lot of the fruit and vegetables being home-grown. Bicycles are available and this is a region that is popular for hot-air ballooning. Jules can arrange flights for anyone who is interested.

Situated 12km/8 miles south of Dijon. Nearest international airports: Geneva at 200km/120 miles and Lyon at 180km;/110 miles. Nearest station (TGV): Dijon.

Additional information:

Openall year. 5 bedrooms three of which have private bathrooms, two with a shared bathroom. Price Ff300-FF350 per night for a double room including breakfast. Dinner Ff95. Information in English sent on request. NB. A three-bedroom self-catering cottage will be ready for 1993.

Hostellerie du Vieux Moulin
21420 Bouilland
Tel 80 21 51 16, Fax 80 21 59 90

Restaurant with rooms

Hidden deep in the Burgundy countryside on the Route des Grands Crus de Bourgogne, Le Vieux Moulin is an attractive stone-built house featuring an interesing galleried granary. From the outside all is rustic charm,but the superb cooking of Jean-Pierre Silva is far from simple. With two Michelin rosettes, this is one of the finest restaurants in the region. The elegant dining room is surprisingly modern with striking black and white furnishings, and vast windows overlooking woods and gardens. Bedrooms are in a separate building and are tastefully furnished in traditional style. Guests can be sure of a warm welcome from Madame Isabelle Silva who speaks English. Le Vieux Moulin makes an extremely pleasant and peaceful stop-over for food and wine lovers.

Situated 46km/28 miles south-west of Dijon and 17km/10 miles north-west of Beaune via D2. Nearest international airport: Paris at 300km/180 miles. Nearest national airport: Dijon. Nearest station: Beaune.

Additional information:

Open all year except January 4 - 28. 24 bedrooms all with private shower or bath/WC. Price FF380 single, FF500-FF800 double. Breakfast FF70. Lunch and dinner FF190-FF450 or a la carte (restaurant closed all day Wednesday and Thursday lunch). Heated and covered swimming pool. Tennis court. Billiarn room. Eurocard, Mastercard and Visa. Full colour brochure in French and English sent on request.

Hôtel Le Parc
Levernois, 21200 Beaune
Tel 80 22 22 51

Hotel **

Le Parc has the best of both worlds — within a few minutes' drive of the Burgundy wine-centre town of Beaune, yet placed on the edge of the small village of Levernois. The rooms are divided between two attractive ivy-clad buildings which open onto a pretty courtyard with views of the park and stately old chestnut trees beyond. Bedrooms are light and spacious, each with its own personality. No restaurant but there is a choice of eating places in the village including a Michelin two-rosette restaurant next door. For golfers, Golf de Beaune-Levernois is at 200 metres/yards. The owner, Madame Oudot, speaks a little English. This is a charming and popular small hotel and advance booking is advisable.

Situated 4km/2.5 miles south-east of Beaune via D970. Nearest international airport: Lyon at 130km/80 miles. Nearest national airport: Dijon at 45km/27 miles. Nearest station: Beaune.

Additional information:

Open all year except the first two weeks in March and mid-November to mid-December. 26 bedrooms most with private shower or bath/WC; telephone. Price FF150-FF400 single or double. Breakfast FF32. Carte Bleue, Eurocard and Mastercard. Further information sent on request.

Hôtel de la Halle
Place de la Halle, 71640 Givrey-en-Bourgogne
Tel 85 44 32 45

Hotel with restaurant

Givrey is a small town in the heart of the Burgundy vineyards and on the Route des Vins de Beaune. Right in the centre next to the fascinating Halle Ronde (round market hall) is Hôtel de la Halle — a very traditional small French family-run hotel offering comfortable accommodation, good food and a friendly atmosphere

47

at most affordable prices. Le patron, Christian Renard, in his younger days was a chef on the transatlantic passenger liners and speaks a little English. The Renards have been in Givrey for 31 years and know the area well. They have information on walking, cycling and driving tours around the surrounding countryside and, of course, details of the local wines. Hôtel de la Halle makes an excellent inexpensive base for exploring this area of Burgundy.

Situated 65km/39 miles north of Mâcon on D981. Nearest international airport: Lyon at 130km/80 miles. Nearest national airport: Dijon at 73km/43 miles. Nearest station: Givrey or Le Creusot (TGV) at 37km/22 miles.

Additional information:

Open all year except November 15-30. 10 bedrooms most with private shower or bath/WC; telephone. Price FF175-FF195 single or double. Breakfast FF25. Lunch or dinner FF50-FF200 (restaurant closed Sunday evening and all day Monday). All major credit cards accepted. Colour brochure in French and English sent on request. Suitable for visitors without a car.

Château du Sassangy
Sassangy, 71390 Buxy
Tel 85 96 12 40, Fax 85 96 11 44

Château/Vineyard chambres d'hôtes/Bed & Breakfast

This classic Burgundian *château* is both a working farm raising the renowned Charolais beef cattle and a

Barge-hotel holidays in Burgundy

The rivers and canals of Burgundy are remarkable for their scenic beauty and have changed little over the last 200 years. Here life moves at a leisurely pace, far away from the hustle and bustle of the 20th century ... and what better way to explore this unspoilt area than by barge-hotel?

The 'Luciole' was designed and built under the direction of John Liley, an English waterway specialist and author of several books. He conceived the 'Luciole' as a purpose-built craft for the inland waterways of Burgundy, offering a very high standard of guest accommodation. At just over 30 metres/100 ft overall, she is the maximum possible size for certain locks and her cabin profile permits her to pass under all bridges on the itinerary while giving normal headroom in the saloon. Accommodation has been carefully planned to provide six double or twin-bedded cabins and two with single berths. Beds are all full length and each cabin has private shower/WC. On board the 'Luciole', the ratio of crew (all English-speaking) is high and great emphasis is placed on the quality of both food and wine.

Two main cruising routes are available: The Nivernais Route along the Canal du Nivernais which passes through vineyards, cherry orchards, ancient

villages and attractive market towns; and the Canal de Bourgogne Route which sweeps through the Burgundian hills passing by the Château de Tanlay (one of the most impressive in France) and the Abbey of Fontenay, founded by St Bernard at the beginning of the 12th century and remarkably preserved.

The weekly cruises begin on Wednesdays from mid-April to mid-October. Guests assemble at a selected hotel in central Paris for a rendezvous with a crew members who escorts the party by TGV (high speed train) to Montbard (80km/48 miles north-west of Dijon), The 'Luciole's' bus then links up with the barge..

Prices are approximately FF13,000 perperson per week which includes six nights accommodation, all meals and wines served on board, local excursions using the barge's mini-bus, transfers between Paris and the barge. Bicycles are kept on board for the use of guests. Group charter rates are also available on request.

For further information please contact:
Inland Voyages Ltd
23 Adlington Road
Bollington, Macclesfield
Cheshire SK10 5JT
UK
Tel/Fax: (0) 625 576880

vineyard producing quality red and white wines. The house is set in its own extensive park and the good-sized bedrooms are furnished with antiques offering every comfort. A lounge and library are at the disposition of house guests and an evening meal using farm produce and wine from the estate is available on request. The owner, Monsieur Marceau, speaks perfect English and he and his wife will be happy to help their guests discover the many places of interest in the vicinity together with the best restaurants.

Situated 80km/48 miles south-west of Dijon and 7km/4 miles west of the village of Buxy via D977. Nearest international airport: Lyon at 140km/86 miles. Nearest national airport: Mâcon at 60km/36 miles. Nearest station: Le Creusot (TGV) at 15km/9 miles.

Additional information:

Open April to October. 6 bedrooms all with private bath/WC; telephone. Price FF350-FF500 single, FF450-FF600 double including breakfast. Dinner FF80-FF120. Mastercard and Visa. Colour brochure in French and English sent on request.

Hôtellerie du Val d'Or
Grande-Rue, 71640 Mercurey-en-Bourgogne
Tel 85 45 13 70, Fax 85 45 18 45

Restaurant with rooms

Without doubt the Val d'Or's main claim to fame is the cooking of its owner Jean-Claude Cogny. His restaurant has been awarded a Michelin rosette and offers first-class French cuisine and wines at prices that are very reasonable for the quality. The hotel is situated in the centre of Mercurey on one of the region's premier wine routes. The bedrooms are comfortable and restfully decorated in pastel tones. English is spoken.

Situated 72km/44 miles north of Mâcon and 13km/7 miles west of Chalon-sur-Saône. Nearest international airport: Lyon at 140km/86 miles. Nearest national airport: Dijon at 60km/36 miles. Nearest station: Chagney at 11km/6 miles or Le Creusot (TGV) at 30km/18 miles.

Additional information:

Open all year except one week mid-May, one week early September and mid-December to mid-January. 13 bedrooms all with private shower or bath/WC; telephone; TV. Price FF300-FF380 single or double. Breakfast FF45. Lunch and dinner FF150-FF360 or a la carte (closed all day Monday and Tuesday lunch). Carte Bleue, Eurocard, Mastercard and Visa. Colour brochure in French and English sent on request.

Les Récollets
Place du Champ-de-Foire, 71110 Marcigny
Tel 85 25 03 34/85 25 05 16, Fax 85 25 06 91

Chambres d'Hôtes/Bed & Breakfast

The attractive stone village of Marcigny is in the region known as the Brionnais — an area well-known for fine food and warm hospitality. In the centre of the village yet overlooking pleasant countryside, Les Récollets is an imposing 18th century house that was originally a convent. The accommodation is extremely comfortable and tastefully decorated with many

Tasting and buying Burgundy wines

The opportunities for sampling and buying local wines in Burgundy are almost overwhelming. From the prestigious headquarters of the internationally famous wine merchants to the impressive châteaux of important producers to village cooperatives, the choice of places in which to enjoy a dégustation or tasting are endless. Serious wine enthusiasts will no doubt have very clear ideas of exactly where they go and who they see; but for visitors who may not be so well-informed, here is a selection of a few caves where English is spoken and/or where clients are welcome to taste a variety of wines with no obligation to purchase. In some establishments, an entrance fee covers the cost of dégustation; in others snacks are available to accompany the wine. If you wish to buy wines after tasting, there is no need to purchase a complete case. It is perfectly acceptable to take just one or two bottles. Most merchants will also arrange to have orders sent abroad.

Marché aux Vins
**Rue Nicholas-Rolin
21200 Beaune
Tel: 80 22 27 69**
Open daily 9.30-1200; 14.30-18.30. From November to March, on Sundays and public holidays closes at 16.00.
The city of Beaune is the 'capital' of Burgundy wines and the marché is a permanent display of the best the region has to offer at all levels. It is the perfect place to obtain an introduction into the

local wines. Up to 40 wines are available
to taste ... so beware! Entrance fee.

La Grande Cave
21640 Vougeot
Tel: 80 61 11 23
Open daily 9.00-12.00, 14.00-18.00.
In the same village as the famous
Château Clos-de-Vougeot set in its own
walled vineyard (open daily 9.00-12.00;
14.00-18.00). Full range of wines available
for tasting.

Château de Corton André
21920 Aloxe-Corton
Tel: 80 26 44 25
Open daily 9.30-18.00.
A fine château in one of the most famous
Burgundy wine villages. It has the
additional advantages of being open
non-stop all day ... even over lunchtime!

Château de Meursault
21190 Meursault
Tel: 80 21 22 98
Open daily 9.30-11.30; 14.30-18.00
The château and the cellars, where
thousands of bottles and barrels of wine
lie aging, are open to the public.
Entramce fee for *dégustation*.

Caveau Municipal de Chassagne-Montrachet
21190 Meursault
Tel: 80 21 38 13
Open 10.30-12.30; 14.00-19.30.
A friendly cooperative of 23 local
vignerons offering a full range of
excellent wines. Wines for tasting or sold
to be drunk as an *apéritif* with a piece of
gougère (Burgundian cheese pastry). No
English spoken but very informal.

Caveau St-Pierre
71260 Lugny
Tel: 85 33 20 27
Open daily except Wed 9.00-21.00
March-October
An interesting *caveau* with a pleasant
traditional house where snacks are
served to accompany the local wines,
which are available for tasting, for
drinking on site or to purchase. There is
also an excellent inexpensive restaurant
serving regional specialities.

Caveau Union des Producteurs de Pouilly-Fuissé
71960 Solutré
Tel: 85 37 80 06
Open daily 9.00-12.00; 14.00-19.00.
Of interest to all white wine lovers, this
friendly cooperative specialises in the
superlative Pouilly-Fuissé, which is
available for tasting and sale.

La Chablisienne
8 boulevard Pasteur, 89800 Chablis
Tel: 86 42 11 24
Open Mon-Sat 8.00-12.00; 14.00-18.00.
An important cooperative of 250
vignerons. The famous white Chablis
wine is produced in a very moden winery
incorporating the most up-to-date
technology. Wines for tasting and
purchase. English spoken.

51

antiques. Meals are served in a delightful dining room dominated by striking hand-painted cupboards. Each bedroom is quite individual with views over the extensive garden. Madame Badin is a most attentive hostess and speaks English.

Situated 83km/50 miles west of Mâcon and 30km/18 miles north of Roanne via D482. Nearest international airport: Lyon at 120km/74 miles. Nearest station: Marcigny.

Additional information:

Open all year. 9 bedrooms all with private bath/WC. Price FF300 single, FF400 double including breakfast. Dinner FF200 including wine. No credit cards accepted. Further information in French and English sent on request. Suitable for visitors without a car.

Les Orties

3 rue Edme Jobert, 89700 Saint-Martin-sur-Armançon
Tel 86 75 78 98, Fax 86 75 81 08

Self-catering village farmhouse cottages

Les Orties is an old Burgundian farmhouse set in a typical rural village. The main house and out-buiildings have been cleverly restored and converted to provide three holiday units, each with its own distinctive charm and character but sharing a small swimming pool, parking area, games room and garden, all contained within the original high stone walls. Each unit retains many interesting architectural features and has a private patio area. Les Orties is English-owned and the resident key-holder speaks English.

Situated 45km/28 miles east of Auxerre and 9km/5 miles east of Tonnerre via D954. Nearest airport: Paris at 200km/120 miles. Nearest station: Tonnerre.

Additional information:

Open all year. The Farmhouse — 3 double bedrooms; oak-beamed lounge/diner with large open fireplace and tradtional open-hearth with cooking implements; kitchen; shower/WC. Sleeps 6/7. Price FF1,700 FF2,100 per week. The Granary large lounge/diner with open fireplace/kitchen and mezzanine; double bedroom; bath/shower/WC. Sleeps 2/4. Price FF1,500-FF2,000 per week. The Old Dairy — double bedroom; large lounge with open plan kitchen; shower WC. Sleeps 2/4. Price FF1,300-FF1,800 per week. Prices include gas and electricity, Bed linen can be supplied at an extra charge on request. No credit cards accepted. Colour brochure in English sent on request.

La Rêverie

6 rue Joyeuse, 58150 Pouilly-sur-Loire
Tel 86 39 07 87

Chambres d'Hôtes/Bed & Breakfast

The abbey at Vézelay is one of the most stunning, most-admired and most-loved Romanesque churches in France. Built during the 12th century, it is a great masterpiece of mediæval French art. The hilltop village too is beautifully preserved with original ramparts, town gates and fine views over the surrounding countryside. Vézelay is situated in the département of Yonne (89) east of Avallon. It inevitably attracts many visitors but is well worth a visit.

Although the eastern areas of the *département* of Nièvre (58) are undoubtedly in the heart of Burgundy, the western extremities merge into the Loire Valley and the hills of the Sancerrois. This is certainly vineyard country but the wines produced here are not Burgundy wines but the most delicate and prestigious of the Loire wines — Sancerre and Pouilly-Fumé. Pouilly-sur-Loire is the village around which the latter of these two superb white wines is made and is, of course, the best place in which to taste and buy. La Rêverie, in the centre of the village, is the home of Monsieur and Madame Lapeyrade and offers five bedrooms, each decorated with great flair using fine fabrics and authentic antiques. The oak-beamed breakfast room doubles as an art gallery and the walls are adorned with a selection of paintings. Madame Lapeyrade speaks English and guests can be sure of a warm welcome. An evening meal is not provided but there is a choice of excellent restaurants in the village.

Situated 200km/120 miles south-east of Paris, 100km/62 miles west of Auxerre and 15km/4.5 miles south of Cosne-sur-Loire via N7. Nearest international airport: Paris. Nearest national airport: Bourges at 60km/36 miles. Nearest station: Pouilly-sur-Loire.

Additional information:

Open April to mid-November or other times on request. 5 bedrooms all with private bath/WC and one with Jaccuzi; telephone; TV. Price FF250-FF420 single or double. Breakfast FF35. No credit cards accepted. Further information in French and English plus colour photos sent on request. Suitable for visitors without a car.

Le Castel
Place de l'Eglise, 89590 Mailly-le-Château
Tel 86 81 43 06, Fax 86 81 49 26

Hotel ** with restaurant

Nicely placed next to the church in a small village, this welcoming small hotel is surrounded by gardens and shaded by lime trees. Rooms are comfortably furnished and the popular restaurant offers good regional cooking at very reasonable prices. In the summer meals are served on a pleasant garden terrace. English is spoken.

Situated200km/120 miles south-east of Paris and 30km/18 miles south of Auxerre. Nearest international airport: Paris. Nearest station: Mailly-le-Château.

Additional information:

Openmid-March to mid-November. 12 bedrooms all with private shower or bath/WC; telephone. Price FF200-FF300 single or double. Breakfast FF35. Lunch or dinner FF75-FF170. Eurocard and Visa. Colour brochure in French and English sent on request. Suitable for visitors without a car.

La Roseraie
71220 La Guiche
Tel 85 24 67 82, Fax 85 24 61 03

Chambres d'Hôtes/Bed & Breakfast

La Roseraie is an imposing house of great character built in the 18th century with parts dating back to the 16th century. Set in the heart of the lovely rolling hills of southern Burgundy and the vineyards of the Chalonais — famous for white wines — this is home to a friendly and welcoming English couple, John and Roz Binns. They offer homely accommodation in rooms that are very comfortably and tastefully furnished with antiques. There is a large lounge for guests and an outside terrace for sunbathing. Roz is an excellent cook and evening meals are served around the long communal dining room table. La Roseraie makes a convenient centre for exploring this interesting region and the Binns have lots of tourist information at the disposal of their guests. In addition there are facilities for golf, tennis, fishing and riding nearby.

Situated 40km/24 miles north-west of Mâcon and 25km/15 miles south-east of Montceau-les-Mines. Nearest international airport: Lyon or Geneva at 200km/120 miles. Nearest national airport: Mâzcon. Nearest station: Le Creusot (TGV) at 30km/18 miles.

Additional information:

Open all year. 7 bedrooms all with private shower or bath/WC. Price FF210-FF295 double including breakfast. Dinner FF120 on request. No credit cards accepted. Further information in English on request.

Hostellerie des Clos
rue Jules-Rathier, 89800 Chablis
Tel 86 42 10 63, Fax 86 42 17 11

Restaurant with rooms

You will find this old *hostellerie* in the centre of the small town of Chablis surrounded by the vineyards that produce the most famous of the Burgundy white wines. Once a *hospice* or almshouse, today it houses the restaurant of Michel Vignaud whose inspired cooking has earned him a Michelin rosette. Understandably his dishes are created to complement the local wines and a hallmark of his cuisine is the way in which he brings a lightness and freshness to traditional recipes. This modern approach is echoed in the decor of both the restaurant and the bedrooms which are bright and airy featuring restful pastel tones. Restaurant prices are very reasonable for this quality of cooking and rates for the smaller bedrooms will not break the bank. Hostellerie des Clos provides a perfect gourmet stop-over or is ideal as a base from which to discover the numerous historic sites of northern Burgundy. English is spoken.

Situated 182km/112 miles south-east of Paris and 20km/12 miles east of Auxerre. Nearest international airport: Paris. Nearest station Tonnerre (TGV) at 16km/10 miles or Auxerre.

Additional information:

Open all year except mid-December to mid-January. 26 bedrooms all with private shower or bath/WC; telephone; TV. Price FF230-FF485 single, FF258-FF520 double. Breakfast FF48. Lunch and dinner FF155-FF395 or a la carte (restaurant closed all day Wednesday and Thursday lunchtime). Amex, Eurocard and Visa. Full colour brochure inFrench and English sent on request.

La Fontaine aux Muses
89116 La Celle-Saint-Cyr
Tel 86 73 40 22, Fax 86 73 48 66
*Hotel ** with restaurant*

This interesting *auberge* is very much a family affair. Built during the 17th century and abandoned after the last war, it was bought and converted into a simple hotel in 1960 by Monsieur Claude Langevin — a musician and composer — and his wife who is a poet. They still run the hotel together with their son who is the chef ... and also a musician. Understandably music continues to play an important part in the life of La Fontaine aux Muses with live performances on week-end evenings either in the restaurant or, during the summer months, in the garden. Local artists exhibit their work at the hotel which in addition has a swimming pool, tennis court and 6-hole golf course. Set in superb rolling countryside close to the famous Chablis vineyards and convenient for the many places of interest in northern Burgundy, this unusual and very friendly hotel makes an ideal base. A little English is spoken.

Situated 150km/93 miles south-east of Paris, 36km/22 miles north-west of Auxerre and 7km/4 miles west of Joigny via D943 and then D194. Nearest international airport: Paris. Nearest station: Joigny.

Additional information:

Open all year. 14 bedrooms all with private shower or bath/WC; telephone. Price FF360 single or double. Breakfast FF32. Lunch and dinner FF175 or a la carte (closed all day Monday and Tuesday lunch). Swimming pool. Tennis court. Golf. Carte Bleue and Visa. Colour brochure in French and English sent on request.

LA KORRIGANE
MANOIR DE BLANCHE ROCHE
LA MALOUINIÈRE
DES LONGCHAMPS

St Malo

Dinan
LE PRESBYTÈRE

Rennes

35

ILLE-ET-VILAINE

LE MONTREL

Loudeac

PENNEREST

56

MORBIHAN

St-Brieuc

22

CÔTES-DU-NORD

Pontivy

KERLEVEHEN GUEST HOUSE

FELEHAN

HOSTELLERIE LES AJONCS D'OR

Guingamp

CHÂTEAU-HOTEL DE BRÉLIDY

HOTEL DE L'ERMITAGE

Carnac

Lorient

RELAIS DE PORS-MORVAN

Quimperlé

29

FINISTERE

KEROLLIVER

KERLOAI

Quimper

HOTEL
KERANSOUER

Brest

Douarnenez

**BRETAGNE
BRITTANY**

Bretagne/Brittany
comprises the following
départements:
   Côtes-du-Nord (22)
   Finistère (29)
   Ille-et-Vilaine (35)
   Morbihan (56)

*B*RITTANY HAS THE REPUTATION OF BEING *a strange , remote , mysterious , magical land with traditions and a culture quite unlike the rest of France. An important centre of activity in prehistoric times, the region was colonised by missionary monks from the Celtic west coast of Britain during the 6th and 7th centuries. The Breton language today is more akin to Welsh than French; the unique religious procession* (**pardons**) *and distinctive churchyards* (closes) *of Brittany are further visible proof of the Celtic past.*

With 1,760 kilometres of coastline — one-third of the total coastline of France — the Bretons have always been seafarers. Quaint fishing villages with quayside restaurants serving the freshest of local Atlantic fish are a popular tourist attraction. The tranquil inland sea of the Morbihan Gulf is perfect for pleasure boats; and Brittany's endless sandy beaches are without equal while the wild cliffs of Finistère are the most ruggedly beautiful inFrance.

Away from the sea, Brittany is a landscape of rolling farmland dotted with forests, rivers and lakes, ideal for walking, cycling and fishing.

Château-Hôtel de Brélidy

22140 Brélidy
Tel 96 95 69 38,
Fax 96 95 18 03

*Château-Hôtel *** with restaurant*

Château Brélidy is a carefully restored authentic Breton castle built in the 16th century on the site of an even older mediæval house,the ruins of which are still visible. Furnishings in the castle are appropriately baronial in style – ornate carved dark oak relieved by light floral tapestry upholstery. The dining room is pretty with tapestry covered chairs and lace table cloths. Set in extensive parkland, Brélidy is centrally placed for discovering the many abbeys and fine houses in the area but is also handy for the delightful fishing villages of the north Brittany coast. Your hostess, Madame Pémezec, is very welcoming and speaks good English.

Situated 47km/29 miles west of St-Brieuc and 14km/8 miles north of Guingamp. Nearest international

airport: Paris at 500km/360 miles. Nearest national airport: Rennes at 150km/100 miles or St-Brieuc. Nearest station: Guingamp.

Additional information:

Open Easter to October. 14 bedrooms all with private shower or bath/WC; telephone. Price FF290-FF610. Breakfast FF45. Dinner Ff165. Amex, Eurocard and Visa. Colour brochure inFrench and English sent on request

---

Le Presbytère
2 rue Quai de Talard, Port de Dinan,
22100 Dinan

Quayside self-catering apartments

Dinan is a most attractive old town and inland port on the River Rance 30km/18 miles south of the point where it meets the sea at St-Malo and Dinard. Beautifully sited, it is very lively with a maze of interesting cobbled streets, quaint mediæval houses, smart boutiques and good restaurants. Le Presbytère is well-placed beside the river and provides immaculately renovated accommodation of a high standard. Accommodation consists of six apartments on three floors. The units are of varying sizes accommodating from two to six people. Each unit has a full bathroom; kitchenette with washing machine and dryer; satellite TV. Furnishings are tastefully simple and modern. The apartments make an ideal base for exploring Brittany. They are within 20 minutes of the Côte Emeraude with miles of quiet golden beaches and excellent water sport facilities, and close to two splendid golf courses. For the convenience of clients, bookings may be made on a daily or weekly basis. Le Presbytère is British-owned and there is an English-speaking representative on site.

Situated 52km/32 miles north-west of Rennes. Nearest international airport: Paris at 400km/240 miles. Nearest national airport: Dinard at 12km/7 miles. Nearest station: St-Malo at 30km/18 miles.

Additional information:

Open all year. 6 apartments sleeping from 4-6 people. Price FF2,950-FF4,450 per week. Daily rates on request. Eurocard, Mastecard and Visa. Full colour brochure sent onrequest from the owner, Roy Stead, 8 Caledonia Place, St Helier, Jersey, UK. Tel (0) 534 33930. Bookings should also be made through the owner. Suitable for visitors without a car.

Le Montrel
Langast, 22150 Ploeuc-sur-Lie
Tel 96 26 84 67

Self-catering cottage

One of the dwellings in a small hamlet, Le Montrel is a traditional 18th century farmhouse which has recently been very tastefully restored, retaining many fascinating features. Providing comfortable accommodation for up to six people, the cottage has three bedrooms – one double and two twins – and a bathroom upstairs; a large living area with effective wood-burning stove and a well-equipped kitchen downstairs. The house and garage stand in an enclosed garden with lawns, patio, barbecue and garden furniture. Le Montrel is a few minutes' walk from the village of Langast which has a restaurant and all shopping facilities. For more extensive shopping the towns of Plouguenast and Plessala are within five minutes by car. The area is ideal for cycling, walking and fishing. Less than half an hour away are numerous uncrowded sandy beaches. The English owner, Patricia Richards, lives next door and will be pleased to help in any way. Baby-sitting and child-minding can be arranged for a small fee.

Situated 50km/31 miles south-west of dinan and 15km/9 miles north-east of the small town of Loudeac. Nearest international airport: Paris at 430km/267 miles. Nearest national airport: Dinard at 60km/37 miles. Nearest station: Loudeac at 15km/9 miles.

Additional information:

Open all year. Christmas by arrangement. 3 double bedrooms. Sleeps 6 people Price FF2,300 per week July/August/September; FF2,000 per week the rest of the year. Price includes all electricity, gas and logs. bed linen and towels can be supplied on request. Information in English sent on request.

Hôtel Ker-Ansquer
Lababan, 29710 Pouldreuzic
Tel 98 54 41 83

Country hotel *** with restaurant

A most attractive stone house built in the regional style and situated in quiet countryside close to the sea. The interior decoration is interesting and the furnishings have been specially made by local craftsmen, as has the china used in the restaurant where, not surprisingly, seafood is the
speciality. Prices are very reasonable and English is spoken.

Situated25km/15 miles west of Quimper, 17km south of Douarnenez and 3km/1.8 miles north-west of Pouldreuzic via D40. nearest international airport: Paris at 583km/355 miles. Nearest national airport: Quimper. Nearest station: Douarnenez.

Additional information:

Open Easter to the end of September.11 bedrooms all with private shower or bath/WC; telephone. Price FF280 single or double. Half board FF280 per person per day (3 days minimum). Breakfast FF30. Dinner Ff160-FF290. All major credit cards accepted. Further information sent on request.

Kerollivier
29180 Plogonnec
Tel 98 91 82 14

Chambres d'Hôtes/Bed & Breakfast

Kerollivier is a recently-restored farmhouse idyllically set in 3 hectares/8 acres of woodland and meadows with a private trout lake. The English owners, Paul and Muffet Visser, offer hospitality in bedrooms providing luxurious accommodation furnished with a mixture of antique furniture and fresh new pine. Rooms also have tea and coffee-making facilities. Muffet prepares substantial breakfasts for house guests. Evening meals are not available but the

fascinating old town of Locronan, with its handsome Renaissance houses, is only a few minutes away.

Although the traditional Breton costume with its distinctive tall coiffe *or headdress is becoming a rarity for all but special occasions, it can still be seen in the villages of the Bigouden area of Finistère, west of Quimper between Audierne and Pont l'Abbé..*

Situated 220km/136 miles west of Rennes and 10km/6 miles north-west of Quimper via D39. Nearest international airport: Paris at 570km/400 miles. Nearest national airport: Brest at 70km/42 miles or Quimper. Nearest station: Quimper.

Additional information:

Open March to October. 2 bedrooms with private shower or bath/WC, tea and coffee-making facilities. Price Ff200-FF230 including breakfast. No credit cards accepted. Further information in English and a photo sent on request.

La Korrigane
39 rue Le Pomellec, 35400 Saint-Malo
Tel 99 81 65 85, Fax 99 40 40 50

Town hotel ***

The Korrigane is one of those very special small hotels that manage to retain the intimate atmosphere of a private family house. Situated in the coastal suburb of St-Servan-sur-Mer, this

elegant 19th century mansion is within walking distance of the old walled town of Saint-Malo, from where Jacques Cartier set sail on his voyages of discovery to the New World. The bedrooms and public rooms are all beautifully and luxuriously decorated with period furnishings and antiques; everything has been arranged with immaculate taste. An attractive small garden at the rear of the house serves as a summer breakfast room and your charming hostess, Madame Le Bourhis, speaks English. Advance booking strongly advised.

Situated 70km/42 miles north-west of Rennes in the centre of Saint-Malo. Nearest international airport: Paris at 400km/240 miles. Nearest national airport: Dinard at 10km/6 miles. Nearest station:Saint-Malo.

Additional information:

Open mid-March to mid-November. 10 bedrooms all with shower or bath/WC; telephone; TV. Price FF350 single, FF400-FF600 double. Breakfast FF50. Limited parking. Amex, Carte Bleue and Diners. Colour brochure in French and English sent on request. Suitable for visitors without a car.

Relais de Pors-Morvan
29127 Plomodiern
Tel 98 81 53 23

Hotel *** with crêperie

This old farm dating from 1833 is situated in the far west of Brittany close to magnificent sandy beaches and in an area offering many tourist attractions. The *relais* benefits from a quiet rural position and is set in a well-maintained garden with tennis court. The accommodation is contained within an attractive range of long low farm buildings opening onto a central courtyard. Bedrooms are comfortable and simply furnished in rustic style. No true restaurant but there is an excellent *crêperie* attached to the hotel where the traditional *crêpe Bretonne* (Brittany pancake) is served. A friendly hotel where English is spoken.

Situated 200km/120 miles west of Rennes and 20km/12 miles north-east of Douarnenez via D107 and D63. Pors-Morvan is 3km/1.8 miles east of the village of Plomodiern. Nearest international airport: Paris at 550km/340 miles. Nearest national airport: Quimper at 35km/21 miles. Nearest station: Douarnenez.

Additional information:

Open March to October. 12 bedrooms with shower or bath/WC. Price FF270-FF290 single or double. Breakfast FF32. Tennis court. Carte Bleue and Visa. Colour brochure in French and English sent on request.

Hôtel de l'Ermitage

Route du Pouldu, 29130 Quimperlé
Tel 98 96 04 66, Fax 98 39 23 41

Country hotel *** with restaurant

The Ermitage consists of a group of five buildings just south of the pleasant town of Quimperlé at the edge of the Carnoët Forest. The main house is an old manor house –Manoir de Kerroch – standing in 5 hectares/2 acres of wooded parkland with a heated swimming pool. The bedrooms are divided between the various buildings, some of which are of more modern construction, Rooms are nicely furnished and many open onto a courtyard terrace. The restaurant serves traditional cuisine with speciality seafood dishes. Prices at the Ermitage are very reasonable for three-star comfort; it is conveniently placed for exploring this popular southwestern corner of Brittany and is only 8km/5 miles from the coast. Guests can expect a warm welcome from their young English-speaking hosts, Monsieur and Madame Ancelin.

Situated 162km/100 miles south-west of Rennes and 5km/3 miles south of Quimperlé via D49. Nearest international airport: Paris at 500km/300 miles. Nearest national airport: Lorient at 15km/9 miles. Nearest station: Quimperlé.

Additional information:

Open all year. 28 bedrooms all with private shower or bath/WC; telephone; TV. Price Ff320-FF380 single or double. Breakfast Ff30. Dinner FF100. Swimming pool. Amex, Eurocard and Visa. Colour brochure inFrench and English sent on request.

Kerloaï

29390 Scaer
Tel 98 59 42 60

Chambres d'Hôtes/Bed & Breakfast

Scaer is a friendly small town in western Brittany that is conveniently placed for exploring the southern Finistère coast. Just outside the town, Monsieur and Madame Penn receive guests in their charming white-washed Breton farmhouse with its traditional furnishings Bedrooms are very comfortable and

Prehistoric monuments in Brittany

The area around Carnac on the Morbihan Gulf (56) has a greater concentration of prehistoric stone monuments, or megaliths, than anywhere else in Europe.. Menhirs, dolmens and cromlechs from between 4,000 and 1,800 BC abound here and remain somthing of a mystery. What is their significance? What were they really for? And perhaps strangest of all, how were these massive rocks physically moved into their distinctive alignments and table-top structures?

For enthusiasts, the following are the most important sites in Brittany.

Carnac (56)

Just outside the lively holiday resort of Carnac, a staggering 3,000 menhirs have been placed in two main alignments 30 metres wide. which stretch more than a kilometre in length . These two lines – Menec and Kerlescan – lead up to a semi-circular apse-like ring of menhirs which are orientated towards the position of the sun and moon at the equinox and solstice..

Locmariaquer (56)

Outside this fishing village is the 'Witches' Stone' – an enormous rock which was originally more than 20 metres high and 350 tons in weight, raised on end. Now shattered, it lies broken into five pieces. At this site too, the Merchant's Table composed of three granite slabs resting on 17 stone supports; and a series of fine tumuli or burial chambers.

Tumulus de Gavrinis (56)

Carved burial chambers on an island in the Morbihan Gulf. Accessible by boat from Larmor-Baden.

Lagatjar (29)

On the south side of the Aunine estuary south of Brest near Camarat, an intersecting alignment of more than 100 stones.

Brignogan Plage (29)

The 'Miracle Stone' – a menhir in the form of a cross on the coast west of Roscoff.

Barnenez Tumulus (29)

East of Roscoff on the Morlaix estuary, a series of 11 connected burial chambers.

La Roche-aux-Fées (35)

The 'Fairies' Rock' – a covered gallery of slate stones situated near Marcillé-Robert, 35km south-east of Rennes.

Madame Penn provides a generous breakfast. No evening meal, but plenty of restaurants and *crêperies* nearby. The Penns speak English.

Situated 200km/124 miles west of Rennes, 30km/18 miles east of Quimper and 4km/2 miles west of Scaer. Nearest international airport: Paris at 500km/300 miles. Nearest national airport: Rennes or Quimper. Nearest station: Quimper or Rosporden at 14km/8 miles.

Additional information:

Open all year4 bedrooms all with shower/WC. Price Ff180 single, FF230 double including breakfast. No credit cards accepted.

Manoir de Blanche Rocher
35430 Saint-Jouan-des-Guérêts
Tel 99 82 47 47

Chambers d'Hôtes/Bed & Breakfast

This very striking 19th century house built in mellow brick is the home of Magali Mérienne, who speaks English and welcomes guests with typical Breton hospitality. Breakfast is the traditional meal of *crêpes* (pancakes), home-baked cakes and fresh fruit. Magali will also prepare an evening meal on request. At five minutes from St-Malo, this lovely manor house is ideal for exploring the north Brittany coast, including Mont-St-Michel.

Situated 65km/39 miles north-west of Rennes, 5km/3 miles south-east of St-Malo. Nearest

63

international airport: Paris at 400km/240 miles. Nearest national airport: Dinard at 10km/6 miles. Nearest station: St-Malo

Additional information:

Open all year. 5 bedrooms all with private bath/WC. Price FF280 single, FF300 double including breakfast. Dinner Ff80. No credit cards accepted. Colour brochure in French and English sent on request.

La Malouiniére des Longchamps
35430 Saint-Jouan-des-Guérêts
Tel 99 82 74 00, Fax 99 82 74 14

Hotel** with restaurant

La Malouiniére is a striking very long low stone building topped by a steep blue-tiled roof and attractive dormer windows along its entire length. Conveniently placed just outside the bustling sea-port of Saint-Malo on the wide estuary of the River Rance, it makes an agreeable base for exploring the northern Brittany coastline. The restaurant specialised in traditional family cooking and the owner, Madame Goger, is very welcoming. English is spoken.

Situated 5km/3 miles south of the centre of St-Malo on the right bank of the River Rance via N137. Nearest international airport: Paris at 400km/240 miles. Nearest national airport: Dinard at 10km/6 miles. Nearest station: Saint-Malo.

Additional information:

Open all year. 14 bedrooms all with shower/WC; telephone; TV. Price FF290-FF370 single and double. Breakfast FF30. Dinner FF130. Swimming pool. Tennis. Parking. Eurocard and Visa. Colour brochure in French and English sent on request. suitable for visitors without a car.

Kerlevehen Guest house
56480 Cleguerec
Tel 97 38 07 36

Chambres d'Hôtes/Bed & Breakfast and self-catering cottages

In 1989 an English couple, Dave and Anne Corfield, bought a small hamlet consisting of nine houses in Brittany. Restoration of some of the houses is now completed, offering attractive accommodation full of character with old exposed beams and original stone walls. Log fires and antique furniture help to create a cosy cottage atmosphere. Anne is an excellent cook and Dave has a well-stocked wine cellar so, whether guests are simply looking for a restful few days or a point from which to explore this lovely part of Brittany, Kerlevehen with its peapceful location and good food, is an ideal place. For walkers, the region has miles of well-defined pathways. For cyclists and fishermen, there are bikes and rods available on site. Golfers too will find Kerlelvehen interesting for the Corfields are also part-owners of a new 9-hole course nearby at Renaison. The Corfield's son manages the course and clubhouse, and the English-speaking pro comes from Jersey.

The self-catering cottage is also part of the hamlet complex and has two double bedrooms, lounge, kitchen/diner and shower/WC (sleeps 4). A further semi-detached cottage has a large open-plan bed/sitting room and sleeps 2. Guests in the cottages may have dinner if they wish.

Situated 130km/80 miles west of Rennes, 80km/50 miles south-west of St-Malo and 2km/1 miles from the village of Cleguerec. Nearest international airport: Paris at 450km/280 miles. Nearest national airport: Rennes. Nearest station: Auray at 20km/12 miles.

Additional information:

Open all year. 5 bedrooms, some with private shower or bath/WC. Price FF120-FF200 per person per night including breakfast. Dinner FF80 including a carafe of wine. The self-catering cottages are let weekly from Saturday to Saturday. Price FF1,500-FF3,000 depending on unit and season. Price includes all gas, electricity, heating, bed linen and towels. Further information in English sent on request.

Pennerest
56920 Noyal Ponticy
Tel 97 38 35 76

Self-catering cottages and Chambres d'Hôtes/Bed & Breakfast

A traditional 17th century Breton farmhouse, Pennerest has been completely renovated by an English couple, Pat and Peter Roberts, to provide a variety of

attractive accommodation set in 1 hectare/2.5 acres of lawns, gardens and orchard. The cottages and bedrooms are all very prettily furnished combining modern faciities with typical Breton character and charm. Five self-catering units have been created from the old barn and other out-buildings, each different but retaining many original features. The smallest is suitable for two people and the larger cottages can sleep up to five people. In the main house, the Roberts offer a double bedroom and a suite of two double rooms both with private bathrooms for Bed & Breakfast. Evening meals are not provided but your enthusiastic hosts can suggest numerous good restaurants nearby including some offering remarkable value for money.

Situated 100km/62 miles west of Rennes, 60km/36 miles south of St-Brieuc and 8km/5 miles south-east of

Pontivy via D764. Nearest international airport: Paris at 450km/270 miles. Nearest national airport: Rennes. Nearest station: Pontivy.

Additional information:

Open all year. Self-catering cottages — Price FF600-FF2,500 depending on unit and season. Price includes electricity and water. heating extra. Bed linen and towels supplied on request at an extra charge. Letting weekly Sunday to Sunday. Bed & Breakfast — 2 bedrooms with private shower/WC. Price FF100 per person per night including breakfast. No credit cards accepted. further information in English sent on request.

Felehan
St-Barthelemy, 56150 Baud
Self-catering country cottage

Felehan is a recently-converted traditional Breton cottage built of stone with a slate roof. It has all modern amenities yet retains its rustic charm. On the ground floor is a living room with beamed ceiling, kitchenette with washing machine, and a granite fireplace with wood-burning stove. Upstairs is a bedroom and bathroom. The cottage has a small garden with barbecue and is located in a tiny hamlet of only three houses, surrounded by open countryside and not far from the beautiful Blavet River. There are facilities nearby for golf, fishing, riding and canoeing. The area is rich in places of architectural and archælogical interest; to the south are the glorious beaches of the Gulf of Morbihan with watersports and numerous little islands that can be visited using the regular ferry services. The English owners live nearby and are on hand to assist in any way.

Situated 110km/70 miles west of Rennes, 20km/12 miles south-west of Pontifvy and 6km/3.5 miles from the village of Baud. Nearest international airport: Paris at 460km/277 miles. Nearest national airport: Rennes. Nearest station: Auray at 20km/12 miles.

Additional information:

Open all year. Sleeps 2/3. Price FF1,800-FF2,500 weekly (Saturday to Saturday) depending on season. Bed linen can be supplied at extra charge. No crdit cards accepted. Brochure in English and photo from Jill Newton, La Couarde, St-Nicholas-en-Bieuzy-les-Eaux, 56310 Bubry, Tel 97 51 82 15, Fax 97 27 91 88.

Hostellerie Les Ajoncs d'Or
Kerbachique, 56720 Plouharnel
Tel 97 52 32 02, Fax 97 52 32 04
Hotel ** with restaurant

Les Ajoncs d'Or is as pretty as a picture postcard – a Breton farmhouse consisting of a group of buildings built in mellow stone. Set amid a delightful country cottage garden at the edge of a small village, it is only 2km/1 miles from the seaside town of Carnac and within walking distance

of the famous prehistoric stone 'alignments'. Bedrooms are simple but comfortable; the restaurant is charmingly rustic serving regional specialities including plenty of seafood dishes. This is a traditional family-run hotel where visitors can be sure of a warm welcome and where English is spoken.

Situated 140km/74 miles south-west of Rennes, 35km/21 miles south-east of Lorient and 2km/1 miles north-west of Carnac via D781. Nearest international airport: Paris at 500km/300 miles. Nearest national airport: Rennes or Lorient. Nearest station: Carnac.

Additional information:

Open all year except mid-November to mid-February. 20 bedrooms all with shower or bath.WC; telephone. Price FF250-FF275 double. Breakfast FF25. Lunch and dinner FF90-FF140 or a la carte. Carte Bleue and Visa. Colourbrochure in French and English sent on request.

Readers' comments are always appreciated. Please let us know about any accommodation that you particularly enjoyed. Suggestions for new entries, too, are very welcome. Write to Meg Jump, La Maison Blanche, 04320 Entrevaux, France.

Charleville-
Mézières

**08
ARDENNES**

Champagne/Ardennes
comprises the following
départements:
Ardennes (08)
Aube (10)
Marne (51)
Haute-Marne (52)

Reims

**51
MARNE**

Épernay
HOTEL LES BERCEAUX

Etoges
CHÂTEAU D'ETOGES

Chalons-
sur-Marne

Troyes

**10
AUBE**

Chaumont

**52
HAUTE-MARNE**

CHAMPAGNE / ARDENNES

*T*HE AREA LYING NORTH-EAST OF PARIS *up to the Belgian border consists of the great forests of the French Ardennes, famous for wild boar (boar-hunting is still a popular sport) and rich rolling countryside. Parts of it are attractive enough but it has little really to attract the overseas visitor æ with one very notable exception: Champagne. The most northerly vineyards in France, producing the world's most famous and prestigious wine, are contained within the Marne département whose largest city, Reims, is also the regional capital. Some of the* grande marque *champagne houses have their headquarters here: others are at Ay, but the ancient town of Epernay is undisputedly the champagne capital. All along its main thoroughfare — avenue de Champagne — stately 18th and 19th century mansions bear outward testimony to the prosperity that fizzy wine has brought to the area. Beneath them however, a fascinating maze of tunnels, corridors, chambers and galleries stretching over 150 kilometres, contain millions of bottles of champagne wine that lie patiently aging. Visitors come to Epernay to tour one … or more, for each has its own individual story to tell … of these gargantuan cellars; to learn about the region and the history of wine; to sit at one of the many downtown cafés sipping a flute of the famous bubbly, watching the world go by.*

The two addresses in Epernay included here offer contrasting bases from which to discover the Champagne area (la Champagne is the area, le champagne is the wine). Both have full information on the main wine routes, visiting hours for the main cellars etc (some, not all, are open on Saturday and Sunday) and English-speaking staff who will ensure that your trip to Champagne is as memorable as the wine itself.

Hôtel Les Berceaux
13 rue des Berceaux, 51200 Epernay
Tel 26 55 28 84, Fax 26 55 10 36

*Hotel *** with restaurant*

Ideally situated in the old town of Epernay, Les Berceaux is within easy walking distance of the champagne houses that make Epernay famous. In this traditional hotel/restaurant, which is owned by chef Luc Maillard and his English wife Jill, there is a definite emphasis on fine food. The hotel's *restaurant gastronomic* concentrates on sophisticated cooking and has a very comprehensive wine list offering more than 60 types of champagne. For more informal wining and dining, the Wine Bar has a set menu at FF100 plus a wide selection of champagnes sold by the glass. Staff are friendly and English is spoken.

Situated 140km/85 miles north-east of Paris in the centre of Epernay. Nearest international airport: Paris. Nearest station: Epernay.

Additional information:

Open all year. 29 bedrooms all with private shower or bath/WC; telephone; TV. Price FF285 single, FF295-FF335 double. Half board FF385-FF575 per person. Breakfast FF33 or FF50 for a buffet breakfast. Lunch or dinner FF100 in the Wine Bar (closed Sunday lunch and all day Tuesday), FF140-FF300 in the restaurant (closed Sunday evening and all day Monday). All major credit cards accepted. Further information in English sent on request. Suitable for visitors without a car.

Château d'Etoges
51270 Etoges
Tel 26 59 30 08,
Fax 26 59 35 57

Château-Chambres d'Hôtes/Bed & Breakfast

What more appropriate way to visit the Champagne vineyards than to stay in a splendid 17th century castle and discover the *art de vivre champenois*? Your hostess at Château d'Etoges is Anne Filliette-Neuville, whose family has lived here for more than 100 years; this was in fact her childhood home. Anne, who speaks excellent English, personally supervised the recent total renovation of the *château* which has now been restored to its former glory, providing impeccable

Dom Pérignon

Dom Pérignon, the famous blind cellar master from the Abbey of Hautvillers, is known as 'the father of champagne'. It is debatable if he actually invented fizzy white wine (the wine-makers of Limoux in south-western France who produce fizzy Blanquette de Limoux, dispute this) but, during the late 17th century, he certainly perfected blending techniques to improve the overall quality of the wine immeasurably, and his innovations still form the basis for methods used today. He is also credited with being the first to use corks in the bottling process. In order to keep the bubbles in the bottle, he tied the corks down with string. Dom Pêrignon is buried in the village churchyard at Hautvillers, just outside Epernay.

Champagne Bottles

In addition to the normal 75cl bottles, half bottles and quarter bottles, champagne is sold in

Magnum (2 bottles)

Jeraboam (4 bottles)

Mathusalem (8 bottles)

Salmanazar (12 bottles)

Balthazar (16 bottles)

Nebuchadnezzar (20 bottles)

accommodation in gracious surroundings. Guests are invited to dine in the original *salle à manger* where regional dishes are served accompanied by a fine selection of wines. Although the castle is undeniably grand, the atmosphere is warm and welcoming. Full information is available on the famous wine cellar tours together with details of other places of interest in the locality.

Situated 120km/74 miles east of Paris and 20km/12 miles south-west of Epernay via D51 1nd D33. Nearest international airport: Paris. Nearest station: Epernay.

Additional information:

Open all year. 19 bedrooms all with private bath/WC; telephone; TV. Price FF300 single, FF450-FF600 double. Half board FF450-FF700 per person. Breakfast FF45-FF60. Dinner FF140-FF220. No credit cards accepted. Full colour brochure in French and English sent on request.

DOM PERIGNON
1638 - 1715

71

FRANCHE - COMTÉ

70
HAUTE SAONE

Belfort

90
TERRITOIRE-DE-BELFORT

○Vesoul

•CHÂTEAU DE RIGNY

○
Gray

Besancon
○

HOTEL TAILLARD•

Goumois○

25
DOUBS

Dole
○

CHEZ PICARD•

Arbois
⊙
JEAN-PAUL JEUNET

39
JURA

○
Lons-le-Saunier

Franche-Comté
comprises the following
départements:
    Doubs (25)
    Jura (39)
    Haute Saône (70)
    Territoire-de-Belfort (90)

*E*AST OF BURGUNDY, STEADILY RISING UP THROUGH THE FOOTHILLS *of the Alps to the Swiss border, is Franche-Comté. The Saône Valley country to the north is a land of dramatic contrasts: endless plains that merge into the Vosges mountains, are matched by great forests that cover almost half of the département. For most travellers, however, it is the more southerly region and the Jura mountains that are likely to be a real discovery. With a temperate climate that is snowy in winter, hot and sunny in summer, plus invigorating fresh unpolluted air, it is a land of lush green Alpine meadows, dense pine-perfumed forests, deep wooded valleys, clear rushing streams, amazing waterfalls, gorges, caves, lakes and vast unknown uplands. For sportsmen it is a sheer delight — fishing, walking, sailing, riding, swimming in summer; skiing in winter. Such healthy exercise builds hearty appetites ... so it will be no surprise that the Comptois are well-known for their good food, fine wines and generous hospitality.*

Chez Picard

3 rue du Puits, 39100 Gevrey
Tel 84 71 05 93

Chambres d'Hôtes/ Bed & Breakfast

Daniel and Rolande Picard welcome guests into their comfortable traditional farmhouse with its fascinating collection of old regional furniture. Surrounded by its own wooded gardens, the Picards' house is in the centre of the pleasant village of Gevrey, just outside Dole - birthplace of Louis Pasteur. Rolande is an excellent cook and her evening meals of local specialities are highly recommended. The Picards speak English.

Situated 50km/30 miles south-west of Besançon and 6km/3.6 miles south-west of Dole via N73 and N5. Nearest international airport: Basel/Mulhouse at 140km/85 miles or Geneva at 150km/90 miles. Nearest station: Dole.

Additional information:

Open all year. 7 bedrooms all with private bath/WC. Price FF130 single, FF180 double including breakfast. Dinner FF90 including wine. Visa. Further information sent on request.

Hôtel Taillard
25470 Goumois
Tel 81 44 20 75, Fax 81 44 26 15

Hotel *** with restaurant

Set in the idyllic forested hillsides of the Jura,
overlooking the Doubs Valley, the Taillard is close to
the Swiss border in quiet countryside at 600
metres/1,800 feet. This typical Alpine chalet offers
comfortable accommodation, flower-decked balconies
and a sunny terrace with stunning views for outside
dining. Monsieur Taillard's cooking has won wide
acclaim and has earned him a Michelin rosette. A
wide choice of mountain activities can be arranged
from the hotel – fishing, walking, riding, kayaking –
and at a nearby fitness centre there is a gymnasium,
ice rink, swimming pool and sauna. The hotel is
centrally placed for excursions into the Swiss Jura,
Germany, Austria and Italy. English is spoken and
guests receive a warm welcome.

**Situated 92km/55 miles east of Besançon. Nearest
international airport: Basel/Mulhouse at 80km/48 miles.**

Additional information:

Open March to mid-November. 17 bedrooms all with private shower
or bath/WC; telephone; TV. Price FF260-FF400 single or double. Half
board FF320-FF360 per person (3 days minimum). Breakfast FF40.
Lunch and dinner FF130-FF310 restaurant closed all day Wednesday).
Amex, Diners and Visa. Colour brochure in French and English sent
on request.

Jean-Paul Jeunet
9 rue de l'Hôtel-de-Ville, 39600 Arbois
Tel 84 66 05 67, Fax 84 66 24 20

Restaurant with rooms

You will find Jean-Paul Jeunet's restaurant— which
has been awarded a Michelin rosette — in Arbois, an
attractive old town that was home to Louis Pasteur
and is also the centre of the Jura wine industry. Like
the Jura wines produced from grapes grown on the
slopes of Alpine foothills, Monsieur Jeunet's cooking
is recognized by its lightness, freshness and purity.

Vin Jaune

*Most famous and distinctive of the
interesting wines from the Jura
département of Franche-Comté is
undoubtedly the celebrated* Vin Jaune *or
Yellow Wine. Produced from Savagnin
grapes that are left on the vine until
extremely ripe, then pressed and
fermented in the normal way, the white
wine is stored in oak casks for six years.
By the end of this period it has aquired
sherry-like characteristics — very
perfumed, nutty and deep gold in colour.
It is served like a red wine rather than a
white — at room temperature, having
been opened some time in advance to
release its heady bouquet. Once opened it
can be kept in the bottle for up to a
month.* Vin Jaune *is sold in squat 62cl
bottles, not the more usual 75cl bottles.*

To sample Vin Jaune *at its very best,
drink it in the Jura where it is made. Try
it with the excellent local cheeses or
charcuterie that has been dried in the
fresh mountain air. Look out too for
another local speciality — Poulet au Vin
Jaune (chicken cooked in Yellow Wine).*

The restaurant decor is a fitting backdrop for his delicate cuisine, with creamy stone walls, natural stripped ceiling beams and furnishings in pastel tones. The elegantly simple bedrooms are divided between the main building and an annexe 150 metres/yards away with a pretty internal garden. English is spoken.

Situated 50km/30 miles south-west of Besançon. Nearest international airport: Geneva at 150km/90 miles. Nearest national airport: Dijon at 85km/52 miles. Nearest station: Arbois.

Additional information:

Open all year except December and January. 18 bedrooms all with private bath/WC; telephone; TV; minibar. Price FF300-FF350 single, FF350-FF450 double. Breakfast FF55. Lunch and dinner FF200-FF500 (restaurant closed all day Tuesday and Wednesday lunch). Lift. Garage. Diners and Visa. Full colour brochure in French and English sent on request. Suitable for visitors without a car.

Château de Rigny

70100 Gray
Tel 84 65 25 01,
Fax 84 65 44 45

*Château-Hotel ***
with restaurant

Superbly situated on the banks of the River Saône with well-tended parkland reaching down to the water's edge, Château de Rigny enjoys a very privileged position. If its setting is magnificent, its interior is equally splendid. An imposing entrance hall, strikingly decorated, leads to two lovely dining rooms and a bar which opens onto a sunny terrace with extensive views over the wooded grounds. Bedrooms are divided between the main building and an annexe but all are furnished to the same high standard. Your hosts, Monsieur and Madame Maupin, are warmly welcoming and speak English.

Situated 44km/27 miles north-west of Besançon and 4km/2.4 miles north of Gray via D70 and D2. Nearest international airport: Basel/Mulhouse at 120km/73 miles. Nearest national airport: Dijon at 50km/30 miles. Nearest station: Gray.

Additional information:

Open all year. 23 bedrooms all with private bath/WC; telephone; TV. Price FF300 single, FF360-FF500 double. Breakfast FF48. Lunch and dinner FF180-FF290 or à la carte. Swimming pool. Tennis court. Helipad. Amex, Carte Bleue and Diners. Full colour brochure in French and English sent on request.

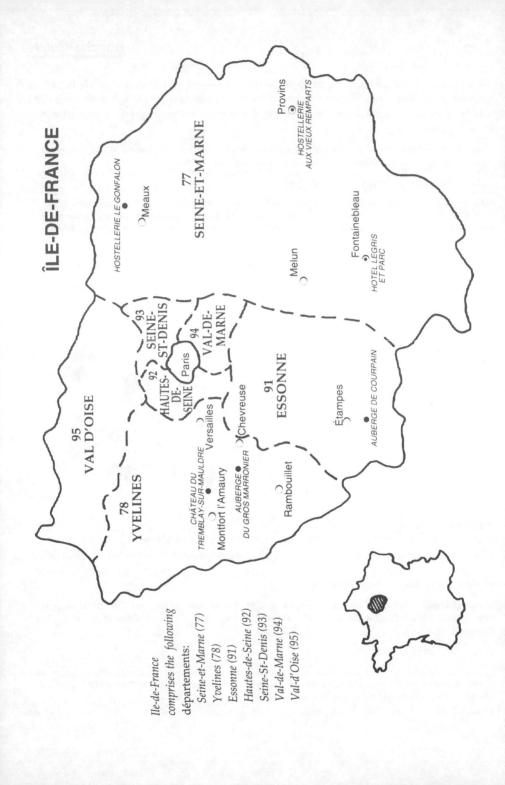

ÎLE-DE-FRANCE

SEINE-ET-MARNE

77

Provins ●
HOSTELLERIE
AUX VIEUX REMPARTS

HOSTELLERIE LE GONFALON ●
○Meaux

Fontainebleau

Melun ○
HOTEL LEGRIS
ET PARC ●

93
SEINE-
ST-DENIS

94
VAL-DE-
MARNE

VAL D'OISE

95

92
HAUTES-
DE-
SEINE

Paris

91
ESSONNE

AUBERGE DE COURPAIN ●

Étampes ○

78
YVELINES

CHÂTEAU DU
TREMBLAY-SUR-MAULDRE ●
Versailles ○
Montfort l'Amaury ○
AUBERGE
DU GROS MARRONIER ●
○Chevreuse

Rambouillet ○

Ile-de-France
comprises the following
départements:
Seine-et-Marne (77)
Yvelines (78)
Essonne (91)
Hautes-de-Seine (92)
Seine-St-Denis (93)
Val-de-Marne (94)
Val-d'Oise (95)

*W*ITH PARIS AS ITS HEART, ILE-DE-FRANCE *was for centuries the powerhouse from which French kings extended their suzerainty and controlled the whole of France. It was here among the great natural forests that served as their hunting preserves, that successive monarchs built their incomparable châteaux — Versailles, Fontainebleau, Malmaison, Rambouillet, Rosny, Vaux-le-Vicomte. It was here too, all along the lovely banks of the River Seine, that the mid-19th century painters — Monet, Manet, Renoir, Seurat, Gaugin, Sisley — found the inspiration that gave birth to Impressionism. Today the busy inner départements (the départements périphériques — 92, 93 and 94) which reach up to the Boulevard Périphérique, encircling Paris itself, have been swallowed into the suburban sprawl, but the outer départements still have much to interest the independent visitor — historic old towns, pretty villages, ancient abbeys, set in gently undulating countryside and vast expanses of virgin woodland. Nowhere is more than 80km/48 miles from the centre of the capital; road and rail communications are excellent; and there is a wide choice of charming small hotels with restaurants offering the finest cuisine at very reasonable prices*

Hôtel Legris et Parc

36 rue du Parc, 77300 Fontainbleau
Tel (1) 64 22 24 24 Fax (1) 64 22 22 05

Hotel *** with restaurant

The bustling town of Fontainbleau makes a good base from which to discover not only the famous Château de Fontainbleau — one of the most distinctive and original of all the royal palaces around Paris — and the surrounding forest, but also the many places of interest south-east of the capital. Right in the centre of town, close to the palace, is the

Legris, an old 17th century residence that once housed the bodyguard of Louis XV. Today it has been transformed into a comfortable hotel with an attractive courtyard garden and fine restaurant serving classic French cuisine.English is spoken.

Situated 65km/40 miles south-east of Paris. Nearest international airport: Paris/Charles-de-Gaulle. Nearest station: Fontainbleau.

Additional information:

Open all year except mid-December to mid-January. 31 bedrooms all with private shower or bath/WC; telephone; TV. Price

FF380-FF440 single or double. Breakfast FF40. Lunch and dinner FF100-FF160 or à la carte (restaurant closed Sunday evening and all day Monday in low season). All major credit cards accepted. Colour brochure in French and English sent on request. Suitable for visitors without a car.

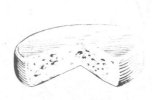

Hostellerie Aux Vieux Remparts
3 rue Couverte, 77160 Provins
Tel (1) 64 08 94 00, Fax (1) 60 67 77 22

Hotel *** with restaurant

Romantically located in the heart of the mediæval town of Provins, the Vieux Remparts is a pleasing and appropriate blend of past and present. Originally a gastronomic restaurant of some repute, bedrooms were added in 1989 in a newly-built adjoining block. Architecturally and æsthetically, the two buildings relate to each other well and provide modern luxury in an authentic olden-days atmosphere. The restaurant retains its rustic charm with exposed beams, antique oak dressers and rush-seated chairs. In summer, meals are also served outside in the attractive - and surprisingly peaceful - shaded internal courtyard garden. The cuisine is sophisticated and of a high quality. Bedrooms are comfortable and English is spoken.

Situated 86km/52 miles south-east of Paris and 55km/33 miles east of Melun, in the centre of the *haute ville* or upper town. Nearest international airport: Paris/Charles-de-Gaulle or Paris/Orly, both at 90km/54 miles. Nearest station: Provins.

Additional information:

Open all year. 25 bedrooms all with private shower or bath/WC; telephone; TV; minibar. Price FF320-FF390 single, FF380-FF510 double. Half board FF430-FF510 per person per day. Breakfast FF50. Lunch and dinner FF180-FF340. Amex, Carte Bleue, Diners and Visa. Full information and colour brochure in French and English sent on request. Suitable for visitors without a car.

Brie

Brie, one of France's most famous cheeses, is also one of the oldest. It originated in the Ile-de-France and came to fame when it was acclaimed 'king of cheeses' by a jury of experts at the Vienna Congress in 1814. It is traditionally made in large flat discs 25-35 centimetres in diametre and 2.5 centimetres thick. At its very best it is a soft creamy cheese with a full nutty, yet very subtle, flavour. Brie de Meaux and Brie de Melun (Meaux and Melun are in département Seine-et-Marne) are each produced in a clearly defined region and are entitled to an Appellation d'Origin Contrôlée (AOC) classification which guarantees their quality.

Provins

East of Paris, on the borders of Ile-de-France and Champagne, lies the fascinating ancient town of Provins. As part of the historic Duchy of Champagne and strategically placed on one of the principal European trade routes, the town prospered and grew during the 12th and 13th centuries. After the union of Champagne with France at the end of the 13th century, it gradually lost its importance but Provins has remained remarkably intact with massive encircling ramparts, a labyrinth of narrow streets and mediæval houses, a splendid tythe barn, three fine early churches and an interesting maze of underground passages. Rising above the town is the great landmark - the 12th century Tower of Caesar.

Throughout the summer months, Provins organizes many popular tourist events, festivals and pageants including Son et Lumière performances in June, an antique market on the third Sunday of every month and a fête de la moisson (harvest festival) on the last Sunday in August.

For actual dates and further information in English, contact Office de Tourism, Place Honoré de Balzac, 77160 Provins. Tel (1) 64 00 16 35.

Hostellerie Le Gonfalon

2 rue de l'Eglise, 77910 Germigny-l'Evêque
Tel (1) 64 33 16 05

Restaurant with rooms

Just outside the town of Meaux, famous for its creamy Brie cheese, is the village of Germigny-l'Evêque, prettily set on the banks of the River Marne. The riverside restaurant - Le Gonfalon - enjoys a prime position with a lovely terrace overlooking the river, where guests can linger over a pre-dinner cocktail. Inside, the Louis XIII style dining room is attractively furnished with ceramic tiled floors and oriental carpets, tapestry-covered chairs and pretty lace table cloths. Chef/patron Line Colubi specializes in seafood dishes and the restaurant has a reputation for fine cooking. Bedrooms are very comfortably equipped and some have a private balcony with river views. English is spoken.

Situated 50km/30 miles east of Paris and 8km/5 miles northeast of Meaux via N3 and D97. Nearest international airport : Paris/Charles-de-Gaulle at 35km/21 miles. Nearest station: Meaux.

Additional information:

Open all year except January 1 to mid-February. 10 bedrooms all with private bath/WC; telephone; TV. Price FF280-FF340 single or double. Breakfast FF40. Lunch and dinner FF250-FF330 or à la carte. Amex, Diners and Visa. Full colour brochure in French and English sent on request.

Château de Tremblay

Tremblay-sur-Mauldre, 78490 Montfort l'Amoury
Tel (1) 34 87 92 92, Fax (1) 34 87 88 23

Château-Hotel *** with restaurant, golf course and golf academy

Château de Tremblay has a lot to offer golfers but is also a very civilized and convenient base near Paris. Located just outside the interesting mediæval town of Montfort l'Amoury (home of the composer Ravel) in the Forest of Rambouillet, and close to Versailles, the

imposing 17th century mansion is set in a country estate of 40 hectares/90 acres. Completely renovated in 1989, it offers spacious and luxurious accommodation. The magnificently furnished reception rooms are nonetheless welcoming with log fires in winter; the dining room has tall windows and fine views over parkland; bedrooms are comfortable and well-equipped and some have open fireplaces for log fires in winter. English is spoken.

The Golf Academy welcomes players on a 'pay as you play' basis. The nine-hole course has been cleverly created to cater for players at different levels of expertise. The circuit called 'Le Parc Anglais' provides a short game situation; alternatively 'Château Bertin' is a classic course. Six teeing surfaces and two greens per hole give a total length of 3,100 metres/yards. Other facilities include a driving range with 100 mats, a pitching green and a three-plateau putting green. Golf clubs and trolleys may be hired.

Situated 40km/24 miles west of Paris, 20km/12 miles north of Rambouillet and 4km/2.5 miles east of Montfort l'Amoury via D13. Nearest international airport: Paris/Charles-de-Gaulle at 60km/36 miles. Nearest station: Montfort l'Amoury.

Additional information:

Open all year except Christmas week. 28 bedrooms all with private shower or bath/WC; telephone; TV; some with open log fire. Price FF500-FF1,100 single or double. Breakfast FF48. Lunch and dinner FF250-FF450 (restaurant closed Saturday and Sunday evening). Amex, Diners and Visa. Full colour brochure in French and English sent on request.

Auberge du Gros Marronier
3 Place de l'Eglise, 78720 Senlisse
Tel (1) 30 52 51 69

Village hotel ** with restaurant

The little village of Senlisse (not to be confused with Senlis which is north of Paris) is hidden in the lush wooded countryside of the regional park in the Chevreuse Valley. Conveniently located close to Versailles, the *auberge* offers simple accommodation in a mellow stone house that was once a presbytery, next to the village church. The cooking too is without pretention but of an excellent quality. In summer meals are served outside in the private garden. Only a little English is spoken but your hostess, Madame Trochon, is very welcoming and is happy to advise her guests on local walking and riding. She will also provide picnic lunches and can arrange the hire of bicycles.

Situated 50km/30 miles south-west of Paris, 20km/12 miles south-west of Versailles and 5km/3 miles west of Chevreuse via D58. Nearest international airport: Paris/Orly at 30km/18 miles or Paris/Charles-de-Gaulle at 90km/54 miles. Nearest station: Chevreuse.

Additional information:

Open all year. 14 bedrooms all with private shower/WC; telephone. Price FF295-FF315 single or double. Half board FF320 single and FF490 double per day (2 days minimum). Breakfast FF35. Lunch and dinner FF75-FF275. Amex, Carte Bleue, Diners and Visa.

Auberge de Courpain
91690 Fontaine-la-Rivière
Tel (1) 64 95 67 04 Fax (1) 60 80 99 02
Country hotel *** with restaurant

Once an old coaching inn, the *auberge* today consists of an interesting collection of characterful buildings including a beautifully preserved 18th century watchtower. Set in attractive gardens and within easy reach of Paris, Fontainebleau, Versailles and even the Loire Valley, the Courpain is a friendly and comfortable base for touring the Ile-de-France area south of Paris. The hotel - which is under the personal direction of Madame Tewe, who speaks good English - has a reputation for fine traditional and regional cooking. The reception rooms are cosy with open fires in winter and a choice of indoor games; bedrooms are each quite individual and feature period furnishings. Madame Tewe has information on all the many tourist attractions in the neighbourhood and will also explain the best walking in the Forest of Fontainebleau (picnic hampers can be provided), arrange fishing trips, horse riding and visits to private gardens.

Situated 55km/33 miles south-west of Paris and 10km/6 miles south of Etampes via D721 in the direction of Pithiviers. Nearest international airport: Paris/Orly at 35km/21 miles or Paris/Charles-de-Gaulle at 100km/60 miles. Nearest station: Etampes.

Additional information:

Open all year except February. 18 bedrooms all with private shower or bath/WC; telephone. Price FF250-FF350 single, FF350-FF400 double. Breakfast FF45. Lunch and dinner FF130-FF180 or à la carte (restaurant closed Sunday evening and all day Monday). Amex, Carte Bleue and Diners. Colour brochure in French and information in English sent on request.

LANGUEDOC - ROUSSILLON

Languedoc/Roussillon
comprises the following
départements:
  Aude (11)
  Gard (30)
  Hérault (34)
  Lozère (48)
  Pyrénées-Orientales (66)

48
LOZÈRE

)Mende

)Rodez

CHATEAU D'AYRES
●

30
GARD

Millau)

HOTEL D'ENTRAIGUES
●) Uzès
HOSTELLERIE LE CASTELLAS
●

)Albi

Nimes
) ● L'HACIENDA

34
HÉRAULT

Montpellier
●)
LES MIMOSAS LA MAISON BLANCHE
Minerve ●) RELAIS CHANTOVENT
●) RELAIS CHANTOVENT
Beziers
)

CHATEAU DE SAINT-AUNAY
●

Narbonne
●)
Carcassonne) RELAIS
DU VAL D'ORBIEU

Limoux
)
●LE COUSTAL 11
AUDE

66
)PYRÉNÉES Perpignan
ORIENTALES)

Font Romeu ●ROZINANTE
)Prades
)

L'ATALAYA ● Vernet- Céret
● les-Bains LA TERRASSE
AU SOLEIL

*L*ANGUEDOC TAKES ITS NAME *from* langue d'oc *('oc' meaning 'yes') — literally 'the language of oc', which was spoken by the people of southern France in centuries past. The northerners spoke* langue d'oil — oil *or* oui *being the word for 'yes' as it still is. To the original Languedoc region has been added Roussillon in the deep south bordering onto the Spanish frontier, and the wild Cévennes mountains to the north together with the upland plateau of the Causses. Much of the region has strong similarities with Provence on the opposite side of the River Rhône which divides them, for this is a sun-soaked Mediterranean land of endless vineyards, ancient olive groves and parched garrigue. But it is a region of strong contrasts too. Old harbour towns such as Collioure and Banyuls share the coastline with vast modern holiday resorts at Argelés-sur-Mer and Canet Plage in the south and La Grande Motte further north; rising high above the sun-drenched plain of Aude are the snow-capped peaks of the Pyrénées. It is an area with a long history — Roman remains at Nîmes and Pont-du-Gard; amazing Mediæval cities at Aigues-Mortes and Carcassonne; Cathar castles in the Corbiéres foothills; summer palaces of popes and cardinals at Villeneuve-lés-Avignon. With a mild climate and a multitude of attractions, Languedoc/Roussillon has much to offer.*

Château de Saint-Aunay

Domaine de Saint-Aunay, 11700 Puicheric
Tel 68 43 72 20

Château-vineyard Chambres
d'Hôtes/Bed & Breakfast

In the heart of the Minervois, Domaine de Saint-Aunay is a working vineyard where the owners, Jean-Pierre and Simone Berge, receive houseguests in their rather unusual turn-of-the-century home. Dinner is available every evening consisting of simple home-cooked local specialities, accompanied — of course — by wines from the property. The bedrooms are spacious with lovely views but do not have private bathrooms. The Berges are very welcoming and English is spoken. Château de Saint-Aunay is an interesting and friendly place from which to discover the many attractions in the area, of which Madame Berge has full details. Advance booking advised.

Situated 35km/15 miles west of Narbonne and 25km/15 miles east of Carcassonne, north of the autoroute A61. Château de Saint-Aunay is on D111 between Puicheric and Rieux-Minervois. Nearest international

airport: Toulouse at 110km/67 miles or Montpellier at 130km/79 miles or Perpignan at 100km/60 miles. Nearest station: Carcassonne or Narbonne.

Additional information:

Open April to November. 6 bedrooms, some with private shower, none with private WC. Price FF220 single or double including breakfast. Dinner FF85 including estate wine. Swimming pool. No credit cards accepted. Brochure in French and English sent on request.

Relais du Val d'Orbieu
11200 Ornaisons
Tel 68 27 10 27, Fax 68 27 52 44

Country hotel *** with restaurant

In the midst of the sun-baked plains of Languedoc between the ancient town of Narbonne and the fascinating mediæval city of Carcassonne, the Val d'Orbieu is a charmingly converted old mill house. Surrounded by vineyards, the long low buildings are clustered together to form pleasant enclosed gardens. Bedrooms are comfortable and the hotel's restaurant, under the direction of Jean-Pierre Robert, has the reputation of being one of the best in the area. It also has a fine wine cellar. The owners, Jean-Pierre and Agnès Gonzalvez, are extremely attentive hosts and speak good English. A friendly well-run hotel that is ideal as either a one-night stop-over or for a longer stay.

Situated 14km/8.5 miles west of Narbonne, north of autoroute A61. Nearest international airport: Montpellier at 120km/73 miles or Perpignan at 80km/48 miles. Nearest station: Narbonne.

Additional information:

Open all year except February. 22 bedrooms all with private shower or bath/WC; telephone; TV; minibar; some with private terrace. Price FF450-FF610 single, FF520-FF720 double. Half board FF875-FF1,035 single, FF1,370-FF1,570 double. Breakfast FF65. Lunch and dinner FF200-FF420 (closed Sunday evening in low season). Swimming pool. Tennis court. Golf practice. All major credit cards accepted. More information in English sent on request.

Pony-Trekking in Aude

Pony-trekking holidays from three to seven days are organized by English-speaking Bernard and Annick Doucet, from their home near Limoux. The week-long trek covers up to 30km/18 miles per day (up to six hours on horseback) with overnight accommodation in simple country gîtes or chambres d'hôtes. Luggage is transported independently. A daily visit to a place of local interest is also incorporated in the schedule. Treks are made in the company of an experienced guide. These routings are only really suitable for fit and confident riders but the three-day trek, based at the Doucets' home, could be undertaken by less experienced riders, or even beginners. Morning rides last from three to four hours with lunch included; afternoons and evenings are free for relaxing around the pool or exploring the are by car or on foot.

For more information in English please contact Bernard and Annick Doucet, Le Coustal, Saint-Sernin, 11300 Limoux. Tel 68 31 34 10.

Hôtel d'Entraigues

8 rue de la Calade, Place de l'Evêché, 30700 Uzès
Tel 66 22 32 68, Fax 66 22 57 01

Town centre hotel***

Uzès is a most attractive mediæval town with buildings in pale mellow golden stone. In a quiet street near the centre is Hôtel d'Entraigues, a large 15th century townhouse that has been very sympathetically restored. Each bedroom is well furnished and quite individual. A lounge with its original stone vaulted ceiling doubles as a breakfast room and although there is no restaurant, Les Jardins de Castille next door, offering excellent cuisine in sophisticated surroundings, is under the same management. A characterful hotel in a historic and lively town. English is spoken.

Situated 40km/24 miles west of Avignon and 25 km/15 miles north-west of Nîmes, in the centre of Uzès opposite the cathedral. Nearest international airport: Montpellier at 85km/51 miles. Nearest national airport: Nîmes. Nearest station: Uzès.

Additional information:

Open all year. 19 bedrooms all with private shower or bath/WC; telephone; TV. Price FF200 single, FF290-FF400 double. Breakfast FF38. Parking. Carte Bleue, Eurocard and Visa. Colour brochure in French and English sent on request. Suitable for visitors without a car.

Le Coustal

Saint-Sernin, 11300 Limoux
Tel 68 31 34 10

Chambres d'Hôtes/Bed & Breakfast

Bernard and Annick Doucet — both great enthusiasts for the history and traditions of their region —offer a warm welcome to houseguests at their comfortable home near Limoux, an attractive town famous for its sparkling white wine, Blanquette de Limoux. The Doucets have lived in Britain and Australia and speak excellent English. They have very comprehensive information on all the many places of interest nearby and will willingly help guests to find their way around. Annick prepares an evening meal on request, consisting of local specialities such as her home-preserved sweet peppers or chicken cooked in the local white wine. Guests have the use of a swimming pool and pony-trekking can be arranged (see opposite).

Situated 25km/15 miles south of Carcassonne and 12km/7 miles south-east of Limoux via D121 to Bouriège,

then D52 towards Castelreng. Nearest international airport: Toulouse at 90km/54 miles or Perpignan at 100km/60 miles. Nearest station: Limoux.

Additional information:

Open May to October. 4 bedrooms all with private shower and shared WC. Price FF120 single, FF200 double including breakfast. Half board FF200 per person. Cold picnic lunch FF50. Dinner FF90-FF120 including wine. Swimming pool. No credit cards accepted. Further information in English sent on request.

Hostellerie Le Castellas
Grand' Rue, Collias, 30210 Remoulins
Tel 66 22 88 88, Fax 66 22 84 28

Village hotel *** with restaurant

At only seven kilometres from the famous Roman three-tiered viaduct, Pont du Gard, in the old village of Collias, is Le Castellas. The hotel has been cleverly converted from two substantial village houses to create a central patio with a swimming pool. The interior decoration is traditional and authentic; the restaurant opens onto a terrace and a pretty courtyard garden. For those who like something a little different, ask for the room with 'the bathroom'! Your friendly hosts, Monsieur and Madame Aparis, speak English.

Situated 30km/18 miles west of Avignon, 25km/15 miles north of Nîmes and 7km/4 miles west of Remoulins via D981 and D3. Nearest international airport: Montpellier at 70km/35 miles or Marseilles at 130km/80 miles. Nearest national airport: Nîmes. Nearest station: Remoulins.

Additional information:

Open all year except January and February. 14 bedrooms all with private shower or bath/WC; telephone; TV; minibar. Price FF395-FF480 single and double. Special weekend full board rate FF1,500 per person. Breakfast FF50. Lunch and dinner FF160-FF350 or à la carte (restaurant closed Wednesday in low season). Swimming pool. Amex, Carte Bleue, Diners and Visa.

L'Hacienda
Mas de Brignon, 30320 Marguerittes
Tel 66 75 02 25, Fax 66 75 45 58

Hotel *** with restaurant

For anyone intending visiting the Roman monuments in Nîmes and Arles, this delightful hotel — convenient for both — would make a perfect country base away from the city bustle. Built around a large patio with swimming pool, L'Hacienda was an old mas or farmhouse which has been completely renovated and stands in attractive gardens. Meals are served in the poolside restaurant and at lunchtime, a special menu of salades and grills is offered ... so sensible in the heat of the southern mid-day sun. The main menu features regional specialities using fresh local produce. For guests who have spent a hard day sight-seeing, there is the possibility of relaxing in the hotel's sauna or, for the more active, bicycles can be rented. There are also facilities on site for boules and archery. Tennis courts and a golf driving range are less than one kilometre away and there is a

Home on the road

This is a little different ... a mobile home ... a campervan. Go where you like, when you like. Tour the south of France ... or all of France ... in a mobile campervan in a choice of sizes that can accommodate from three to six people. Lettings are very flexible from a few days to a few weeks. The modern diesel-driven motor homes are well-maintained and equipped with chemical WC; cookery, washing-up and cleaning kits; comprehensive insurance; 100km/60 miles free mileage per day. Optional extras include unlimited mileage; bedding kit i.e. sheets, blankets, pillows and towels; bicycles; wind surfing rack; camping table and chairs; snow chains. Prices start at FF3,500 per week.

For more information in English contact FMR Evasion, Z. A. la Biste, RN113, 34670 Baillargues-Montpellier. Tel 67 87 21 21, Fax 67 87 24 78.

golf course within eight kilometres. Your hosts, Monsieur and Madame Chauvin, speak only a little English but receive their guests as family friends.

Situated 6km/3.6 miles east of Nîmes via autoroute exit Nîmes-Est, then N86 and D135. Nearest international airport: Montpellier at 50km/30 miles or Marseilles at 100km/60 miles. Nearest station: Nîmes.

Additional information:

Open all year. 11 bedrooms all with private shower or bath/WC; telephone; TV; minibar. Price FF360-FF460 single and double. Half board FF370-FF550 per person. Breakfast FF50-FF60. Dinner FF130-FF290 or à la carte. Swimming pool. Sauna. Carte Bleue, Eurocard, Mastercard and Visa. Colour brochure in French and English sent on request.

Relais Chantovent
34210 Minerve
Tel 68 91 14 18

Restaurant with rooms

The intriguing old village of Minerve — once a Cathar stronghold — has had a violent past but today is peaceful and picturesque, enjoying a magnificent setting on a rocky outcrop between two rivers. In the centre of the village, the *relais* has a splendid terrace with fine views over the Gorges du Brian. The restaurant is simply decorated with rustic furniture, exposed beams and fresh ceramic-tiled floors. The cuisine concentrates on regional cooking at its best, using the freshest of local products. In keeping with the general ambiance, bedrooms are simply but attractively furnished. Some are in the main building, others in a nearby village house which has recently been refurbished. The owner, Madame Evenou, speaks only a little English but is as charming and welcoming as any visitor could wish.

Situated 44km/27 miles west of Béziers via D11 and D607. Nearest international airport: Montpellier or Toulouse both at 130km/80 miles. Nearest station: Béziers.

Additional information:

Open all year except mid-January to mid-March. 7 bedrooms all with private shower or bath/WC. Price FF180-FF220 single or double. Breakfast FF25. Lunch and dinner FF85-FF200. Half board FF260 per person. Carte Bleue, Eurocard and Visa.

Les Mimosas

avenue des Orangers, 34460 Roquebrun
Tel and fax 67 89 61 36

Chambres d'Hôtes/Bed & Breakfast and self-catering apartments

The attractive village of Roquebrun on the banks of the River Orb is known as the 'gateway' to the Regional Park of Haut Languedoc. It is also in the heart of a wine-growing area and just half an hour from the Mediterranean coast. In the centre of the village, Les Mimosas is a substantial 19th century *maison de maître* offering flexible accommodation that can be used for Bed & Breakfast or as self-catering units. Your hosts are a friendly English/New Zealand couple, Denis and Sarah La Touche, who left New Zealand in 1992 to settle in the village. They know the area well and have lots of information on local places of interest, walks in the Regional Park and the excellent fishing in the River Orb. Sarah is an enthusiastic cook and guests are invited to dine en famille. Les Mimosas makes a charming base from which to explore this unspoilt and little-known area which is sadly lacking in attractive tourist accommodation.

Situated 100km/60 miles south-west of Montpellier and

The Cathars and their Castles

The doctrine of the Cathar Church had complex and obscure origins in the Middle East but basically it preached a purer form of Christianity. It spread into Europe during the 11th and 12th centuries and by 1160 was particularly entrenched in Languedoc, where the Cathars — and the Albigensians with similar beliefs — built many castles and fortified villages. Eventually the Catholic Church deemed both these sects to be heretical. The Albigensian Crusade was launched by Simon de Montfort and his son in 1209-1224, and by King Louis VIII in 1226-1229, with the intention of eradicating the heretics. The crusades led to the brutal destruction of many towns and villages, and to the massacre of local inhabitants. Castles were beseiged and then the Cathari resisters were burnt at the stake. The last Cathari stronghold to fall was Montsequi in 1224, where all 207 defendants were burnt alive in a field below the castle. Perhaps it is the little town of Minerve, however, that is best remembered for its gallant stand in 1210. A stone marks the spot where 180 villagers perished.

The Cathari castles — often strikingly set on rocky outcrops in a stark and remote landscape — remain evocative and dark monuments to a savage and bloody past.

Huîtres

The Bassin de Thau is a large natural salt lake on the Mediterranean coast 20 kilometres/12 miles south of Montpellier, famous for its huîtres or oysters. The little town of Bouzigues is the main centre and Huîtres de Bouzigues eaten at one of the many stalls in the town or along the road to Mèze — accompanied perhaps by an ice-cold bottle of Picoul de Pinet, the local light white wine — is a rare treat.

In Bouzigues, as well, is the Musée de la Conchyliculture (shellfish museum) which is open daily 10.00-12.00 and 14.00-19.00.

30km/18 miles north-west of Béziers via D14. Nearest international airport: Montpellier. Nearest station: Béziers.

Additional information:

Open all year. 2 bedrooms and 2 apartments (sleeping 2-4 people) all with private bath/WC. Apartments have a kitchenette/dining room. Price FF190-FF220 single or double, FF320 for four people. Breakfast FF20-FF45. Lunch and dinner FF75 including wine. No credit cards accepted. Further information in English sent on request.

La Maison Blanche

1796 avenue de la Pompignane, 34000 Montpellier
Tel 67 79 60 25, Fax 67 79 53 39

Town centre hotel *** with restaurant

The inspiration for this delightful and unique hotel comes straight from the old traditional plantation houses of Louisiana, all sparkling white slender columns and airy balconies. Set in a pleasant shaded garden, it is within minutes of the port, city centre and airport. If a town centre hotel is what you are looking for in the lively town of Montpellier, look no further. The service is efficient and friendly and the restaurant — not surprisingly — always has Creole specialities from the Franco/American deep south on the menu. English is spoken.

Situated in the centre of Montpellier, 10 minutes from the autoroute exit for Montpellier-Est and the airport. Please note that the hotel entrance is actually on rue de Salaison, not avenue de la Pompignane. Nearest international airport and station: Montpellier.

Additional information:

Open all year. 38 bedrooms all with private bath/WC; telephone; TV; minibar. Price FF400 single, FF450 double. Half board FF390 per person. Breakfast FF38. Lunch and dinner FF120 or à la carte (restaurant closed August 1-14 and Sunday). Garage parking. Amex, Mastercard and Visa. Full colour brochure sent on request. Suitable for visitors without a car.

Château d'Ayres
48150 Meyrueis
Tel 66 45 60 10, Fax 66 45 62 26
Château-Hotel *** with restaurant

Set in extensive parkland dominated by
magnificent hundred-year-old oak trees,
this lovely mansion of mellow stone is a
rather special place to stay. Dating back to
the 18th century and built on the site of a
12th century Benedictine monastery,
it retains many original features.
The reception rooms are
beautifully furnished with
antiques and — although
undeniably grand — proportions are
on a homely scale, creating a friendly and
intimate atmosphere. Bedrooms are spacious, each one being individual. This is very much a
family-run hotel; the owner, Monsieur de Montjou, speaks good English. The excellent cooking is
the responsibility of Madame Chantal de Montjou, assisted by her son. Château d'Ayres is ideally
placed for the impressive Tarn Gorges and for discovering the wild beauty of the National Parc
des Cevennes.

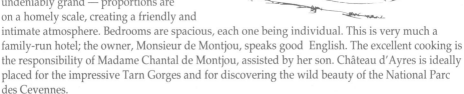

**Situated 100km/60 miles north-west of Montpellier and 40km/24 miles north-east of Millau. Nearest
international airport: Montpellier. Nearest station: Millau.**

Additional information:

Open April 1 to November 2. 24 bedrooms all with private shower or bath/WC; telephone; TV; some with minibar. Price
FF360-FF660 single and double. Breakfast FF52. Lunch and dinner FF132-FF290. Swimming pool. Tennis court. Jacuzzi. Amex,
Diners and Visa. Colour brochure in French and English sent on request.

L'Atalaya
Llo, 66800 Saillagouse
Tel 68 04 70 04, Fax 68 04 01 29
Country hotel *** with restaurant

Llo is a pretty village high in the Pyrénées close
to the frontier with Andorra and Spain. This is
the area known as La Cerdagne, a countryside
with stunning scenery, excellent walking and
fishing, hot summers and snow-bound winters.
L'Atalaya, which takes its name from the local
word for the tower of a ruined 11th century
castle dominating the village, is a truly

Roussillon or French Catalonia

Roussillon occupies the southernmost corner of the French Mediterranean coast where it meets northern Spain, and generally corresponds with the département of Pyrénées-Orientales (66). The Pyrénées form the southern boundary with Spain, and the Corbières mountains enclose the plain of Roussillon to the north. Perpignan, the capital city, sits centrally on the banks of the River Têt and it was from here that the Counts of Barcelona ruled over Roussillon and Spanish Catalonia until 1172. The region then passed to the Kings of Aragon, later to become part of the Kingdom of Majorca. The massive fortified Palace of the Kings of Majorca remains a striking edifice on the skyline of Perpignan to this day. In 1463, the Spanish rulers presented Roussillon to Louis XI of France in return for his help in suppressing a Catalan revolt, but it was not until 1659 that the present frontier was decided upon and Roussillon finally and permanently became part of France. Now, more than 300 years later, the Catalan people both sides of the border share a common culture and a language which is still widely spoken; and Catalan poetry, literature and music are thriving.

delightful stone auberge that has been restored with great flair and style by the owners, Hubert and Ghislaine Toussaint, who speak English. Monsieur Toussaint was in fact born and raised in London. Meals are served in the cosy dining room or outside on a geranium-filled terrace. Bedrooms have traditional furniture — some with four-poster beds — and light floral cotton fabrics. From the hotel guests can enjoy rambling, fishing, golf, and in the winter, downhill and cross-country skiing.

Situated 100km/60 miles south-west of Perpignan, 12km/7 miles south of Font-Romeu and 3km/1.8 miles east of Saillsagouse via D33. Nearest international airport: Perpignan. Nearest station: Font-Romeu.

Additional information:

Open all year except November 5 to December. 13 bedrooms all with private shower or bath/WC; telephone; TV; minibar. Price FF450-FF550 single and double. Breakfast FF46. Lunch and dinner FF150-FF330 or à la carte (restaurant closed all day Monday and Tuesday lunch in low season). Swimming pool. Carte Bleue, Eurocard and Visa. Colour brochure in French and English sent on request.

La Terrasse au Soleil
Route de Fontfrède, 66400 Céret
Tel 68 87 01 94, Fax 68 87 39 24

Country hotel **** with restaurant

La Terrasse au Soleil could be described as unadulterated luxury in simple surroundings. Situated just outside the interesting old town of Céret close to the Spanish border, the hotel is nicely placed on a hillside with commanding views over wooded countryside and Mont Canigou. Once a typical Catalan farmhouse in the midst of cherry trees for which Céret is famous, the original structure has been completely renovated and extended to provide first-class accommodation and amenities including air-conditioning in the bedrooms. Furnishings reflect the strong Spanish influence that is a feature of this area — French Catalonia — and outside a vast dining terrace takes advantage of the fine views and the 300 days of sunshine a year that the region is claimed to enjoy. A large heated swimming pool, floodlit tennis court, golf practice range and attractive gardens are also available to guests. Meals are served in the Spanish-style restaurant or, for much of the year, outside where candle-lit dinners on sultry summer evenings will be a memorable experience. Your hosts, Monsieur and Madame Leveille-Nizerolle, have created an atmosphere that is luxurious, welcoming and informal. English is spoken.

Situated 35km/21 miles south-west of Perpignan and 2km/1.2 miles south of Céret via D13F in the direction of Fontfrède. Nearest international airport: Perpignan. Nearest station: Perpignan with a bus connection to Céret.

Additional information:

Open all year except January and February. 26 bedrooms all with private bath/WC; telephone; TV; minibar; hairdryer; safe. Price FF460-FF640 single and double. Half board FF690-FF870 single, FF920-FF1,100 double (minimum two days). Breakfast FF60. Lunch and dinner FF120-FF200 or à la carte. Swimming pool. Tennis court. Golf practice range. Mastercard and Visa. Colour brochure in French and English sent on request.

Rozinante
Fuilla, 66820 Vernet-les-Bains
Tel 68 96 34 50

Chambres d'Hôtes/Bed & Breakfast

English-born Gene Barter and her family hold open house in their large comfortable villa set in striking Pyrénéan foothill country, just a short walk from the small village of Fuilla and less than 15 minutes' drive from the bustling market town of Prades. The spa town of Vernet-les-Bains and the walled mediæval town of Villefranche-de-Conflent are also nearby. The atmosphere at Rozinant is informal and relaxed. There is a swimming pool and boules pitch in the garden, which has magnificent views over Mont Canigou. Gene is an enthusiastic cook, providing delicious dinners of local specialities which family and houseguests eat together around a long table. The area offers exceptional walking and during the last week of July and the first two weeks of August every year, the Pablo Cassals festival takes place in Prades, where the Spanish-born cellist spent the last years of his life. The event attracts many world-famous musicians. Gene has full details; visitors interested in staying at Rozinante for the festival should book early.

Situated 40km/25 miles west of Perpignan. Nearest international airport: Perpignan. Alternatively Toulouse, Montpellier and Barcelona (Spain) are all at 150km/93 miles. Nearest station: Villefranche-de-Conflent. There is also a daily service on the 'little yellow train' between Perpignan and Andorra which passes close to the house.

Additional information:

Open all year. 3 bedrooms sharing a large bathroom. Price FF150 single or double. Breakfast FF25. Dinner FF80. Information in English sent on request.

*L*IMOUSIN IS THE HIDDEN HEARTLAND OF *FRANCE* — *a little-known area at the crossroads between north and south, between the famed Loire Valley and popular Dordogne. Poitou lies to the west and stretches across almost to reach the Atlantic Ocean. It is a verdant country of gentle hills, secret valleys and vast forests that is traversed by five fine rivers — the Dordogne, Creuse, Cher, Corrèze and Vienne. There are mediæval castles, Romanesque churches, pretty villages and bustling market towns ... but above all there is total peace and perfect tranquility, for Limousin and Poitou truly are off the well-beaten tourist tracks.*

La Maison Anglaise
Saint-Robert, 19310 Ayen
Tel 55 25 19 58

Village hotel with restaurant

The delightful village of Saint-Robert sits on the borders of Dordogne and Corrèze, on top of a plateau with commanding views over both *départements*. With a 12th century church and a collection of fine 16th century town houses, Saint-Robert is a member of *Plus Beaux Villages de France* — an association of the most attractive villages in France. On the edge of the village stands La Maison Anglaise — an early 19th century *bourgeoise* residence that has been restored to its former glory by the English owners, Dawn and Eddy Baldwin. There are polished wooden floors throughout and open fires in all the public rooms. Bedrooms are bright and airy, traditionally furnished and have tea/coffee making facilities – something that you will not find in many French hotels. Dawn is responsible for the cooking ... which is

resolutely French despite the name of the hotel! The hotel has a swimming pool, bicycles may be hired and there are public tennis courts in the village. All water sports are available on a nearby lake plus pot-holing, hang-gliding, rock climbing and archery. On local rivers there is excellent trout and coarse fishing.In addition Saint-Robert is centrally placed for sight-seeing in the Dordogne and lesser-known Corrèze. At Christmas the festivities are celebrated in traditional English style while New Year is typically French.

Situated 55km/33 miles east of Périgueux, 30km/18 miles north-west of Brive-la-Gaillarde and 3km/1.8 miles west of Ayen via D5. Nearest international airport: Toulouse or Bordeaux at 200km/120 miles. Nearest

LIMOUSIN / POITOU

Limousin/Poitou
comprises the following
départements:
  Corrèze (19)
  Creuse (23)
  Haute-Vienne (87)
  Vienne (86)
  Deux-Sèvres (79)

79
DEUX-SÈVRES

Parthenay
LES BELLES ETOILES

Niort

Poitiers

86
VIENNE

L'Isle Jourdain
CHEZ MAIRINE   *LES BREGERES*
        Bellac

87
HAUTE-VIENNE
        Limoges

Angoulême

CHEZ COURTAUD
  LES OURGEAUX

Nontron

Guéret

23
CREUSE
        Aubusson
              Crocq
  LA BASSE

19
CORRÈZE

Périgueux   *LA MAISON*
            ANGLAISE   Tulle

        Brive-la-Gaillarde

national airport: Brive-la-Gaillarde. Nearest station: Brive-la-Gaillarde with a bus connection to the village.

Additional information:

Open all year. 6 bedrooms all with private shower, some with private WC. Price FF150-FF300 single or double. Half board FF270-FF400 single, FF400-FF520 double (minimum 2 days). Weekly rate FF1,900-Ff2,800 single, FF2,800-FF3,000 double. Breakfast FF35 or Full English breakfast FF55. Dinner FF58-FF178 or à la carte. Swimmingpool. Tea and coffee making facilities. All major credit cards accepted. Colour brochure in English sent on request. Suitable for visitors without a car.

La Basse
Poussanges, 23500 Felletin
Tel 55 66 49 79

Self-catering country cottage

Sue Bowden's cottage is in a small hamlet in a totally unspoilt and little-known area of the Creuse *département*. Set in gently undulating countryside, the traditional stone-built house is close to the attractive old town of Crocq between Limoges and Clermont-Ferrand. There is a small walled garden and an adjoining barn which can be used as a garage. Sue lives nearby and is on hand to help and advise. An ideal holiday house for those looking for somewhere really off the beaten track.

Situated 100km/61 miles east of Limoges and 100km/61 miles west of Clermont-Ferrand. Nearest international airport: Bordeaux at 250km/152 miles. Nearest national airport: Limoges or Clermont-Ferrand.

Additional information:

Open all year. Sleeps 4/5. 2 bedrooms, bath/WC, sitting/dining room with sofa bed, kitchen. Washing machine. Central heating. Price FF1,000-FF2,000 per week including electricity, logs, bed linen and towels. TV optional extra. No credit cards accepted. Further details in English from Sue Bowden at the above address.

Chez Courtaud
Ballerand, Marval,
87440 Saint-Mathieu
Tel 55 78 71 38,
Fax 55 78 76 76

Chambres d'Hôtes/Bed & Breakfast and self-catering apartments

In the midst of the beautiful forest of Ballerand, between the villages of Marval and Abjat in the *département* of Haute Vienne, Chez Courtaud is a 500-year-old farmhouse that has been restored by the English owners, John and Jenny Wisdom. The actual farmhouse is furnished to a high standard and is used as bed and breakfast accommodation. In the extensive surrounding gardens there is a swimming pool, a field for games and a lawned area overlooking a pretty lake. In nearby outbuildings are three self-catering units, all fitted to a similar high standard, with shared use of the swimming pool. Your friendly hosts are on hand to help make their guests feel at home and assist in any possible way. Chez Courtaud is centrally placed for visiting the Dordogne, Limoges, Cognac and the many attractive market towns and villages in this little-known corner of France.

Situated 60km/36 miles east of Angoulême, 57km/34 miles south-west of Limoges and 12km/7 miles south of Saint-Mathieu via D67. Nearest international airport: Bordeaux at 170km/103 miles. Nearest national airport: Limoges. Nearest station: Nontron at 35km/21 miles.

Additional information:

Open all year. Bed & Breakfast: 3 bedrooms, one with private bath/WC, two with shared bath/WC. Price FF150-FF180 double. Breakfast FF20. Dinner FF65. Studio (sleeps 2) with bedroom, sitting room, kitchen, shower/WC. Price FF1,000-FF2,500 per week. Stable apartment (sleeps 2/4) with bedroom, sitting room with corner kitchenette and sofa bed, shower/WC. Price FF1,000-FF2,500 per week. Cottage (sleeps 6) with 2 bedrooms, shower/WC, sitting room, kitchen/dining room. Price FF1,800-FF3,000. All units share a laundry room with washing machine and ironing facilities. Swimming pool. No credit cards accepted. Further information in English sent on request.

Les Ourgeaux

Pageas, 87230 Chalus
Tel 55 78 50 97, Fax 55 78 54 76

Restaurant with rooms

It takes a certain amount of courage for an English couple to open a restaurant in France ... but John Higham and Vanessa McKeand have done just that. After 25 years in the classical music business in Britain, John and Vanessa bought Les Ourgeaux — an

Aubusson

The small town of Aubusson, pleasantly sited in a wooded river valley, gained fame in the late Middle Ages when Flemish weavers settled here in the 14th century, bringing with them the art of tapestry weaving. The name of Aubusson soon became synonymous with the finest tapestries and the town was granted the right to be a manufacture royale. *At its height, there were 1,600 craftsmen weaving here and at neighbouring Felletin (11km south). During the 17th century many of the Protestant workers fled from religious persecution to seek safer havens elsewhere in Europe, and by the end of the 19th century the art of tapestry weaving had largely fallen into decline. In the 1930s, under the inspirational guidance of Jean Lurçat, weaving skills were revived and today business is once again thriving. There are frequent exhibitions featuring some outstanding contemporary tapestries, demonstrations and several workshops open to the public at both Aubusson and Felletin.*

Aubusson is situated in the *département* of Creuse 45km/27 miles south-east of Guéret.

18th century farmhouse set in open countryside — in 1989. After extensive renovation work, they originally offered bed and breakfast with dinner. However the evening meals cooked by Vanessa proved to be so popular that the couple changed direction slightly and decided to concentrate their efforts on a restaurant instead — a venture which has won encouraging approval from their local French clientele. Les Ourgeaux is situated on the borders of Haute Vienne and Dordogne, in the peaceful green landscape of the Tardoire Valley. It makes a convenient country base for trips to the porcelain factories of Limoges as well as for sight-seeing in the Dordogne. The famous National Stud at Arnac-Pompadour is also within easy reach and has regular race meetings during the summer months.

Situated 30km/18 miles south-west of Limoges and 3km/1.8 miles north of Chalus via N21. Nearest international airport: Bordeaux at 250km/152 miles. Nearest national airport: Limoges. Nearest station: Limoges.

Additional information:

Open all year. 3 bedrooms all with private shower or bath/WC. Price FF250-FF300. Breakfast FF25. Dinner FF105-FF135. Eurocard and Mastercard. Further information in English sent on request. Suitable for visitors without a car as there is a bus service into Chalus.

Les Brégères
87330 Saint-Barbant
Tel 55 60 40 21 or 55 60 41 03

Farmhouse Chambres d'Hôtes/Bed & Breakfast

Les Brégères is a working sheep farm which lies just outside the tiny village of Saint-Barbant in Haute Vienne. A young English couple, Julian and Inge Bunce, run the farm and also produce ewes' milk cheese. Guest accommodation is provided by Inge's mother, Joy Waters, who lives in a cottage next door. Les Brégères is ideally suited to travellers seeking a convenient overnight stop when driving to or from south-western France, or it is perfect for anyone looking for really friendly, homely accommodation in order to explore this unspoilt area. Joy's home-cooking is excellent and evening meals can be supplied on request.

Situated 60km/36 miles south-east of Poitiers, 60km/36 miles north-west of Limoges and 25km/15 miles north-west of Bellac via D951 to Méziers and then D4 to Saint-Barbant. Nearest international airport: Paris at 340km/200 miles. Nearest national airport: Poitiers or Limoges. Nearest station: Bellac.

Additional information:

Open all year. 3 bedrooms with shared bathroom. Price FF110 single, FF165 double including breakfast. Weekly rate FF900 per person. Dinner FF70 including wine. Central heating. No credit cards accepted. Further information in English sent on request.

Chez Mairine
86430 Luchapt
Tel 49 48 89 65

Farmhouse Chambres d'Hôtes/Bed & Breakfast

Chez Mairine is a small farm in an unspoilt rural area of the Vienne *département*, breeding red deer commercially. It was started in 1983 by an English couple, Roger and Joanna Fredenburgh, as the first such enterprise in France. Today they have around 300 deer at any one time, including 150 breeding hinds. This is a region that will appeal to nature lovers as there is an abundance of wild life, but the pleasant market town of L'Isle Jourdain is close by with water-skiing, wind-surfing and sailing. During July an excellent open-air theatre takes place at L'Isle Jourdain on the banks of the River Vienne, and an international folk dance festival is held nearby in August. The Fredenburghs extend a warm welcome to guests seeking a quiet country base from which to explore this little-known area that has barely been touched by tourism

Situated 35km/21 miles south-east of Poitiers, 28km/17 miles north-west of Confolens and 6km/3.6 miles south-east of L'Isle Jourdain via D11. Nearest international airport: Paris at 340km/200 miles. Nearest national airport: Poitiers or Limoges at 60km/36 miles. Nearest station: Bellac at 30km/18 miles.

Additional information:

Open Easter to October. 2 bedrooms with shared shower/WC. Price FF120 single, FF200 double including breakfast. No credit cards accepted. Further information in English sent on request.

Leisure Courses at Le Palland

A range of 'learn at leisure' courses are available at Le Palland, a waterside mansion dating from the 17th century which is approached via an impressive 200-year-old oak-lined avenue. The house is surrounded by its own home farm with a herd of Limousin beef cattle, yet is only 5km/3 miles from the mediæval market town of St-Léonard-de-Noblat and half an hour from Limoges.

Fly fishing courses are offered throughout the year with instruction in English. The course tutor is a prize-winning local French lady fishing expert who has had considerable experience of fly fishing all over Europe. She demonstrates the old traditional method - Pêche à l'Arbelete -

Residential French Cookery Courses

Pat Cove, a professional cook and qualified teacher, conducts courses in regional French cooking at Gourgé, a small village near Parthenay in the département of Deux-Sèvres. The atmosphere of the courses is very relaxed in groups of no more than seven students, allowing for informal discussion on the particular dishes being demonstrated. Recipes tend to be simple, showing how the use of local ingredients reflects historical and cultural changes in the different regions. Appropriate wines to accompany menus are available for tasting. The courses are in English and

their skills and approach to sketching, still life and landscape painting in oils or watercolours. Professional English-speaking tutors conduct the painting courses and non-participating partners are welcome.

Price for a 5-day fishing or painting course is FF4,500 per person including tuition, materials and full board in bedrooms which all have private shower or bath/WC. Non-participating partner FF2,500.

For further information in English please contact Boel Norman, Le Palland, Moissannes, 87400 St-Léonard-de-Noblat. Tel 55 75 36 62, Fax 55 75 36 49 or Learn at Leisure Ltd, Blunts Hill Farm, Porchfield, Newport, Isle of White PO30 4LL, United Kingdom. Tel and fax (0)983 821155.

which is particular to this region. Rods, lines, materials for fly-tying, waders and fishing permits are all supplied to course members. Please note that experienced fishermen who may wish to fish without participating in the course are also welcome.

Painting courses are available during the summer months and are designed to cater for both inexperienced and advanced students who are interested in developing

recipe sheets are provided. Mornings are generally free with daily sessions beginning mid-afternoon. Each lesson lasts about three hours, during which time the evening meal is prepared with demonstrations and group participation. There is then time to relax with an apéritif before dinner at 8pm. On one evening each week, dinner is at a local restaurant.

The lessons and accommodation are at Les Belles Etoiles, which is actually two adjoining houses that have been converted to create a single residence. The area is totally unspoilt and there are few tourists. The gently undulating countryside is ideal for cycling and walking. Parthenay - the nearest town

which is 13km/8 miles away - has the second largest cattle market in France and there are many excellent country markets in other nearby towns.

Occasional painting, patchwork and wine courses are also offered at Les Belles Etoiles.

Weekly courses run from Sunday to Saturday. Price approx FF3,000 per person including full board and instruction. There is a 20% reduction for non-participating partners.

For further information in English please contact Pat Cove at 14 Thorpewood Avenue, London SE26 4BX, United Kingdom. Tel (0)81 699 3437.

VALLÉE DU LOIRE / CENTRE
CENTRAL LOIRE VALLEY

*Loire/Centre
comprises the following*
départements:
   *Cher (18)
   Eure-et-Loir (28)
   Indre (36)
   Indre-et-Loire (37)
   Loir-et-Cher (41)
   Loiret (45)*

Paris

Chartres

**28
EURE-ET-LOIR**

**45
LOIRET**

LE MANOIR DE LA FORÊT   Orléans

Vendôme

HOTEL DE LA SOLOGNE
Beaugency

CHÂTEAU DE
LA VOUTE   CHEZ LANGLAIS

LE CLOS SAINT-ANDRE

Blois
LE MOULIN   LUTAINE
NEUF   LA CAILLÈRE   **41
LOIR-ET-CHER**

Tours   Chenonceau   **18
CHER**

Bourgeuil   Langeais   Montrichard
LE GRAND MONARQUE   HOTEL DU
Azayale-Rideau   BON LA BOUREUR
Montsoreau   LE CLOSE PHILIPPA   Bourges
Chiron
HOTEL   PALLUS
DIDEROT   LES GRANGES   **36
INDRE**

**37
INDRE-ET
-LOIRE**

Châteauroux

Châtellerault

Poitiers   Le Blanc
DOMAINE DE L'ETAPE

*T*HE LOIRE IS A GREEN AND FERTILE LAND *of lush hunting forests, orderly vineyards, picture-book farmyards with red-tiled roofs, historic towns with half-timbered houses and old cobbled streets. At its heart is Tourraine — the mellow countryside around the great city of Tours — known as the 'Garden of France'. Flowing across it is the mighty Loire, a fickle unpredictable river that man has never really tamed. The longest river in France, it is also one of the best-known, for along it is to be found the greatest collection of 15th, 16th and 17th century châteaux — or castles — anywhere in the world. They are quite unique and consequently attract many tourists. The châteaux of the Loire are second only to Paris in the number of visitors received. Outside the Loire Valley, the region is much less known. To the south are the mysterious marshlands of the Sologne, an area called the land of a thousand lakes; to the east is the old Kingdom of Berry, its capital the fine mediæval city of Bourges; to the north, the vast wheat-growing lands of Beauce from which the imcomparable cathedral at Chartres rises to dominate the endless horizon.*

Domaine de l'Etape
Route de Mélâbre, 36300 Le Blanc
Tel 54 37 18 02

Country house hotel** with restaurant

Far away from the tourist track ... just outside the little market town of Le Blanc on the banks of the River Creuse ... on the edge of the marshlands east of Poitiers - 'the land of a thousand lakes' - is a nicely old-fashioned hotel called Domaine de l'Etape. With horses, fishing, boating and a home farm that provides fresh produce for the restaurant, it's a friendly sort of place. The main house, built in the 19th century, is set in 130 hectares/300 acres. Bedrooms here are simple and comfortable but for a more rustic setting, choose the rooms at the nearby farm. The area is not really within striking distance of the main Loire *châteaux* but the great Benedictine abbey of Fontgombault is close by, plus an impressive castle at Azay-le-Ferron and delightful market towns at Le Blanc and Argenton-sur-Creuse. English is spoken.

Situated 63km/38 miles east of Poitiers, 50km/30 miles south-east of Châtellerault and 5km/3 miles south-east of Le Blanc via D10. Nearest international airport: Paris at 300km/180 miles. Nearest national airport: Poitiers. Nearest station: Le Blanc.

Additional information:

Open all year. 31 bedrooms all with private shower or bath/WC; telephone;TV. Price FF185-FF340 single or double. Breakfast FF38. Dinner FF110 or à la carte. Amex, Diners and Visa. Colour brochure in French and English sent on request.

Hôtel Diderot
4 rue Buffon, 37500 Chinon
Tel 47 93 18 87 Fax 47 93 37 10
*Hotel ***

The fine old town of Chinon sits on the banks of the River Vienne surrounded by vineyards. Well-known as the birthplace of the 16th century French humanist writer Rabelais, the area was the setting for much of his work. Located in a quiet residential area very close to the town centre, the Diderot is a splendid 18th century house clad in ivy. There is a beamed breakfast room with a 15th century fireplace, where *petit déjeuner* (including a selection of Madame's delicious home-made jams) is served. There is no restaurant at the hotel but there is an excellent choice of places to eat in the town. Monsieur and Madame Kazamias are very welcoming and speak English.

Situated 47km/28 miles south-west of Tours. Nearest international airport: Paris at 250km/158 miles. Nearest national airport: Tours. Nearest station: Chinon.

Additional information:

Open all year except mid-December to mid-January. 25 bedrooms all

Cycling Holidays in the Loire Valley

Cycling holidays in the Loire are based in Chinon with a choice of seven, nine, 12 or 14-day itineraries. The gently rolling countryside is not too taxing for cyclists and offers many interesting rides through vineyards and quiet country roads. Routes include 'Plantagenet France' and the tomb of Richard the Lionheart at Fontevraud Abbey, the troglodyte houses carved into hillsides and ... of course ... the famous châteax.

Holidays are available from early June to late September and prices start at approximately FF3,500 per person per week, which includes half board at all hotels on the route and use of a specially manufactured six-speed bicycle.

General information:

Cycling holidays are organized by a UK-based company, Cycling for Softies, which operates in nine different French regions. The total package can include air fares from the UK to and from the main airport in each French region or, alternatively, clients may arrange their own transport to the base hotel.

The basic formula for every holiday is the same. The first two nights are spent at

the home-base hotel and the last two nights will also be back there. The total duration of the holiday may be from seven to 14 days, allowing complete flexibility in between. Itineraries are decided in advance and overnight accommodation booked. Each region has its own characteristic geography which determines what cycling to expect, therefore holidays are given a 'terrain coding' - easy, variable or harder.

For full information in English contact Cycling for Softies, 2&4 Birch Polygon, Rusholme, Manchester M4 5HW, United Kingdom. Tel (0)61 248 8282, Fax (0)61 248 5140.

with private shower or bath/WC; telephone. Price FF210-FF260 single, FF260-FF335 double, Breakfast FF30. All major credit cards accepted. Colour brochure in French and English sent on request. Suitable for visitors without a car.

Le Clos Philippa
10 rue Pineau, 37190 Azay-le-Rideau
Tel 47 45 26 49

Chambres d'Hôtes/Bed & Breakfast

Located in the centre of the village, Le Clos Philippa is an 18th century residence overlooking the park of the famous *château*. Although surrounded by high walls on the roadside, the house has a very pretty garden at the rear. Your hostess, Bernadette Wilmann, has furnished her home in traditional style with period furniture, and there is a dining room and salon for the use of guests. No evening meal, but this is no problem as there is an excellent selection of restaurants in the village. Madame Wilmann speaks English.

Situated 26km/16 miles south-west of Tours. Nearest international airport: Paris at 260km/158 miles. Nearest national airport: Tours. Nearest station: Azay-le-Rideau.

Additional information:

Open all year. 4 bedrooms all with private shower/WC. Price FF250 single, FF270-FF330 double including breakfast. Parking. No credit cards accepted. Further information in English sent on request. Suitable for visitors without a car.

Le Clos Saint-André
Ingrandes-de-Touraine, 37140
Bourgueil
Tel 47 96 90 81

Vineyard Chambres d'Hôtes/Bed & Breakfast

Just outside Bourgueil – the only red wine producing area in the Loire Valley – is Le Clos Saint-André, a working vineyard with a *maison de maître* from the 18th century plus outbuildings from the 16th century. Your friendly English-speaking hosts, Michel and Michèle Pinçon, offer houseguests an evening meal of local specialities ... accompanied, of course, by the house wine. A convenient base for all the main *châteaux*; the Pinçons also have bicycles for hire and they can arrange fishing nearby.

Situated 38km/23 miles west of Tours and 10km/6 miles east of Bourgueil via D35. Nearest international airport: Paris at 280km/170 miles. Nearest national airport: Tours. Nearest station: Langeais at 10km/6 miles.

Additional information:

Open all year. 5 bedrooms all with private bath/WC. Price FF220 single, FF250-FF300 double including breakfast. Dinner FF90-120. No credit cards accepted. Further information in English sent on request.

Hôtel du Bon Laboureur et du Château
37150 Chenonceaux
Tel 47 23 90 02 Fax 47 23 82 01

Hotel *** with restaurant

Chenonceaux is arguably the most beautiful - and certainly one of the most popular – of all the fabulous *châteaux* along the Loire Valley. It is also one of the busiest which means that guests staying at the Bon Laboureur, just 200 metres from the castle gates, have the distinct advantage of arriving early to miss the crowds, or lingering later in the day when everyone else has gone. Bedrooms are comfortable and the food is very good indeed. Choose between the gastronomic restaurant or the more informal grill room, serving local specialities. In summer meals are served in the hotel's attractive shaded gardens. Expect a warm welcome from the Jeudi family who have owned the hotel for four generations. English is spoken.

Situated 33km/19 miles east of Tours. Nearest international airport: Paris at 234km/140 miles. Nearest national airport: Tours. Nearest station: Chenonceaux.

Additional information:

Open mid-February to mid-December. 40 bedrooms all with private shower or bath/WC; telephone; TV. Price FF280-FF400 single, FF320-FF600 double. Breakfast FF40. Lunch and dinner FF100 in the grill, FF175-FF300 or à la carte in the restaurant. Swimming pool. Tennis court (at 300 metres). Parking. Amex, Diners and Visa. Colour brochure in French and English sent on request. Suitable for visitors without a car.

Le Moulin Neuf
33 rue du Vieux Calvaire, 37390 Mettray
Tel 47 54 47 62, Fax 47 41 53 37

Chambres d'Hôtes/Bed & Breakfast

This immaculately preserved 18th century water mill stands in grounds of 2 hectares/4.5 acres

through which the River Choisille flows. The interior is beautifully furnished and two large glass windows display the original mill mechanism. Houseguests have the use of a swimming pool and an all-weather tennis court. No evening meal but there is a good choice very nearby or in Tours. Your charming hostess, Madame Annick Samuzeau, speaks only a little English but her daughter spent some time in the United States and speaks English well.

Situated 6km/3.6 miles north of Tours via N138 and D76. Nearest international airport: Paris at 240km/146 miles. Nearest national airport: Tours. Nearest station: Tours.

Additional information:

Open all year. 3 bedrooms all with private shower or bath/WC. Price FF370 single, FF400 double including breakfast. Swimming pool. Tennis court. No credit cards accepted. Further information in English sent on request.

Le Grand Monarque
3 Place de la République, 37190 Azay-le-Rideau
Tel 47 45 40 08, Fax 47 45 46 25

*Hotel ** with restaurant*

At the heart of the Loire *châteaux* circuit and almost at the gates of Azay-le-Rideau, this ivy-clad manorhouse offers comfortable bedrooms and excellent cooking. There is a pleasant rustic restaurant but during the summer months meals are served on the lovely garden terrace, shaded by tall trees. A good selection of Loire wines are stocked and English is spoken.

Situated 26km/16 miles south-west of Tours. Nearest international airport: Paris at 260km/158 miles. Nearest national airport: Tours. Nearest station: Azay-le-Rideau.

Additional information:

Open all year but restaurant closed November to March. 28 bedrooms all with private shower or bath/WC; telephone; some with TV. Price FF235-FF400 single, FF270-FF500 double. Half board FF300-FF570 per person. Breakfast FF40. Lunch and dinner FF150-FF410 or à la carte. All major credit cards accepted. Colour brochure in French and English sent on request. Suitable for visitors without a car.

Pallus

Cravant-les-Coteaux, 37500 Chinon
Tel 47 93 08 94, Fax 47 98 43 00

Chambres d'Hôtes/Bed & Breakfast

Pallus is a delightful *maison tourangelle* – a house in the style around Tours – built during the 18th century. Today it is the charming home of Bernard and Barbara Chauveau, who are both specialists in antiques. It is no surprise then that the bedrooms are beautifully and tastefully furnished with period pieces, each room with an individual personality. A large salon is at the disposal of guests and there is also an attractive garden with views across the vineyards of Chinon. Delicious breakfasts and the Chauveaus speak English.

Situated 50km/30 miles south-west of Tours and 8km/4.8 miles east of Chinon via D21. Nearest international airport: Paris at 280km/170 miles. Nearest national airport: Tours. Nearest station: Chinon.

Additional information:

Open all year. 3 bedrooms all with private bath/WC. Price FF450-FF500 double including breakfast. Swimming pool. No credit cards accepted. Further information in English sent on request.

Les Granges

37220 Parcay-sur-Vienne
Tel 47 58 54 62

Chambres d'Hôtes/Bed & Breakfast

Les Granges is an attractive manorhouse with its own home-farm, set in 25 hectares/56 acres of private land. It has been in the family of the American owner, Germaine Kling, since 1830 and Ms

Châteaux of the Loire

Along both banks of the middle reaches of the River Loire, between Orléans in the east and Angers in the west, is the most fabulous collection of assorted castles to be found anywhere in the world. Built of the local 'tufa' - a limestone that whitens with age - they vary from massively grandiose, to bewitchingly pretty, to incredible follies.

In centuries past, the Louvre in Paris had traditionally been the foremost royal palace but it had never really been popular with the French kings. They preferred to spend as much time as possible on their country estates, and the excellent hunting available in the forests along the River Loire was a great attraction. It was from the royal residences at Amboise and Blois that monarchs held court from the Middle Ages to the 17th century ... and wherever the king went, so went his courtiers. As successive sovereigns built grander and grander palaces on the banks of the Loire, so their aristocratic subjects constructed fine houses for themselves close to their king. This continued from the 15th to the 17th century when the magnificent new palace at Versailles won royal favour.

There are literally hundreds of châteaux along the Loire Valley, many open to the public. Some stood empty for many decades ... even centuries ... and not all are furnished. Internally some may be a slight disappointment but externally they are pure magic. Everyone has his or her favourites; these are some of the better-known and best-loved:

Blois (41)

Not the most attractive of Loire

châteaux, *a vast royal palace of great architectural interest and variety with a notable spiral staircase. Son et lumière performances in English.*

Amboise (37)

The other great royal residence, where François I brought Leonardo de Vinci from Italy to spend his last years living and working in France. He is buried here. See also the Leonardo apartments and drawings; and the royal staterooms.

Azay-le-Rideau (37)

An irresistible fairytale castle surrounded by water on the edge of the River Indre. Beautifully decorated and furnished interior.

Chenonceaux (37)

One of the loveliest and most romantic of the Loire châteaux: a Renaissance castle on the River Cher, with a long gallery in the form of a covered bridge that spans the river. Known as the Castle of the Six Ladies, it reflects the unerring instinct and good taste of its successive mistresses.

Chaumont (41)

Beautifully sited in wooded parkland high above the Loire, it has an imposing fortified exterior with later Renaissance additions. Well furnished inside.

Chambord (41)

A breathtakingly beautiful château *built in a forest clearing. Conceived on an unrealistically enormous scale – it has 440 rooms and 365 chimneys – it was never really lived in and became something of a 'white elephant'.*

Cheverny (41)

An untouched period piece that has been in the same family since it was built in the 17th century. Original decor.

Langeais (37)

An early castle from the 15th century with an interesting collection of mediæval furnishings and paintings.

Ussé (37)

Said to be the setting for the original story of Sleeping Beauty, this is a delightful white stone château *with a mass of turrets and towers.*

Villandry (37)

A large 16th century castle that is especially famous for its formal gardens, which were recreated at the beginning of this century from original plans and drawings.

Kling now lives here throughout the year. Les Granges makes a very convenient base from which to explore the Loire Valley and guests can be sure of a warm welcome.

Situated 50km/30 miles south-west of Tours and 10km/6 miles south-east of Chinon via D760 to L'Ile-Bouchard and then D18. Nearest international airport: Paris at 285km/153 miles. Nearest national aiport: Tours. Nearest station: Chinon.

Additional information:

Open from spring to autumn. 4 bedrooms all with private bath/WC. Price FF450 including breakfast. No credit cards accepted. Further information in English sent on request.

Le Manoir de la Fôret
Fort-Girard, 41160 La Ville-aux-Clercs
Tel 54 80 62 83, Fax 54 80 66 03

*Country hotel ** with restaurant*

Built as a hunting lodge in the Forest of Fréteval during the last century, this ivy-clad country house is set in 2 hectares/5 acres of park and surrounded by woodland. For those seeking a peaceful retreat away from the main tourist areas, but within easy reach of them, it is perfect. Traditionally furnished throughout in period style, it offers extremely comfortable accommodation, a gourmet restaurant and pleasant forest walks. Service is attentive and a little English is spoken.

Situated 70km/42 miles west of Orléans and 15km/9 miles north of Vendôme via N10 and D141 to La Ville-aux-Clercs. Nearest international airport: Paris at 140km/85 miles. Nearest station: Vendôme (TGV).

Additional information:

Open all year. 19 bedrooms all with private shower or bath/WC; telephone; TV. Price FF300-FF420 single or double. Breakfast FF32. Lunch and dinner FF135-FF255 or à la carte (restaurant closed Sunday evening and all day Monday in low season). Mastercard and Visa. Colour brochure in French and English sent on request. Suitable for visitors without a car as it is only 40 minutes by TGV from Paris and guests can be collected from Vendôme station.

Chez Langlais
46 rue de Meuves, 41150 Onzain
Tel and fax 54 20 78 82

Chambres d'Hôtes/Bed & Breakfast

Centrally placed between Blois and Tours, in the heart of 'châteaux country' and close to Chaumont, Chez Langlais is a pretty 19th century house with a delightful flowery garden. Bedrooms are nicely decorated with delicate floral prints and there is a cosy sitting room with an

Mushroom growing

Some 70% of all mushrooms cultivated in France come from the caves in the Saumur area of the Loire. At Monsoreau, one of these fascinating mushroom farms is open to the public. From the outside it appears to be a group of troglodyte houses, but the facade conceals vast underground galleries, dug out during the 15th century when the limestone was used in the building of the numerous castles and abbeys in the locality. Guided tours explain the various stages of cultivation and the excellent mushrooms may be purchased. Only a little English is spoken but explanatory leaflets in English are available. There is also a specialist restaurant serving mushroom dishes.

Séjourné-Robineau, Route de Saumur, 49730 Monsoreau. Tel 41 51 70 30. Open daily from March to mid-November 10h-18.30h. Adults FF15, children FF10. Restaurant open daily July and August for lunch except Monday. Sunday lunchtime only in June and September.

open fire in winter. Madame's home-made jams are a feature of the generous breakfasts. Martine Lamglais is a warm and welcoming hostess ... and she speaks English. A charming and friendly base for sight-seeing in the Loire.

Situated 16km/9 miles south-west of Blois. Nearest international airport: Paris at 200km/120 miles. Nearest national airport: Tours. Nearest station: Onzain.

Additional information:

Open all year. 5 bedrooms all with private shower or bath /WC. Price FF310-FF350 double including breakfast. No credit cards accepted. Further information in English sent on request. Suitable for visitors without a car.

Lutaine
Route de Seur, 41120 Cellettes
Tel 54 70 48 14

Chambres d'Hôtes/Bed & Breakfast

The Marquise de Chevigné invites guests to stay in her restored farmhouse in the grounds of the Château de Lutaine. The house is just on the edge of the Forest of Russy, a few kilometres south of Blois and within easy reach of the main Loire *châteaux*. Perched on a wooded hillside with lovely views, Lutaine offers very comfortable accommodation with breakfast taken in the garden during the summer months. No evening meal but plenty of restaurants at different price levels nearby. Rénée de Chevigné speaks

English and has information on the many nearby places of interest.

Situated 8km/4.8 miles south-east of Blois via D765 to St-Gervais-la-Fôret and then D956. Nearest international airport: Paris at 190km/115 miles. Nearest national airport: Tours at 60km/36 miles. Nearest station: Blois or Vendôme (TGV).

Additional information:

Open all year. 4 bedrooms all with private shower or bath/WC. Price FF300 double including breakfast. No credit cards accepted. Further information in English and a photograph sent on request.

Château de la Voûte
41800 Troo
Tel 54 72 52 52
*Château-Chambres
d'Hôtes/Bed & Breakfast*

Château de la Voûte is owned by two antique dealers, Monsieur Clays and Monsieur Vernon, who have restored and furnished their lovely 16th century house with impeccable taste and exquisite style. Bedrooms are really splendid – spacious yet comfortable, each evocative of a period in French history such as 'Pompadour', 'Empire' and 'Louis XIII'. Many of the antiques incorporated into the furnishings are quite valuable, so the owners prefer not to accept small children. Antique lovers will enjoy browsing around the treasure trove in the antique sales and showroom which is also housed in the *château*. Château de la Voûte makes a refined and appropriate base for sight-seeing in the Loire Valley. English is spoken and although an evening meal is not available, there is an excellent restaurant in Troo just a few minutes walk away.

Situated 50km/30 miles north of Tours and 22km/13 miles west of Vendôme. Nearest international airport: Paris at 200km/120 miles. Nearest national airport: Tours. Nearest station: Vendôme (TGV).

Additional information:

Open all year. 5 bedrooms all with shower or bath/WC. Price FF350-FF550 single or double including breakfast. Visa. Further information in French and English sent on request.

Troglodyte Houses

Troglodyte houses, dug out of soft limestone rock, are a curiosity of the Loire region. Cosily furnished, they are still lived in today. See them in the quaint historic village of Troo, along Rue Gouffier where each house has its own neat front garden. Similar cave dwellings are to be found in the villages of Genille, Les Roches and Trhet, all in the département of Loir-et-Cher (41).

La Caillère

36 Route de Montils, 41120 Candé-sur-Beuvron
Tel 54 44 03 08, Fax 54 44 00 95

Restaurant with rooms

Ideally located for sight-seeing being between Amboise and Blois, this ivy-covered farmhouse dates back to the mid-18th century. Sited on the outskirts of a small village it has a pretty garden with lawns, flowers, fruit trees and a terrace area where drinks and meals are served during the summer months. The dining room, decorated in pastel shades, has exposed beams and polished wooden floors. The refined cuisine of chef/owner Jacky Guindon has won him wide acclaim and his restaurant, with three Michelin knives and forks, is one of the *bonnes tables* of the region. In summer, salmon dishes are a speciality, as are the *brochet* or pike dishes that are so typical of the local cuisine. La Caillère is a very welcoming place and English is spoken.

Situated 14km/8 miles south-west of Blois on the opposite side of the River Loire, via D751 in the direction of Montrichard for 5km/3 miles and then D173. Nearest international airport: Paris at 200km/120 miles. Nearest national airport: Tours. Nearest station: Blois.

Additional information:

Open all year except mid-January to end of February. 14 bedrooms all with private bath/WC; telephone. Price FF270-FF370 single and double. Breakfast FF45. Lunch and dinner FF98-FF308 or à la carte (restaurant closed all day Wednesday). Diners, Eurocard and Visa. Further information in French and English sent on request.

Hôtel de la Sologne

Place Saint-Firmin, 45190 Beaugency
Tel 38 44 50 27, Fax 38 44 90 19

Hotel **

At the eastern end of the main Loire Valley between Orléans and Tours, Beaugency is one of the more attractive towns on the banks of the Loire. It retains much of its mediæval flavour and has many fine buildings including a splendid old stone bridge and an 11th century keep. There are grander hotels in Beaugency but none is more friendly and charming than the Solognate. With flowers in window boxes, a covered terrace/winter garden, a rustic salon with an open fire and nicely furnished rooms, this is a comfortable and unpretentious place to stay. Madame Rogue is a thoughtful hostess and although there is no restaurant, she will be happy to recommend those in town. She speaks only a little English.

Situated 30km/18 miles west of Orléans and 36km/22 miles east of Blois. Nearest international airport: Paris at 150km/91 miles. Nearest national airport: Tours at 100km/60 miles. Nearest station: Beaugency.

Additional information:

Open all year except New Year. 16 bedrooms all with private shower or bath/WC; telephone. Price FF160 single, FF220-FF280 double. Breakfast FF38. Carte Bleue, Eurocard and Mastercard. Colour brochure in French and English sent on request. Suitable for visitors without a car.

Vendôme

For those who have had their fill of fabulous castles, a trip to Vendôme might be a welcome relief. No royal châteaux here, but a picturesque floating town built on adjoining islands in the River Loir (without an 'e'), which flows into the the mighty River Loire (with an 'e') further west, south of Angers. Streams, rivulets and weirs trickle through the town and the naturally-moated central area is approached through a richly-decorated 14th century gateway. The flamboyant abbey church is remarkable for its elaborate window tracery and the soaring bell-tower reaches 85 metres/260 feet.

Vendôme is situated 33km/20 miles north-west of Blois and is 40 minutes from Paris via TGV.

Readers' comments are always appreciated. Please let us know about any accommodation that you particularly enjoyed. Suggestions for new entries, too, are very welcome. Write to Meg Jump, La Maison Blanche, 04320 Entrevaux, France.

MIDI-PYRÉNÉES

46 LOT

●LAFUSTE

Cahors
○
LA SOURCE BLEUE

12 AVEYRON

Villefranche- Rodez
○ de-Rouergue ○
HÔTEL LONGCOL

Millau
○

82 TARN-ET-GARONNE

Montauban ○

Cordes ○

HOTEL MIDI-PAPILLON

LES TOURNESOLS TOUPINE
Albi ○

LES MAGNOLIAS

Condom ●
HÔTEL DES TROIS LYS

HOTEL DE BASTARD

Gaillac ○

DOMAINE DES JULIANNES

81 TARN

Auch ○

32 GERS

Toulouse ○

Castres ○
CHÂTEAU FONTGUITARD

31 HAUTE-GARONNE

Tarbes ○

65 HAUTE-PYRÉNÉES

09 ARIEGE

Foix ○

Midi-Pyrénées
comprises the following
départements:
   Ariège (09)
   Aveyron (12)
   Haute-Garonne (31)
   Gers (32)
   Lot (46)
   Haute-Pyrénées (65)
   Tarn (81)
   Tarn-et-Garonne (82)

*T*HIS IS ONE OF THE LARGEST REGIONS IN FRANCE, *a vast inland area stretching from the Spanish border in the south to the Dordogne in the north, meeting at the great limestone plateaux of Causses. Two mighty rivers, the Lot and the Garonne, have etched out deep paths through the limestone creating picturesque gorges, chasms and caves. Further south the central area offers a gentler landscape, a quiet countryside that is noted for its Armagnac brandy. Further south again, the* départements *of Ariège, Haute-Pyrénées and a thin wedge of Haute-Garonne rise high into the Pyrénées where a handful of mountain bears — the last remaining in western Europe — find sanctuary. The whole region is steeped in history and contains many superb mediæval villages and towns, including some splendid examples of fortified* bastides *traditionally built around a central market place. It is however its gastronomy that is the region's main claim to fame for, as every Frenchman knows, this is where some of the finest food in France is to be found. Like the landscape, like the people who live here, the cooking is hearty and robust ... rich, flavoursome dishes that are the perfect partners for the region's full-bodied wines.*

Hôtel Longcol

La Fouillade,
12270 Najac
Tel 65 29 63 36,
Fax 65 29 64 28
*Country hotel ****
with restaurant

In open countryside with commanding views, the Longcol gives the impression of being a small independent hamlet or village. It is in fact a collection of old buildings that have been sympathetically restored snd converted into a characterful and comfortable hotel, set in 25 hectares/55 acres of grounds. The architecture is distinctive and typical of the region — stone-built with interesting steep roofs in blue-grey natural slate. Inside the decor is predominently rustic with lots of exposed beams, tiled floors, oriental rugs and period furniture. Bedrooms are all different and feature attractive fabrics and antique furniture. On site facilities include a swimming pool, tennis court, fishing, jogging and walking. In addition, the area is particularly rich in places of interest — the Gorges du Tarn, Albi and many delightful unspoilt villages and bustling market towns. English is spoken.

Situated 20km/12 miles south of Villefranche-de-Rouergue, 50km/30 miles north of Albi and 7km/4 miles north-east of Narjac via D39. Nearest international aiport: Toulouse at 120km/73 miles. Nearest national airport: Rodez at 70km/42 miles. Nearest station : Villefranche-de-Rouergue.

Additional information:

Open mid-March to mid-November. 14 bedrooms all with private shower or bath/WC; telephone; TV; minibar. Price FF380-FF700 single and double. Half board FF390-FF525 per person. Breakfast FF45. Lunch and dinner FF110-FF260 or à la carte. Swimming pool. Tennis court. Amex and Visa. Colour brochure in French and English sent on request.

Hôtel Midi-Papillon
St-Jean-de-Bruel, 12230 La Cavalerie
Tel 65 62 26 04, Fax 65 62 12 97

*Hotel ** with restaurant*

The Hôtel du Midi-Papillon has been in the same family for four generations. Today it is Jean-Michel Papillon and his wife Maryse who continue the tradition. Their hotel is situated in a pleasant village

Armagnac ... the other French brandy

Armagnac is France's other great brandy, cognac being perhaps the better known. Its history however extends back even further than that of cognac, for brandy has been made in the rugged Gascony countryside of south-western France since the 15th century. The département of Gers is the most important area of production, the three main sub-regions being Bas-Armagnac to the south and west of Eauze, Ténarèze based at Condom, and Haut-Armagnac around the provincial capital of Auch.

Unlike cognac with its more organized and centralized production methods, armagnac production is still basically a cottage industry with individual farmers distilling their own brews. After distillation the young, raw, colourless brandy is aged in black oak casks made with special wood from the Forest of Monlezun, which imparts to the brandy a very distinctive flavour. Brandies from various years are then blended to produce a subtle and rounded taste.

Armagnac producers in the region offer tastings and sell direct to the public. Your local hosts will have full information and will suggest their favourite chais (cellars for storing wines and spirits — produced 'shay') but listed below are producers where English is spoken.

Janneau Fils

50 avenue d'Aquitaine, 32100 Condom. Tel 62 28 24 77. Open Monday to Saturday 09.00-12.00 and 14.00-18.00.

Château de Cassaigne

Cassaigne, 32100 Condom. Tel 62 28 04 02. Open daily 09.00-12.00 and 14.00-19.00..

Château de Lacaze

Parlebosq, 40310 Gabarret. Tel 58 44 33 65. Open Monday to Friday 09.00-12.00 and 14.00-17.30.

Marquis de Caussade

avenue de l'Armagnac, 32800 Eauze. Tel 62 09 94 22. Open daily 10.00-12.30 and 15.00-17.30.

on the banks of the River Dourbie, providing guests with comfortable country accommodation and excellent cooking. Jean-Michel's cuisine is based on his own home-grown fruit and vegetables together with home-raised poultry and *charcuterie maison*. Maryse is in charge of the dining room which is cosily rustic; in summer meals are served outside on the terrace that overlooks the river. The Midi-Papillon makes a friendly quiet base from which to discover the Aveyron *département*, the Gorges du Tarn and the famous caves where Roquefort cheese is produced. The River Dourbie is well-known for its superb fishing and Maryse can arrange permits for keen fishermen. English is spoken and guests can be sure of a warm welcome at this delightful small hotel.

Situated 40km/24 miles south-east of Millau via N9 and D999. Nearest international airport: Toulouse at 200km/120 miles or Montpellier at 100km/60 miles. Nearest station: Millau.

Additional information:

Open Easter to November. 19 bedrooms, some with private shower or bath/WC. Price FF75-FF95 single, FF100-FF200 double. Breakfast FF25. Lunch and dinner FF70-FF185 or à la carte. Carte Bleue, Mastercard and Visa.

Les Magnolias
12550 Plaisance
Tel 65 99 77 34

Restaurant with rooms

Hidden deep in little known countryside, Les Magnolias is lovely ... a gracious mellow 14th century village house, impeccably restored retaining many original features and furnished with carefully chosen antiques. A charming intimate garden with an ancient magnolia tree; the artistic and light cuisine of Francis Roussel; the warm welcome of his wife, Marie-France complete the scene. With only six bedrooms, advance booking is advised. The Roussels speak a little English ... and they are working hard to improve!

Situated 42km/25 miles east of Albi via D999 to St-Surnin-sur-Rance and then D33 northwards in the direction of Réquista. Nearest international airport: Montpellier at 170km/103 miles. Nearest national airport: Albi. Nearest station: Albi.

Additional information:

Open mid-March to mid-November. 6 bedrooms all with private bath/WC; telephone; TV. Price FF250-FF350 single and double. Breakfast FF35. Lunch and dinner FF68-FF300 or à la carte. Amex, Carte Bleue, Eurocard, Mastercard and Visa. Colour brochure in French and English sent on request.

Hôtel des Trois Lys
38 rue Gambette, 32100 Condom
Tel 62 28 33 33, Fax 62 28 41 85

Town centre hotel***

For lovers of fine brandies, a visit to Condom, capital of the armagnac-producing area of Gers, is a special treat. Located close to the town centre and very near to the Musée de l'Armagnac is a gracious 18th century mansion whose perfectly-proportioned facade opens onto a large swimming pool, floodlit by night. This is the Trois Lys, retaining the atmosphere of a prestigious family home. Rooms are very spacious and prettily furnished in period style. Long classic windows, festooned in delicate floral prints, allow in plenty of light.

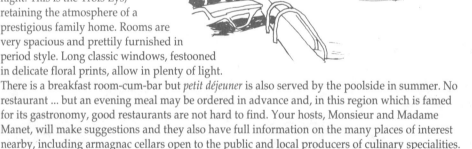

There is a breakfast room-cum-bar but *petit déjeuner* is also served by the poolside in summer. No restaurant ... but an evening meal may be ordered in advance and, in this region which is famed for its gastronomy, good restaurants are not hard to find. Your hosts, Monsieur and Madame Manet, will make suggestions and they also have full information on the many places of interest nearby, including armagnac cellars open to the public and local producers of culinary specialities. A selection of the best of these is on sale at the hotel. A little English is spoken.

Situated 140km/85 miles north-west of Toulouse. Nearest international airport: Toulouse or Bordeaux at 140km/85 miles. Nearest national airport: Agen. Nearest station: Condom.

Additional information:

Open all year. 10 bedrooms all with private shower or bath/WC; telephone; TV. Price FF250 single, FF350-FF500 double. Breakfast FF38. Swimming pool. Parking. Carte Bleue, Eurocard, Mastercard and Visa.

Hôtel de Bastard
rue Lagrange, 32700 Lectoure
Tel 62 68 82 44, Fax 62 68 76 81
*Hotel ** with restaurant*

The splendid fortified hilltop village of
Lectoure is in the region of south-
western France that produces armagnac,
the rival brandy to cognac which is
made further north. Just on the edge of
town, the Bastard is an imposing 18th
century mansion with a fine
monumental front doorway. Elegantly
furnished reception rooms open onto a
vast terrace that overlooks the
Lectouroise countryside. In the vicinity
are facilities for golf and tennis. Information on local footpaths for walking is available as well as
details on guided visits around the armagnac cellars. English is spoken.

**Situated 35km/21 miles south of Agen and 21km/12 miles east of Condom. Nearest international airport:
Toulouse at 114km/69 miles. Nearest national airport: Agen. Nearest station: Agen (TGV) with a bus
connection to Lectoure.**

Additional information:

Open all year except January, February and Christmas. 29 bedrooms all with private shower or bath/WC; telephone; TV. Price
FF175-FF255 single, FF210-FF300 double. Half board FF300-FF340 single, FF250-FF300 per person double. Breakfast FF30.
Lunch and dinner FF80-FF300 or à la carte (restaurant closed Friday evening, Saturday lunch and Sunday evening in low
season). Swimming pool. Garage parking. Amex, Diners and Visa. Colour brochure in French and English sent on request.
Suitable for visitors without a car.

La Source Bleue
Touzac, 46700 Puy-l'Evêque
Tel 65 36 52 01, Fax 65 24 65 69

*Riverside hotel *** with restaurant*

Idyllically sited on the left bank of the River Lot in
a garden of giant cedar trees, weeping willows and
bamboo, the Source Bleue was originally a paper
mill with foundations going back to the 11th
century. The present owners, Monsieur and
Madame Bouyou, who speak English, have totally
restored the mill with imagination and flair,
providing comfortable and characterful
accommodation in this superbly tranquil setting.

119

The cooking is refined and service courteous, either in the charming rustic restaurant or on the riverside terrace. Fishing can be arranged, there are two golf courses nearby and wine lovers will enjoy discovering the robust wines along the Cahors wine route.

Situated 37km/22 miles west of Cahors, 40km/24 miles north-east of Villeneuve-sur-Lot and 6km/3.6 miles west of Puy-l'Evêque via D8. Nearest international airport: Bordeaux or Toulouse at 150km/91 miles. Nearest national airport: Agen. Nearest station: Puy l'Evêque.

Additional information:

Open April to November. 12 bedrooms all with private bath/WC; telephone; TV; some with private terrace or patio. Price FF250-FF410 single and double. Half board FF550-FF710 double (3 days minimum). Breakfast FF35. Lunch and dinner FF130-FF200 (restaurant closed Tuesday). Swimming pool. Sauna. Colour brochure in French and English sent on request.

Lafuste
Marminiac, 46250 Cazals
Tel 65 22 89 15

Self-catering country apartments

In a lovely and peaceful part of the Lot *département*, Lafuste is an attractive old farmhouse that has recently been converted to provide three separate apartments. Each is centrally heated for year-round occupation and is furnished and equipped to a high standard. A communal utility room has a washing machine, iron and deep freeze; guests also have use of a large swimming pool. The English owners, Mike and Sandra Colwill, live at Lafuste and have full information on sight-seeing, restaurants, sporting facilities etc. Sandra will prepare a welcome dinner on arrival if ordered in advance.

Situated 70km/35 miles north-east of Villeneuve-sur-Lot, 30km/18 miles north-west of Cahors and 3km/1.8 miles north-west of Cazals via D13. Nearest international airport: Toulouse at 120km/73 miles. Nearest station: Cahors.

Additional information:

Open all year. 3 apartments each sleeping 4/6 people in 2 bedrooms, one with a double bed and one with 3 singles (a fourth bed can be added on request); bathroom; kitchen; sitting room. Price FF2,000-FF3,000 per week (Saturday to Saturday) including bed linen (not towels), electricity and gas. Dinner on arrival FF60. No credit cards accepted. Further information in English sent on request.

Toupine
81630 Montdurausse
Tel 63 33 55 13

Chambres d'Hôtes/Bed & Breakfast

Toupine is a typical Tarn farmhouse with a striking long low roof that nestles snugly in a hollow surrounded by gently rolling farmland.

The English owners, Carole and Wally Handsley — both medical micro-biologists before moving to France some years ago — have arranged two pretty guestrooms that are tucked in under roof beams. Both have a washbasin/vanity unit and share a shower/WC that has been created from the traditional *pigeonnier* or dovecote. Carole is a keen cook and offers guests an evening meal which usually includes regional dishes. Special diets can be catered for if ordered in advance. Toupine makes an ideal base for discovering the well-known bastide villages and is within easy reach of Cahors, Albi, Toulouse and Carcassonne.

Situated 19km/12 miles east of Montauban and 3km/1.8 miles from Monclar-de-Quercy. Nearest international airport: Toulouse at 50km/31 miles. Nearest station: Montauban.

Additional information:

Open March to October. 2 bedrooms with shared shower/WC. Price FF100 per person including breakfast. Dinner FF80. Information in English sent on request.

Cordes

The remarkably well-preserved and restored hilltop village of Cordes, situated 25km/15 miles north-west of Albi, was built in the 13th century by the Counts of Toulouse. Within 100 years it had become a prosperous centre for weaving and leather work, attracting wealthy merchants who constructed the numerous handsome Gothic townhouses that give Cordes such character. Other fine buildings include an impressive covered market square, two interesting churches dating from the 12th and 14th centuries, fortified ramparts and monumental gateways. In recent years, artists and craftsmen have again returned, producing creative work of a high standard, revitalizing the town and adding to its charm.

Various festivals are held during the summer months, for which mediæval costumes may be hired. The Fête du Grand Fauconnier is on July 14/15 and Fête de la Bonne Vie on either the third or fourth Sunday in September.

For more information contact the Syndicat d'Initiative, Maison du Grand Fauconnier, 81170 Cordes. Tel 63 56 00 52. English is spoken.

Domaine des Juliannes
Paulinet, 81250 Alban
Tel 63 55 94 38
Riding school/stables with Chambres d'Hôtes/Bed & Breakfast

The Domaine des Juliannes consists of an estate of 80 hectares/180 acres in unspoilt countryside close to the Gorges de l'Oulas, offering a choice of fine bridle paths and a cross-country riding course. The school is professionally directed with qualified instructors, a covered ring and a good selection of horses and ponies. Bed & Breakfast accommodation of a high standard is available for both riders and non-riders in the well-renovated 17th century farmhouse. Bedrooms are spacious and comfortable; the home-cooking is plentiful and delicious; there is a swimming pool and bicycles may be hired on site. With a golf course 35km/21 miles away, a wind-surfing lake at 12km/7 miles and towns such as Albi, Castres and Cordes nearby, Juliannes makes an interesting and action-packed holiday base. Your hospitable hosts, Marc and Claudine Choucavy, speak English and also have a self-catering gîte for eight people.

Situated 42km/25 miles north of Castres, 35km/21 miles south-east of Albi and 8km/5 miles south-west of Alban via D86. Nearest international airport: Toulouse at 90km/54 miles. Nearest national airport: Albi. Nearest station: Albi.

Additional information:

Open March to December. 3 bedrooms and 2 apartments (slepping 4/5 people) all with private bath/WC. Price FF250 single, FF280-FF410 double including breakfast. Additional nights are at a reduced rate. Weekly rates FF1,250-FF2,400. Gîte FF1,800-FF2,700 per week depending on season. Lunch buffet FF60. Dinner FF100. Riding instruction FF65 per hour. Riding FF60 per hour, FF120 per half day, FF280 per full day. Swimming pool. Bikes FF30 per hour, FF100 per day. Eurocard accepted. Further information in French and English sent on request.

Les Tournesols
La Ratayrie , 81170 Livers-Cazalles

Self-catering manorhouse

Set on a hillside overlooking the popular mediæval village of Cordes, Les Tournesols is something quite exceptional. Built from hand-cut limestone blocks in the 18th and 19th centuries, this superb manorhouse has been totally restored and modernized by the owners, Aymon and Anne-Marie Playe. Furnished throughout with antiques and old paintings, it has over 300 square metres/900 square feet of living space and 3,000 square metres/half an acre of garden. All the rooms retain their original character, including large open fireplaces in the living and dining rooms. The kitchen is fully-equipped with a washing machine, washing-up machine and microwave. A colour television and hi-fi equipment are supplied in the lounge; and various games are available — boules, badminton, croquet, table tennis — and there is a swimming pool. Tennis courts and hire bicycles can be found in Cordes, together with all shopping including a Saturday morning market. In the larger town of Gaillac, the wine-producing centre of the region, there are major supermarkets and a big Friday market. As an activity holiday base or for a family gathering, Les Tournesols (sunflowers) offers exciting possibilities. The owners speak English.

Situated 70km/42 miles north-east of Toulouse, 20km/12 miles north-west of Albi and 3km/1.8 miles east of Cordes via D600 towards Albi. Nearest international airport: Toulouse. Nearest station: Vindrac at 8km/5 miles.

Additional information:

Open all year. 6 twin-bedded rooms; 1 double-bedded room; 2 bathrooms; 1 shower room; 4 WCs; lounge; dining room; outside dining terrace; swimming pool; garage; barn with indoor games; optional telephone; central heating. Price FF7,000-FF14,000 per week depending on season, including bed linen but not towels. Laundering and maid service extra.

For full information in English, contact the owners Aymon and Anne-Marie Playe, 24 chemin de Bazardens, 31270 Cugnaux. Tel 61 92 83 84, Fax 61 92 87 30.

Château Fontguitard
Cambounet-sur-le-Sor, 81580
Puylaurens
Tel 63 71 74 08

Country house hotel

The English owners of Château Fontguitard, John and Jean Tibbles, have decided on a rather unusual formula for their holiday hotel. Their imposing 18th century mansion has been divided into suites of one to three bedrooms, which are then let on a weekly basis. Not really a hotel, not really Bed & Breakfast, not self-catering units ... Château Fontguitard is more like a country house party. Houseguests have the freedom of 3 hectares/6 acres of gardens and woodland with a swimming pool, tennis court and badminton area. There is table tennis in the conservatory and a small library with books and magazines in French and English. A buffet-style breakfast is served in the dining room, snacks and light meals are served at the bar, barbeques or cheese and wine evenings are held during the week, and picnic hampers are popular for a take-away lunch. The Tibbles know the area well and have lots of information on local atrractions. They can also arrange hunting and fishing in a neighbouring estate. Although no evening meals are served (except for the evening events once or twice a week), there is an excellent selection of restaurants at all price levels within easy driving distance.

Situated 70km/42 miles east of Toulouse and 12km/7 miles west of Castres via N126 and D14. Nearest international airport: Toulouse. Nearest station: Castres.

Additional information:

Open Easter to November and for a Christmas house party. 6 suites accommodating 2-6 people, all with private bath/WC. Price FF1,500-FF3,500 per suite per week depending on season. Breakfast FF35. Barbeque FF60 including wine. Swimming pool. Tennis court. Visa accepted. Brochure in English sent on request from the above address. From January to March, the Tibbles should be contacted at 1 Silver Court, 68 Park Lane, Blunham, Beds MK44 3NJ, United Kingdom. Tel (0)767 40190.

NORMANDIE
NORMANDY

Normandie/Normandy
comprises the following
départements:
  Calvados (14)
  Eure (27)
  Manche (50)
  Orne (61)
  Seine-Maritime (76)

*W*ITH 600 KILOMETRES OF COASTLINE, THE SEA *has always played an important part in the history of Normandy. It was from these shores that William, Duke of Normandy, set sail to conquer England in 1066; and it was on these same beaches that the Allied forces landed to liberate France on June 6, 1944. Today the coastline is popular with visitors who enjoy its picturesque fishing villages and modern pleasure ports. Inland, Normandy's prestigious past is apparent everywhere — distinctive Norman architecture in squat early churches, elegant Gothic cathedrals, formidable castles and sophisticated country houses. Normandy has long been a prosperous part of France. Its people have a reputation for hard work and being strategically placed between Paris and the Channel coast, communications with the capital were always of prime importance. The lush green countryside provides excellent pasturage and delectable Norman cuisine is rich in cream and butter. These same green fields also make perfect grazing for horses, and Normandy is the principal horse-breeding and racing region of France, attracting owners and trainers from all over the world.*

Hostellerie du Haras da la Hanquerie

Quetteville, 14130 Pont-l'Evêque
Tel 31 64 14 46, Fax 31 64 24 52

Hotel** with restaurant

An *haras* is the name given to
the famous Norman stud farms
for breeding race horses. This
hostellerie is an authentic *haras*
where Monsieur Lombard
continues to raise horses. It is Madame Lombard who runs the hotel although her husband is often there to welcome guests. The hotel is part of the 20 hectare/45 acre farm and is surrounded by the fields and meadows where the horses are exercised. A recent extension blends in very well with the original family house and now offers good comfortable accommodation at a reasonable price. English is spoken.

Situated 70km/43 miles west of Rouen and 10km/6 miles east of Pont-l'Evêque on RN175 3km/1 1/4 miles west of Beuzeville. Nearest international airport: Paris at 200km/120 miles. Nearest national airport: Caen at 50km/30 miles. Nearest station: Pont-l'Evêque.

Additional information:

Open all year. 20 bedrooms all with private shower or bath/WC; telephone; minibar. Price FF250-FF350 single or double. Breakfast FF33. Lunch or dinner FF120-FF280 or à la carte (closed Thursday except July and August). Eurocard, Mastercard and Visa. Further information sent on request.

Château de la Rapée

27140 Bazincourt-sur-Epte
Tel 32 55 11 61

Château-Hôtel*** with restaurant

This very distinctive château is much in the style of an English Victorian-Gothic country mansion. It might seem imposing at first glance, but once inside, you will find a family atmosphere and a very warm welcome. It is Madame Bergeron who greets her guests (her English is limited but her son speaks it well) while Monsieur looks after the catering. The house, which was built in 1825, was taken over by the Bergeron family in 1973 initially as a restaurant and there is still great emphasis on excellent traditional cuisine. Prices are reasonable and meals are served in a dignified dining room with open fireplace, polished parquet floors and sturdy tapestry-covered chairs or, in summertime, on an airy terrace with pleasant views over 4 hectares/2 acres of wooded parkland. At only an hour's drive from Paris and on the edge of the forest of Gisors, Château de la Rapée is central to various châteaux and museums open to the public, including the Monet house at Giverny.

Situated 70km/42 miles north-west of Paris, 60km/36 miles south-east of Rouen and 6km/3 1/2 miles north of Gisors on D915. Nearest international airport: Paris Charles-de-

The Normandy landing beaches of the Second World War

After four years of German occupation in France, the Allied forces launched their invasion of liberation on June 6, 1944. The largest water-borne armada the world has ever seen assembled in England awaiting ideal tides to facilitate landings on the Normandy beaches. The first airborne troops parachuted in under cover of darkness and then, just before dawn on D-Day, the main invasion began. The American forces landed on 'Utah Beach' on the eastern edge of the Cherbourg Peninsula and at 'Omaha Beach', west of Port-en-Bressin. The British, Canadian, Polish and Free French troops embarked simultaneously on 'Gold Beach' near Arromanches, 'Juno Beach' at Courseulles and 'Sword Beach' at Ouistreham. Casualties were excessively heavy; it is estimated that 10,000 Allied troops lost their lives on that first day alone.

Today there are monuments and War Museums all along the north Normandy coast. War cemeteries are beautifully cared for and in some places, war debris still litters the beaches as a constant reminder of the cost in human lives of June 6, 1944.

For more information in English, please contact either of the following:

Office de Tourism, Place St-Pierre, 14000 Caen. Tel 31 86 27 65.

Office de Tourism, 1 rue Cuisiniers, 14400 Bayeux. Tel 31 92 16 26.

Gaulle at 60km/36 miles. Nearest national airport: Paris Le Bourget at 40km/24 miles. Nearest station: Gisors.

Additional information:

Open all year except mid-January to end-February. 14 bedrooms all with private shower or bath; telephone; TV on request. Price FF300-FF600 single or double. Breakfast FF45. Lunch or dinner FF145-FF195 of à la carte (closed Wednesday except for residents). Amex, Diners and Visa. Colour brochure in French and English sent on request.

Auberge du Vieux Puits
6 rue Notre-Dame-du-Pré, 27500 Pont-Audmer
Tel 32 41 01 48

Hotel ** with restaurant

The Vieux Puits looks almost too good to be true ... but happily it is just as good as it looks! Built in the early 17th century, it was originally a tannery and was transformed into an auberge in 1920 but retained all its authentic charm. The present owner, Monsieur Foltz (who speaks English), took over from his father in 1964 and has continued to collect old furniture and decorations that contribute to the unique atmosphere of this delightful inn. The dining rooms are unashamedly rustic in character with simple wooden tables and chairs, polished oak dressers, open fires, antique china, brass and copper kitchenware. The cooking is traditionally Norman and very good indeed. In summer, meals are served outside in a small flowery courtyard. In keeping with the general ambiance, bedrooms are simple and most are in an adjoining building that has been constructed to harmonize perfectly with the half-timbered auberge.

Situated 50km/30 miles south-west of Rouen and 48km/29 miles south-east of Le Havre. Nearest international airport: Paris at 170km/103 miles. Nearest national airport: Deauville at 40km/24 miles or Rouen. Nearest station: Pont-Audemer.

Additional information:

Open all year except mid-December to mid-January. 12 bedrooms most with private shower or bath/WC; some with TV. Price FF150-FF380 single or double. Breakfast FF36. Lunch and dinner FF170-FF275 of à la carte (restaurant AND hotel closed Monday dinner and all day Tuesday except in July and August). Mastercard and Visa. Further information in English sent on request. Suitable for visitor without a car.

Hotel d'Argouges
21 rue Saint-Patrice, 14400 Bayeux
Tel 31 92 88 86, Fax 31 92 69 16

Hotel **

This friendly, well-run town-centre 18th century hotel is within walking distance of the famous Bayeux tapestry. Completely renovated in 1982, it offers comfortable and quiet accommodation although only 50 metres/yards from the main street.
Bedrooms are divided between two buildings, both of which face onto a central courtyard and garden. The hotel has no restaurant but does have an arrangement with nearby restaurants which offer good cooking at reasonable prices. The owners, Monsieur and Madame Auregan, are very welcoming and Madame speaks English.

Situated in the centre of Bayeux which is 30km/18 miles west of Caen. Nearest international airport: Paris at 270km/143 miles. Nearest national airport: Caen. Nearest station: Bayeux.

Additional information:

Open all year. 25 bedrooms most of which have private bath/WC; telephone; some have TV and minibar. Price FF260-FF380 single or double. Breakfast FF32. Amex, Diners, Mastercard and Visa. Brochure in French and English sent on request. Suitable for visitors without a car.

Ferme de la Rançonnière
Crepon, 14480 Creully
Tel 31 22 21 73, Fax 31 22 98 39

Hotel** with restaurant

This very interesting building is a unique fortified farmhouse dating back to the 13th century. It has recently been renovated and offers comfortable accommodation with many original architectural features. The atmosphere is pleasantly rustic and the service is friendly. The owners speak English.

Situated 23km/14 miles north-west of Caen, 12km/7 miles east of Bayeux in the village of Crepon which is 6km/3 1/2 miles from the sea. Nearest international airport: Paris at 250km/155 miles. Nearest national airport: Caen. Nearest station: Bayeux.

Additional information:

Open all year. 35 bedrooms all with private shower or bath/WC; telephone. Price FF250-FF320 single or double. Half board FF250-FF395 per person. Breakfast FF38. Lunch or dinner FF98-FF235 or à la carte. All major credit cards accepted. Colour brochure in French sent on request.

The Bayeux Tapestry

The incredible Bayeux Tapestry, Normandy's greatest art treasure, is 70 metres long and consists of 58 embroidered panels depicting the Norman conquest of England in 1066. Known in France as the tapisserie de la reine Mathilde after William the Conqueror's queen, Mathilde, it is thought to have been stitched quite soon after the event on the instructions of the Bishop of Bayeux to adorn his cathedral (which is also worth visiting). It is well displayed in a specially designed room at the Centre Guillaume le Conquérant on Rue de Nesmond, opposite the cathedral in Bayeux. The centre is open daily from 09.00-19.00. Entrance fee is FF35.

Château du Baffy

Colombiers-sur-Seulles, 14480 Creully
Tel 31 08 04 57, Fax 31 08 08 29

Château-hotel** with restaurant and sports facilities

Conveniently placed for exploring Normandy and set in 1 hectare/2 acres of private park, Château du Baffy offers its guests a choice of distractions — a swimming pool, tennis courts, archery, cycling, horse-riding and fishing. Nearby there are also facilities for golf and sailing. Accommodation is divided between the main building and Villa Mathilde in the grounds. Bedrooms are simply but comfortably furnished and the hotel has a fine restaurant where home-smoked salmon is a speciality. Prices at Château du Baffy are very reasonable and offer excellent value. English is spoken. Warm welcome.

Situated 26km/16 miles north-west of Caen, 15km/9 miles east of Bayeux and 8km/5 miles from the sea. The village of Colombiers-sur-Seulles is on D35 due east of Douvres-la-Délivrande. Nearest international airport: Paris at 300km/180 miles. Nearest national airport: Caen. Nearest station: Bayeux.

Additional information:

Open all year. 35 bedrooms all with private shower or bath/WC; telephone. Price FF300-FF470 single or double including breakfast. Lunch and dinner FF95-FF160 or à la carte. Swimming pool, tennis, archery. Amex, Mastercard and Visa. Colour brochure in French and English sent on request.

Château de Goville

14330 Le Breuil-en-Bessin
Tel 31 22 19 28, Fax 31 22 68 74

Château-hotel and restaurant

Built in the 18th century, Château de Goville has belonged to the same family since 1813 and it is the present owner, Monsieur Jean-Jacques Vallée, who welcomes guests into his home. Completely renovated and furnished to a very high standard, the

129

atmosphere of the château is essentially that of a much-loved family residence. The bedrooms — each with its own personality — are extremely comfortable and decorated with attractive fabrics and antiques. A private park of 5 hectares/2 acres ensures total privacy and the hotel's gastronomic restaurant, Le Carité, has a reputation for fine food. Château de Goville is within easy reach of the Normandy landing beaches and Bayeux, famous for its tapestry. There is also a 27-hole golf course nearby. The château has an international clientele and a little English is spoken.

Situated 40km/24 miles north-west of Caen and 11km/7 miles west of Bayeux on D5. Nearest international airport: Paris at 300km/180 miles. Nearest national airport: Caen. Nearest station: Bayeux.

Additional information:

Open all year. 15 bedrooms all with private shower or bath/WC; telephone; minibar. Price FF395-FF695 single or double. Breakfast FF45. Lunch and dinner FF115-FF245 or à la carte (closed Tuesday in low season). Amex, Diners and Visa. Full colour brochure in French and English sent on request.

Le Château
Bémecourt, 27160 Breteuil-sur-Iton
Tel 32 29 90 47

Manor house Chambres d'Hôtes/Bed & Breakfast

Built on the site of an old fortified castle, Le Château is not really a château at all but a superb half-timbered manor house with a steep tiled roof and dormer windows. Flanked by two 15th century towers, it is encircled by a moat where guests are invited to try their luck fishing. The garden is a haven of peace and is dominated by stately hundred-year-old

Calvados — Normandy's apple brandy

Normandy's northerly Atlantic climate makes it one of the relatively few regions of France that is not suitable for wine production. Instead Normandy's local drink is cider, made in the apple-growing département of Calvados, which gives its name to a potent spirit distilled from cider. The first distillation produces a spirit that has about 30 per cent alcohol, but a further distillation raises the alcohol level to nearer 60 per cent. This is then kept in oak barrels for up to six months before bottling. By that stage, the Calvados has a pronounced flavour of ripe apples, a subtle bouquet and a pleasantly soft taste. In Normandy, a glass of Calvados is traditionally served halfway through a heavy meal to aid digestion: this is known as the trou Normand — *literally a 'Norman hole', presumably because the fiery liquid burns through the stomach!*

trees. Breakfast at Le Château is something of an occasion which is often more of a 'brunch' with generous portions of fresh farm products. The owner, Madame Lallemand-Legras, speaks excellent English and is very happy to explain all the nearby centres of interest to her guests and to advise on the best restaurants.

Situated 80km/49 miles south of Rouen and 30km/18 miles south-west of Evreux. From Breteuil-sur-Iton take D141 toward Rugles and at 2.5km/1 1/2 miles from the village turn left to Le Château. Nearest international airport: Paris at 120km/73 miles. Nearest national airport: Rouen. Nearest station: Evreux.

Additional information:

Open all year. 3 bedrooms all with shower or bath but shared WC. Price FF350 single or double including breakfast. No credit cards accepted. Further information in English sent on request.

Auberge de l'Abbaye
27800 Le Bec-Hellouin
Tel 32 44 86 02

Village auberge ***
and restaurant

Le Bec-Hellouin is a pretty picture-postcard village that owes its existence to the great abbey dating from the 11th century. Although much-destroyed during the French Revolution, it is still an impressive monument to its past glory. Close by, bedecked with flowers, the 18th century half-timbered auberge is exceedingly attractive and has a formidable reputation for authentic Norman cooking. *Lapin au Cidre* (rabbit cooked in cider) is a house speciality and the chef's *tarte aux pommes* (apple tart), served with lashings of thick Normandy cream, is said to be the best in the region. Local cider is served in distinctive pottery mugs; summertime meals are taken in an open courtyard. Internal decor is cosily rustic with exposed beams, tiled floors and mellow brick or stone walls. Bedrooms are simple but comfortable. English is spoken.

Situated 40km/25 miles south-west of Rouen and 6km/4 miles north of Brionne. The auberge is in the centre o the village. Nearest international airport: Paris at 150km/93 miles. Nearest national airport: Deauville at 50km/31 miles. Nearest station: Evreux at 40km/24 miles and bus connection.

Additional information:

Open all year except January and February. 8 bedrooms all with private bath/WC; telephone. Price FF320-FF350 single or double. Breakfast FF32. Lunch and dinner FF120-FF250 or à la carte (closed Monday evening and all day Tuesday in low season). Mastercard and Visa. Colour brochure in French and English sent on request. Suitable for visitors without a car.

Hôtel de France et des Fuchsias
18 rue Mal-Foch, 50550 Saint-Vaast-la-Hougue
Tel 33 54 42 26, Fax 33 43 46 79

*Hotel** and restaurant*

Saint-Vaast-la-Hougue is famous for its oyster-beds, fishing harbour and, more recently, a new yachting marina. Just behind the port is the justly-named Hôtel de France et des Fuchsias, its walls smothered in hundred-year-old rambling fuchsias. Five years ago the owners acquired a second house to create additional bedrooms and an attractive garden of lawns and stately trees connects the two buildings. Accommodation in the main block is simple and some of the cheaper rooms do not have en suite bathrooms. Bedrooms in the annexe are very comfortable and most open onto the garden. The hotel has an excellent restaurant featuring produce from the family farm. Naturally, fish dishes are a speciality — turbot with oysters, lobster flamed with Calvados, monkfish with fresh pasta — but the chef is also well-known for his desserts. During the last 10 days of August every year, a series of classical music concerts takes place in the courtyard of the hotel. The charming owners, Monsieur and Madame Brix, speak only a little English but they run a delightful hotel in this pleasant coastal area.

Situated 30km/18 miles east of Cherbourg in the centre of Saint-Vaast-la-Hougue. Nearest international airport: Paris at 350km/220 miles. Nearest national airport: Cherbourg (Maupertus) at 30km/18 miles. Nearest station: Valognes at 17km/10 miles.

Additional information:

Open all year except January and February. 32 bedrooms, most with private shower or bath/WC; telephone; TV. Price FF125-FF160 without private WC, FF260-FF365 single or double with private shower or bath/WC. Breakfast FF35. Lunch and dinner FF70-FF220 or à la carte. Amex, Diners, Eurocard, Mastercard and Visa. Full colour brochure in English sent on request. Suitable for visitors without a car by taxi from Valognes.

La Maison Cachée
La Mardière, Saint-Barthélémy, 50140 Mortain
Tel 33 59 53 32

Chambres d'Hôtes/Bed & Breakfast

Norman and Kelly Smith, a retired English couple, believe that their restored 18th century stone cottage on the Normandy/Brittany border is very close to paradise. Facing south, it is surrounded by orchards, meadows and gently rolling countryside. Close to all amenities, it is nevertheless totally peaceful and will appeal to visitors who are looking for a quiet country base from which to explore this lovely region of France. The Smiths know the area well and can offer expert advice on many places of interest. Keen fishermen will be attracted by the excellent trout and salmon fishing; there is also a golf course a few minutes' drive away. Bedrooms are extremely comfortable and an evening meal with wine ... or of course local cider ... is available if ordered in advance.

Situated 55km/34 miles south-west of Caen, 50km/30 miles north-east of Rennes and 4km/2 miles north of

Mortain Nearest international airport: Paris at 250km/155 miles. Nearest national airport: Caen at 55 km/34 miles. Nearest station: Vire at 20km/12 miles.

Additional information:

3 bedrooms all with private bath/WC. Price FF160 per person including breakfast. Evening meal FF100. No credit cards accepted. Full information in English sent on request. Suitable for visitors without a car as the Smiths will collect from Vire.

Manoir du Lys
61140 Bagnoles-de-l'Orne
Tel 33 37 80 69, Fax 33 30 05 80

Country house hotel*** with restaurant

The largest spa town in western France, Bagnoles-de-l'Orne is attractively situated in woodland beside a lake. It has the usual spa resort atmosphere with a gaming casino and a varied choice of hotels and restaurants. Central to many places of interest in the region, it has good sporting facilities and excellent walking in the Andaines forest. Country lovers will also be attracted by the nearby Normandie-Maine Regional Nature Reserve. At only 3km/1 1/2 miles from the town centre, Manoir du Lys is however very peaceful and set in well-kept gardens and surrounded by lush woodland. The half-timbered manor house offers elegant accommodation in bedrooms that are spacious and beautifully furnished. Under the personal control of the owner, Paul Quinton, the cooking is refined and includes adaptations of Norman specialities. There are tennis courts and three golf practice holes at the hotel. Monsieur and Madame Quinton arrange numerous special activity weekends throughout the year: river fishing in spring and early summer; mushroom collecting during September and October. English is spoken.

Situated 90km/58 miles south of Caen. nearest international airport: Paris at 240km/160 miles. Nearest national airport: Caen. Nearest station: Bagnoles-de-l'Orne or Laval (TGV) at 50km/31 miles.

Additional information:

Open all year except January and February. 20 bedrooms all with private shower or bath/WC; telephone; minibar. Price FF290-FF650 single or double. Half board (minimum 3 days) FF500-FF690 single, FF700-FF1,230 double. Breakfast FF40. Lunch or dinner FF110-FF350 or à la carte. Tennis courts, 3-hole golf. Amex, Carte Bleue and Mastercard. Colour brochure in French and English sent on request.

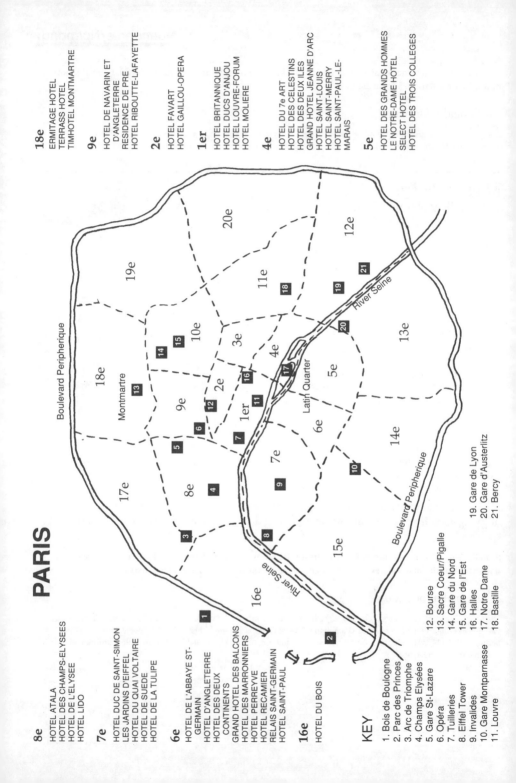

*P*ARIS IS A BIG, BEAUTIFUL CITY *and is a favourite destination for the world's travelling public. Accommodation is therefore much in demand and advance booking – as far ahead as possible – is strongly recommended. Arriving in Paris without a hotel reservation is not a calculated risk. It is a recipe for disaster.*

Another potential nightmare is driving in Paris. This is not simply because of the monumental traffic jams. Neither is it especially on account of the flamboyance of Parisian drivers. The real headache is parking. The available places are only a fraction of those needed for residents and commuters. Car parks are permanently full and double, triple, even quadruple kerbside parking is the norm. There is no indication that the situation will improve in the foreseeable future. It can only get worse.

If private car parking facilities are not required, the choice of hotel accommodation can be totally flexible. Travel around the capital is easy by bus, Métro or RER (the fast train network linking suburbs) and taxi. Paris is a compact city so nowhere is very far away. It is also quite practical to stay outside the central zone. Even just a short distance from the most fashionable quartiers, prices tend to be lower.

For administrative purposes Paris is divided into 20 arrondissements. The first begins on the Right Bank at the Louvre and the following seven spiral round on both banks of the River Seine. The remainder form an outer spiral contained within the boundary of Paris's inner ring road, the Périférique. They are usually referred to by number, the first being written as 1er (premier meaning first) and the rest with 'e' after the number eg 2e (deuxième meaning second), 14e (quatorzième meaning fourteenth). The last two numbers of the postal code indicate the arrondissement, the first two – 75 – being the code for Paris. Thus an address with a postal code of 75008 is in the 8th arrondissement and 75016 is in the 16th.

The following Paris hotels are listed alphabetically by arrondissement or a group of neighbouring arrondissements. Unless stated otherwise, reception staff all speak very adequate English. Most offer a double room for less than FF1,000. Please note that very few Paris hotels, other than grande luxe, have a restaurant although most serve breakfast.

RIVE DROITE — RIGHT BANK
LOUVRE/TUILLERIES/OPÉRA/LES HALLES – 1er AND 2e.

This is just about as central as you can get. It covers the area between the Louvre and the Tuilleries Gardens including the arcaded Rue de Rivoli (where there is a large well-known English bookshop), which is a disconcerting blend of ultra-exclusiveness and blatant tourism. Just to the north is the Belle Epoque *opera house, its surrounding streets packed with duty free shops and travel agents. Between the 1er and 2e* arrondissements *is Forum des Halles - the new extensive underground shopping centre that occupies the site left when the old central food market, Les Halles, was repositioned at Rungis in the outskirts of Paris. There are many cafés and restaurants in and around Les Halles and most of the top designer houses have* prêt-à-porter *boutiques in the centre.*

Hôtel Britannique ***

20 avenue Victoria, 75001 Paris
Tel (1) 42 33 74 59, Fax (1) 42 33 82 65

Built by the English at the turn of the century, the Britannique still retains echoes of its Victorian past. Completely renovated, today it is a very comfortable hotel in an attractive street

40 bedrooms all with private shower or bath; telephone; TV; hair-dryer; minibar. Price FF490 single, FF590-FF680 double. Breakfast FF40. Lift. All major credit cards accepted. Métro: Chatelet. RER: Chatelet-Les Halles.

Hôtel Ducs d'Anjou **

1 rue Sainte-Opportune, 75001 Paris
Tel (1) 42 36 92 24, Fax (1) 42 36 16 63

Next door to Les Halles this light, bright hotel is resolutely modern. The decor is strikingly contemporary incorporating lots of strong clear colours.

38 bedrooms all with private shower or bath; telephone; TV; hair-dryer. Price FF572 single, FF649 double including breakfast. Lift, Amex, Diners, Mastercard, Visa. Métro: Chatelet. RER: Chatelet-Les Halles.

Hôtel Favart ***
5 rue Marivaux, 75002 Paris
Tel (1) 42 97 59 83, Fax (1) 40 15 95 58

A quiet, spacious refined late 18th century hotel with lots of character and attentive service. Easy to find directly opposite L'Opéra Comique.

37 bedrooms all with private shower or bath; telephone; TV; minibar; safe. Price FF495 single, FF600 double including breakfast. Lift. All major credit cards except Diners. Métro: Richelieu-Drouot. RER: Auber.

Hôtel Louvre-Forum ***
25 rue de Bouloi, 75001 Paris
Tel (1) 42 36 54 19, Fax (1) 42 33 66 31

Perfect for shopping situated between Les Halles and Palais Royal, this friendly hotel is in a lively, young quarter but benefits from its position in a quiet side street.

28 bedrooms all with private shower or bath; telephone; TV; minibar. Price FF395 single, FF450 - 480 double. Breakfast FF30. Lift. Amex, Diners, Mastercard, Visa. Métro: Louvre or Palais-Royal. RER: Chatelet-Les Halles.

Hôtel Molière ***
21 rue Molière, 75001 Paris
Tel (1) 42 96 22 01, Fax (1) 42 60 48 68

Close to the Opera, Comedie Francaise and the main shopping streets this pleasant, efficient hotel has associations with Molière who used it for private performances of his plays. Situated on a quiet side street.

33 bedrooms all with private shower or bath; telephone; TV; hair dryer; minibar. Price Ff420 single, Ff530 - 650 double. Breakfast FF30 or a more substantial buffet at FF50. Lift. Amex, Diners, Visa. Métro: Pyramide or Palais-Royal. RER: Auber.

Hôtel Gaillon-Opéra ***
9 rue Gaillon, 75002 Paris
Tel (1) 47 42 47 74, Fax (1) 47 42 01 2

In a shopping area close to the opera this tasteful and comfortable hotel is built around an attractive enclosed patio-garden. Pleasant lounge with exposed stone walls and ceiling beams.

26 bedrooms all with private bath; telephone; TV; hair-dryer; minibar; safe. Price FF650 -750 single, F850 double including breakfast. Lift. All major credit cards accepted. Métro: Opéra or 4 Septembre. RER: Auber.

MARAIS/BASTILLE/BEAUBOURG — 3e AND 4e

The Marais district, situated to the east of the Louvre, was the fashionable centre of 17th century Paris. During the last couple of decades it has been considerably smartened up with many of its lovely old buildings being restored to their former glory especially around the fascinating Place des Vosges. Some houses now contain museums and many are open to the public. On the eastern edge of the Marais is Place de la Bastille, site of the infamous prison, the Bastille, whose storming marked the start of the French Revolution. Nothing remains of the old stronghold and the site is today occupied by an impressive new opera house – the largest in the world. To the west is the Beaubourg area with another unmistakable landmark – the controversial Pompidou Centre. Whatever you may thing about the reactionary architecture, the centre is a hive of activity and should not be missed. Included in the 4e arrondissement is Ile Saint-Louis, the island in mid-river which is the most sophisticated 'village' in Paris.

Hôtel du 7e Art **
20 rue Saint-Paul, 75004 Paris
Tel (1) 42 77 04 03, Fax (1) 42 77 69 10

A friendly, informal hotel in the Marais district whose owners have an unmistakable passion for the seventh art – the cinema. Posters of old films appear everywhere. One of the rare hotels with a bar/restaurant open to the public. Good value; interesting area.

23 bedrooms all with private shower or bath/WC; telephone; TV. Price FF380 – FF430 single or double. Breakfast FF35. All major credit cards accepted. Métro: Saint-Paul or Pont-Marie.

Hôtel des Célestins **
1 rue Charles V, 75004 Paris
Tel (1) 48 87 87 04

A small, friendly hotel full of charm, part of a 17th century convent. Convenient for the Marais and the Bastille; within walking distance of Ile Saint-Louis.

15 bedrooms all with private bath or shower/WC; telephone. Price FF470 single, FF570 double. Breakfast FF37. Mastercard and Visa. Métro: Bastille or Saint-Paul.

Hôtel des Deux Iles ***
59 rue St-Louis-en-Ile, 75004 Paris
Tel (1) 43 26 13 35, Fax (1) 43 29 60 25

A nicely restored 17th century house on the main street of Ile Saint-Louis. Comfortably furnished with a hint of the tropics – exotic fabrics and cane furniture. Cosy lounge/bar in the vaulted cellar.

17 rooms all with private shower or bath/WC; telephone; TV; hair-dryer. Price FF590 single, FF690 double. Breakfast FF37. Lift. No credit cards accepted. Métro: Pont-Marie.

Grand Hôtel Jeanne d'Arc **
3 rue de Jarente, 75004 Paris
Tel (1) 48 67 62 11

Simple, clean, cheap, friendly and very Parisian.

37 bedrooms all with private shower or bath/WC; telephone; TV. Price FF330 single or double. Breakfast FF30. Lift. Mastercard and Visa. Métro: Saint-Paul.

Hôtel Saint-Louis **
75 rue Saint-Louis-en-Ile, 75004 Paris
Tel (1) 46 34 04 80, Fax (1) 46 34 02 13

An elegantly simple and immaculate hotel on the island's main street. Period furnishings. Rooms are comfortable and quiet. The owners have chosen not to put televisions in the bedrooms.

21 bedrooms all with private shower and bath/WC; telephone; hair-dryer; safe. Price FF620 single or double. Breakfast FF42. Lift. No credit cards accepted. Métro: Pont-Marie.

Hôtel Saint-Merry ***
78 rue de la Verrerie, 75004 Paris
Tel (1) 42 78 14 15, Fax (1) 40 29 06 82

The Saint-Merry is not quite like any other Paris hotel. Part of it was originally the presbytery of the neighbouring church of Saint-Merry and this ecclesiastical connection sets the tone. Decor is uncompromisingly Gothic with much heavily-carved and scrupulously-polished woodwork. With only 12 rooms, no lift, no televisions … but a warm welcome, this hotel is a little gem.

12 bedrooms all with private shower or bath, not all with private WC; telephone. Price FF400 - FF700 single or double. Breakfast FF40. No credit cards accepted. Métro: Hôtel-de-Ville or Castelet. RER: Chatelet-Les Halles.

Hôtel Saint-Paul-Le-Marais ***
8 rue de Sévigné, 75004 Paris
Tel (1) 48 04 97 27, Fax (1) 48 87 37 04

In the heart of the Marais close to Place des Vosges, this tasteful hotel has the best of both worlds. The building is a typical 17th century mansion which has been sympathetically renovated to retain many original features; the furnishings are discreetly modern.

27 bedrooms all with private shower or bath/WC; telephone; TV; hair-dryer. Price FF480 single, FF850 double. Breakfast FF40. Lift. All major credit cards accepted. Métro: Saint-Paul.

ETOILE/CHAMPES ELYSÉES — 8e

The 8e arrondissement lies on either side of the Champes Elysées as it descends from the Arc de Triomphe (also called l'Etoile) down towards Place de la Concorde and the river. This is one of the smartest residential districts with select hotels, sophisticated restaurants, haute couture *boutiques and art galleries. Many embassies are found around Rue de Faubourg St-Honoré and Avenue Matignon. To the north is Boulevard Haussman with large department stores and major banks. Understandably hotels in the* arrondissement *tend to be very expensive. A few of the hotels included in this section are just outside the 8e either in the 17e just north of the Arc de Triomphe between Avenue de la Grande Armée and Avenue de Wagram; or in the 16e to the east of the Arc de Triomphe between the main thoroughfares of Avenue Foch, Avenue Victor Hugo and Avenue Kieber.*

Hôtel Atala ****
10 rue Châteaubriand, 75008 Paris
Tel (1) 45 62 01 62, Fax (1) 42 25 66 38

A stone's throw away from the Arc de Triomphe, this understated hotel is spacious, pleasantly decorated and has extremely courteous service. It is slightly more expensive than the other addresses listed here but has a special bonus. In this very sough-after area, it enjoys its own private garden with stately trees and flowering shrubs. A restaurant with lounge opens onto the garden through a series of long windows making it a delightful summer residence.

47 bedrooms all with private bath/WC; telephone; TV; minibar. Price FF800 – FF990 single, FF1200 double.. Breakfast FF50. Lift. All major credit cards accepted. Métro: George V. RER: Charles-de-Gaulle-Etoile.

Hôtel du Bois **
11 rue du Dôme, 75016 Paris
Tel (1) 45 00 31 96, Fax (1) 45 00 90 05

An excellent address if you are looking for a reasonably-priced hotel within striking distance of the Champs Elysées. The access is however via a steep passage and there is no lift in the hotel itself. If this does not deter you, you will find that the staff are friendly ... and the owner is English.

41 bedrooms all with private shower or bath/WC; telephone; TV; minibar. Price FF385 single, FF455 – FF510 double. Breakfast FF40. All major credit cards except Diners. Métro: Etoile or Kléber. RER: Charles-de-Gaulle-Etoile.

Hôtel des Champs-Elysées **
2 rue d'Artois, 75008 Paris
Tel (1) 43 59 11 42, Fax (1) 45 61 00 61

A two-star hotel that offers excellent value for money with well-equipped rooms, a small lounge/bar and a *jardin d'hiver*. Charming owners and a warm welcome.

35 bedrooms all with private shower or bath/WC; telephone; TV; hair-dryer; minibar; safe. Price FF430 single or double. Breakfast FF30. Lift. Mastercard and Visa. Métro: Saint-Philippe-du-Roule.

Hôtel de l'Elysée ***
12 rue des Saussaies, 75008 Paris
Tel (1) 42 65 29 25, Fax (1) 42 65 64 28

This very beautifully decorated hotel is situated close to both the Champs Elysées and Faubourg St-Honoré. There is an elegant bar/lounge and impressive foyer furnished in classical style.

30 bedrooms all with private shower or bath/WC; telephone; TV; hair-dryer. Price FF520-FF800 single or double. Breakfast FF50. Lift. All major credit cards accepted. Métro: Champs Elysées or Miromesnil.

Hôtel Lido ***
4 passage de la Madeleine, 75008 Paris
Tel (1) 42 66 27 37, Fax (1) 42 66 61 23

A quiet elegant hotel in a side street just off Place de la Madeleine and close to the luxury shops on Rue Royale. Every comfort and classical period decor.

32 bedrooms all with private bath/WC; telephone; TV; hair-dryer; minibar; safe. Price FF680 single, FF780 double including breakfast. Lift. All major credit cards accepted. Métro: Madeleine. RER: Auber.

Hôtel Tilsitt-Etoile ***
2 rue Berry, 75017 Paris
Tel (1) 43 80 39 71, Fax (1) 47 66 37 63

Situated just north of the Arc de Triomphe, this is a well-run comfortable hotel. Quietly elegant but friendly and efficient.

39 bedrooms all with private shower or bath/WC; telephone; TV; hair-dryer; minibar. Price FF530 single, FF660-FF700 double. Breakfast FF45. Lift. All major credit cards accepted. Métro: Ternes or Etoile. RER: Charles-de-Gaulle-Etoile.

GRANDS BOULEVARDS — 9e

This area between the Opéra and Montmartre was the centre of Parisian elegance during the 19th century. It fell out of fashion but is now being rediscovered by those who enjoy its local shopping, street markets, pavement cafés and busy night-life. It is also convenient for the main stations – Saint-Lazare, Gare du Nord and Gare de l"Est.

Hôtel de Navarin et d'Angleterre **
8 rue Navarin, 75009 Paris
Tel (1) 48 78 31 80, Fax (1) 48 74 14 09

A simple family-run hotel in a lively area. Not all rooms have private WC and there is no lift but there is a small garden where breakfast is served in the summer.

27 rooms, some with private shower and bath/WC; telephone; some with TV. Price FF240-FF320 single or double. Breakfast FF25. Mastercard and Visa. Métro: Pigalle or Saint-Georges.

Résidence du Pré **
15 rue Pierre-Sémard, 75009 Paris
Tel (1) 48 78 26 72, Fax (1) 42 80 64 83

Excellent value for money in this recently refurbished hotel. Many bedrooms open onto an internal courtyard and a popular bar.

40 bedrooms all with private shower or bath/WC; telephone; TV. Price FF365 single, FF395-FF410 double. Breakfast FF25. Lift. All major credit cards accepted. Métro: Poissonière.

Hôtel Riboutté-Lafayette **
5 rue Riboutté, 75009 Paris
Tel (1) 47 70 62 36, Fax (1) 48 00 91 50

Right in the centre of things, this hotel has recently been renovated. It is quiet and friendly. Only a little English spoken.

24 bedrooms all with private shower or bath/WC; telephone; TV. Price FF380 single, FF420 double. Breakfast FF25. Lift. Amex, Mastercard and Visa. Métro: Cadet.

MONTMARTRE — 18e

Montmartre with its picturesque steep cobbled streets and alleyways, crowned by the great white basilica of Sacré-Coeur, retains its popular appeal. There are still painters busy at their easels in Place du Tertre, a couple of windmills have been preserved and the night-life is as boisterous as in Montmartre's 19th century heyday when this quaint hilltop village was the favourite quartier *of Bohemian artists. If you do not need to be centrally based in Paris, Montmartre might be an attractive idea. Cooler in summer and with fine views over the city, there is a choice of interesting hotels, many very reasonably priced. The lower levels of the Butte (the hill on which Montmartre stands) are served by the métro; a minibus or funicular take passengers right up to Sacré-Coeur.*

Ermitage Hôtel **
24 rue Lanmarck, 75018 Paris
Tel (1) 42 64 79 22, Fax (1) 42 64 10 33

At 200 metres from Sacré-Coeur, the Ermitage must be one of the nicest little hotels in Paris. Only 12 bedrooms and no lift but with its own small garden. Madame speaks excellent English and is absolutely charming. If you book early you can ask for either a room that opens onto the garden or one with 'the view'.

12 bedrooms all with private shower or bath/WC; telephone. Price Ff360-FF400 single or double including breakfast. No credit cards accepted. Métro: Lamarck-Caulaincourt or Château-Rouge. Minibus or funicular to Sacré-Coeur.

Terrass Hôtel ****
12/14 rue Joseph-de-Maistre, 75018 Paris
Tel (1) 46 06 72 85, Fax (1) 42 52 29 11

This large, very traditional French family-run hotel is situated at the foot of the Butte and has a superb roof terrace with stunning views over all of Paris. There are two restaurants – the classic Guerlande (closed during August) and the less formal Albatros.

101 bedrooms all with private bath/WC; telephone; TV: hair-dryer; minibar. Price FF800 single, FF950 double including breakfast. Lift. Amex, Diners and Visa. Métro: Place-de-Clichy.

TimHôtel Montmartre **
11 rue Rivignan, 75018 Paris
Tel (1) 42 55 74 79, Fax (1) 42 55 71 01

A very satisfactory friendly hotel close to the top of the Butte and facing onto a quiet tree-lined square.

64 bedrooms all with private shower or bath/WC; telephone; TV. Price FF303 single, FF388 double. Breakfast FF32. Lift. All major credit cards accepted. Métro: Abbesses or take the minibus.

RIVE GAUCHE — LEFT BANK

LA CITÉ/NOTRE-DAME/QUARTIER LATIN (LATIN QUARTER) — 5e

Ile de la Cité – the larger of the two islands that rise from the Seine – was at the heart of mediæval Paris; and Notre-Dame, the magnificent Gothic cathedral that dominates the riverside landscape, is still the official centre of the capital. All distances nationwide from Paris are calculated from here. The quais on both sides of the island and on the left bank are lined with a fascinating assortment of open-air stalls selling books, prints and bric-a-brac. There is a colourful daily flower market on the island and the area is ideal for leisurely browsing. The old city gradually spread to the left bank and it was here that the great university, the Sorbonne, was created in 1253. The Latin Quarter (named after the language of the scholars) has been devoted to academic and student life ever since.

Hôtel des Grands Hommes ***

17 place du Panthéon, 75005 Paris
Tel (1) 46 34 19 60, Fax (1) 43 26 67 32

This hotel and its sister-hotel next door, the Panthéon, are owned by the same family who are obviously successful and competent hoteliers. Both buildings have been well-restored and decorated in slightly different period styles.

32 bedrooms all with private bath/WC; telephone; TV; hair-dryer; minibar. Price FF630 single, FF720 double including breakfast. Lift. All major credit cards accepted. Métro: Cardinal-Lemoine. RER: Luxembourg.

Le Notre-Dame Hôtel ***

1 quai Saint-Michel, 75005 Paris
Tel (1) 43 54 20 43, Fax (1) 43 20 98 72

On Ile de la Cité in a picturesque setting beside the *quais* of the Seine and with fine views over Notre-Dame. Very comfortably furnished. Charming and attentive reception.

23 bedrooms all with private shower or bath/WC; telephone; TV; minibar. Price FF570-FF770 single or double. Breakfast FF35. Lift. Amex, Diners and Visa. Métro: Saint-Michel. RER: Cluny-Saint-Michel.

Select Hôtel ***
1 place de la Sorbonne, 75005 Paris
Tel (1) 46 34 14 80, Fax (1) 46 34 51 79

Close to Boulevard Saint-Michel, overlooking a tree-lined square, the Select is well-placed for exploring the Latin Quarter. It has a convivial bar which opens onto a pavement terrace during the summer months ... perfect for people-watching.

69 bedrooms all with private shower or bath/WC; telephone; TV. Price FF560-FF690 single or double. Breakfast FF30. Lift. All major credit cards accepted. Métro: Odèon or Saint-Michel. RER: Luxembourg or Cluny-Saint-Michel.

Hôtel des Trois Collèges **
16 rue Cujas, 75005 Paris
Tel (1) 43 54 67 30, Fax (1) 46 34 02 99

A pleasant reasonably-priced hotel situated close to the Sorbonne.

44 bedrooms all with private shower or bath/WC; telephone; TV; hair-dryer. Price FF330 single, FF400-FF460 double. Breakfast FF40. Lift. All major credit cards accepted. Métro: Saint-Michel. RER: Luxembourg or Cluny-Saint-Michel.

LUXEMBOURG/SAINT-GERMAIN-DES-PRÉS — 6e

The Luxembourg Palace (now home of the French Senate or Upper House) with extensive parks and formal gardens lies to the west of the university. Between here and the river is St-Germain-Des-Prés, the more up-market area of the Latin Quarter with fashionable boutiques, art galleries, book and antique shops. This is the artistic and intellectual centre of the Left Bank with a choice of smart cafés and restaurants.

Hôtel de l'Abbaye St-Germain ***
10 rue Cassette, 75006 Paris
Tel (1) 45 44 38 11, Fax (1) 45 48 07 86

A stylishly restored 17th century town house near the Luxembourg Gardens. Breakfast and drinks are served in a pretty paved courtyard.

44 bedrooms all with private bath/WC; telephone. Price FF720-FF1200 single or double including breakfast. Lift. Visa. Métro: Saint-Sulpice, Rennes or Sèvres-Babylone.

Hôtel d'Angleterre ***
44 rue Jacob, 75006 Paris
Tel (1) 42 60 34 72, Fax (1) 42 60 16 93

Pretty bedrooms grouped around a delightful patio covered with rambling greenery. This building was once the British Embassy in Paris … hence the name.

29 bedrooms all with private bath/WC; telephone; TV. Price FF600-FF1000 single or double. Breakfast FF40. Lift. All major credit cards accepted. Métro: St-Germain-des-Prés.

Hôtel des Deux Continents **
25 rue Jacob, 75006 Paris
Tel (1) 43 26 72 46

Situated in the same pleasant street as the Angleterre above, this family-run hotel has been modelled from three old houses, only one of which is served by a lift. The rooms with staircase access are cheaper and offer excellent value in this sought-after area.

40 bedrooms all with private shower or bath/WC; telephone; TV. Price FF380-FF570 single, FF510-FF620 double including breakfast. Lift (see above). Mastercard and Visa. Métro: St-Germain-des-Prés.

Grand Hôtel des Balcons **
3 rue Casimir-Delavigne, 75006 Paris
Tel (1) 46 34 78 50, Fax (1) 46 34 06 27

Well-placed between Boulevard Saint-Germain and the Luxembourg Gardens, this friendly hotel is immediately recognised by its many-balconied facade. An interesting simple hotel.

55 bedrooms all with private shower or bath/WC; telephone; TV. Price FF300-FF380 single or double. Breakfast FF40. Lift. Visa. Métro: Odéon. RER: Luxembourg.

Hôtel des Marronniers ***
21 rue Jacob, 75006 Paris
Tel (1) 43 25 30 60. Fax (1) 40 46 83 56

Yet another hotel in the popular rue Jacob, the Marronniers' main claim to fame is undoubtedly its garden … complete with *marronniers* – chestnut trees.

37 bedrooms all with private shower or bath/WC; telephone. Price FF420 single, FF600 double. Breakfast FF42. Lift. No credit cards accepted. Métro: St-Germain-des-Prés.

Hôtel Perreyve **
63 rue Madame, 75006 Paris
Tel (1) 45 48 35 01, Fax (1) 42 84 03 30

A quiet unpretentious hotel within walking distance of the Luxembourg Gardens.

30 bedrooms all with private shower or bath/WC; telephone; TV. Price Ff380-FF430 single or double.
Breakfast FF35. Lift. All major credit cards accepted. Métro: Rennes.

Hôtel Récamier **
3 bis place Saint-Sulpice, 75006 Paris
Tel (1) 43 26 04 89

Away from the bustle of the main boulevard in a quiet square near the church of Saint-Sulpice,
this homely hotel has a lot of charm.

30 bedrooms most with private shower or bath/WC; telephone. Price FF420-FF500 single, FF450-FF530
double. Breakfast FF30. Lift. No credit cards accepted. Métro: St-Sulpice, St-Germain-des-Prés or Mabillon.

Relais Saint-Germain ***
9 carrefour de l'Odéon, 75006 Paris
Tel (1) 43 29 12 05. Fax (1) 46 33 45 30

This is a rather special little hotel: Just 10 bedrooms, each one different, each one beautifully and
elegantly furnished.

10 bedrooms all with private bath/WC; telephone; TV; hair-dryer; minibar; safe. Price FF1190-FF1380
including breakfast. Lift. Amex, Diners and Visa. Métro: Odéon. RER: Cluny-Saint-Michel.

Hôtel Saint-Paul ***
43 rue Monsieur-le-Prince, 75006 Paris
Tel (1) 43 26 98 64, Fax (1) 46 34 58 60

In the heart of the Latin Quarter this sympathetically restored hotel has considerable character
with exposed beams and personalised bedrooms. Discreet and courteous service.

31 bedrooms all with private shower or bath/WC; telephone; TV; hair-dryer; minibar. Price FF450 single,
FF520 double. Breakfast FF40. Lift. All major credit cards accepted. Métro: Odéon. RER: Luxembourg or
Cluny-Saint-Michel.

FAUBOURG SAINT-GERMAIN/TOUR EIFFEL (EIFFEL TOWER) — 7e

During the 18th century Parisian aristocracy moved away from the Marais on the right bank and built grand houses in Faubourg Saint-Germain. Today this arrondissement *retains much of its former elegance although many of the handsome buildings are now used by foreign embassies and government ministries. Beside the river to the west is the soaring Eiffel Tower surrounded by extensive green open spaces. The rest of the area is exclusive residential or commercial districts.*

Hôtel Duc de Saint-Simon ***
14 rue de Saint-Simon, 75007 Paris
Tel (1) 45 48 35 66, Fax (1) 45 48 68 25

Just off Boulevard Saint Germain this very stylish hotel benefits from an attractive flowery central courtyard. Bedrooms are distinctive and many are decorated with antiques.

34 bedrooms all with private bath/WC; telephone; TV on request; hair-dryer. Price FF950-FF1800 single or double. Breakfast FF60. No credit cards accepted. Métro: Rue-du-Bac. RER: Gare d'Orsay.

Les Jardins d'Eiffel ***
8 rue Amélie, 75007 Paris
Tel (1) 47 05 46 21, Fax (1) 45 55 28 08

An extremely comfortable and well-equipped hotel on the left bank but within easy reach of the Champs Elysées. There is limited private parking at the hotel.

44 bedrooms all with private bath/WC; telephone; TV; hair-dryer; minibar; safe; trouser press. Price FF530-FF690 single, FF630-FF810 double. Breakfast FF35. Lift. All major credit cards accepted.

Hôtel du Quai Voltaire **
19 Quai Voltaire, 75007 Paris
Tel (1) 42 61 50 91, Fax (1) 42 61 62 26

On the opposite side of the river to the Louvre and close to the exciting 20th century art gallery, Musée d'Orsay, this building was part of an old abbey that was destroyed during the French Revolution.

33 bedrooms all with private shower or bath/WC; telephone; TV on request. Price FF440-FF520 single, FF620-FF690 double. Breakfast FF40. Lift. All major credit cards accepted. Métro: Rue-du-Bac. RER: Gare d'Orsay.

Hôtel de Suède ***
31 rue Vaneau, 75007 Paris
Tel (1) 47 05 00 08, Fax (1) 47 05 69 27

Situated in a reasonably quiet street in the embassy district. Rooms at the back overlook the Mâtignon (prime minister's official residence), Period furnishings and wood-panelled lounge.

41 bedrooms all with private shower or bath/WC; telephone. Price FF540 single, FF600 double including breakfast. Lift. Amex, Eurocard, Visa. Métro: Saint-François-Xavier or Sèvres-Babylone.

Hôtel de la Tulipe **
33 rue Malar, 75007 Paris
Tel (1) 45 51 67 21

A simple two-storey hotel with a central paved courtyard onto which most of the bedrooms open.

20 bedrooms all with private shower or bath/WC; telephone; TV; minibar. Price FF378 single, FF458 double. Breakfast FF30. Amex, Eurocard, Mastercard and Visa. Métro: Latour-Maubourg or Invalides. RER: Pont-de-l'Alma.

Readers' comments are always appreciated. Please let us know about any accommodation that you particularly enjoyed. Suggestions for new entries, too, are very welcome. Write to Meg Jump, La Maison Blanche, 04320 Entrevaux, France.

PICARDY / NORD / PAS-DE-CALAIS

Picardy/Nord/Pas-de-Calais
comprises the following
départements:
- Aisne (02)
- Nord (59)
- Oise (60)
- Pas-de-Calais (62)
- Somme (80)

*T*HE NORTHEASTERN CORNER OF FRANCE TENDS TO BE *an overlooked region — a landscape to pass through on the way to somewhere else. But for those who take the time to wander a little, it has a great deal of interest and charm. There are fine abbeys; impressive Gothic cathedrals are to be found at Amiens (the largest in France), Laon, Noyon, Soissons and Senlis; picturesque old towns such as Compiègne (where Joan of Arc was captured and handed over to the English) and Chantilly with its famous race course, stables and château; great forests; wide agricultural plains; wooded valleys and pleasant sparsely populated countryside. The Channel coast offers beautiful sandy beaches and in the extreme north — Pas-de-Calais — on the Belgian border, the Flemish influence is still apparent in the attractive local architecture, museums and art galleries.*

Domaine des Jeanne
rue Dubarle, 02290 Vic-sur-Aisne
Tel 23 55 57 33

Chambres d'Hôtes/Bed & Breakfast

This riverside estate with its fine 17th century mansion was once the property of the Duc de Gaête, Finance Minister to Napoleon I. Today Jean and Anne Martner offer quality bed and breakfast in very comfortable rooms that overlook the 2 hectare/4.5 acre park. There is a swimming pool and a tennis court for the use of guests plus the possibility of fishing in the  River Aisne. Excellent evening meals are available and the Martners speak English. Domaine des Jeanne is convenient for Paris/Charles-de-Gaulle airport and is also central for the many sightseeing attractions north of Paris.

Situated 100km/60 miles north-east of Paris, 25km/15 miles east of Compiègne and 16km/10 miles west of Soissons. Nearest international airport: Paris/Charles-de-Gaulle at 70km/42 miles. Nearest station: Soissons.

Additional information:

Open all year. 5 bedrooms all with private shower/WC. Price FF280-FF300 including breakfast. Dinner FF75 (please order in advance). Swimming pool. Tennis court. Carte Bleue, Eurocard, Mastercard and Visa. Brochure in French and further information in English sent on request.

Les Patrus
02540 L'Epine-aux-Bois
Tel 23 69 85 85

Chambres d'Hôtes/Bed & Breakfast

Set in open countryside between Paris and Champagne, Les Patrus is an old post-house of character dating back to the 17th and 18th centuries. Your friendly English-speaking hosts, Marc and Mary-Ann Royal, now keep horses on the property and offer guests very comfortable accommodation with a country-style breakfast and dinner of good, wholesome home-cooking. Les Patrus is very centrally situated for visiting the champagne houses of Reims and Epernay, Paris (one hour), Fontainbleau and the new Euro-Disneyland.

Situated 45km/27 miles east of Meaux and 10km/6 miles west of Montmirail via D933. Nearest international airport: Paris/Charles-de-Gaulle. Nearest station: Montmirail.

Additional information:

Open all year. 5 bedrooms all with private bath/WC; telephone. Price FF260-FF350 double including breakfast. Dinner FF90-FF130. Eurocard and Mastercard. Further information in English sent on request.

Château de Ligny
Ligny-en-Cambrésis, 59190 Ligny-Haucourt
Tel 27 85 25 84

Château-hotel*** with restaurant

This lovely old castle is conveniently situated within easy access of the main northern autoroutes - A1, A2 and A26 - near the church in a quiet village. Built during the 17th century on the site of an earlier 13th century house, it is surrounded by attractive lawns and gardens. An interesting Renaissance gate leads to a small bridge that spans the original moat. Bedrooms are very comfortable and the reception rooms are tastefully furnished with antiques. A pleasant and civilized stop-over in northern France where your hosts, Monsieur and Madame Boulard, speak English.

Situated 50km/30 miles south-west of Valenciennes and 17km/10 miles south-east of Cambrai via N43 to Beauvois then D74 to Ligny-en-Cambrésis. Nearest international airport: Paris at 200km/120 miles. Nearest national airport: Lille at 80km/48 miles. Nearest station: Cambrai.

Additional information:

Open all year except Christmas and mid-January to mid-February. 9 bedrooms all with private bath/WC; telephone; TV; some with minibar. Price FF460-FF1,100 single or double. Breakfast FF45. Lunch and dinner FF170-FF330 (closed Saturday lunch and all day Monday). Amex, Diners and Carte Bleue. Colour brochure in French and English sent on request.

Auberge de Fontaine

22 Grande Rue, Fontaine-Châalis, 60300 Senlis
Tel 44 54 20 22

*Country auberge ** with restaurant*

A simple country inn located on the very edge of the Forest of Ermonville close to the interesting towns of Senlis, Chantilly and Compiègne yet only 50km/30 miles north of Paris. This is a friendly family-run concern where Monsieur Campion is in the kitchen ... and his cooking is very good indeed! Try his home-made *foie gras* and rabbit dishes. Madame Campion looks after the hotel and has decorated the bedrooms prettily with floral papers and lace curtains. The main buildings of the inn form an internal courtyard where meals are served in the summer, and there is a garden beyond. The Campions speak English and have full information on places of interest in the vicinity, forest walks, riding and fishing.

Situated 50km/30 miles north-east of Paris, 40km/24 miles south of Compiègne and 10km/6 miles south-east of Senlis via D330. Nearest international airport: Paris. Nearest station: Senlis.

Additional information:

Open all year except February. 8 bedrooms all with private shower or bath/WC; telephone. Price FF240-FF300 single or double. Breakfast FF30. Lunch and dinner FF115-FF180 or à la carte (closed Tuesday evening and all day Wednesday). Carte Bleue and Visa. Brochure in French and further information in English sent on request.

Château de Montreuil

62170 Montreuil-sur-Mer
Tel 21 81 53 04 Fax 21 81 36 43

Restaurant with rooms

Château de Montreuil is neither a *château* in the usual sense of the word - it is a large 1930s residence – nor is it *sur mer*. Montreuil was on the coast some centuries ago, but is now about 10 miles inland. There is, however, no confusion concerning the cooking of Christian Germain; it has won him a Michelin rosette. The restaurant is comfortably elegant, decorated in tones of soft blue. During the summer months, meals are served

153

on an outside terrace overlooking pleasant gardens. Bedrooms are luxurious and have 24-hour room service. For those who enjoy sporting activities, there are three golf courses within a short drive and tennis nearby. Madame Germain is English so there are no language problems.

Situated 66km/40 miles south of Calais. Nearest international airport: Paris at 200km/120 miles. Nearest national airport: Le Touquet at 14km/8 miles. Nearest station: Montreuil.

Additional information:

Open all year except mid-December to mid-February. 14 bedrooms all with private shower or bath/WC; telephone; TV. Price FF600-FF930 double. Half board FF1,350-FF1,650 double. Special mid-week half board price out of high season FF500 per person per day. Breakfast FF60. Lunch and dinner FF250-FF350 (restaurant closed Monday in low season and Thursday lunch). Eurocard, Mastercard and Visa. Colour brochure in French and English sent on request.

Grand Hôtel Clément

91 Esplanade du Maréchal Leclerc, 62610 Ardres
Tel 21 82 25 25 Fax 21 82 98 92

*Hotel *** with restaurant*

Originally an old posting inn, the Clément has been in the same family since 1917 and the present chef/owner, François Coolen, is the fourth generation and great-grandson of the first propretor, Paul Clément. François is also a member of the association *Jeunes Restaurateurs de France* and his cooking is very good indeed. Bedrooms are nicely furnished in a charming, rather old-fashioned French style and there is a pleasant garden at the rear of the hotel. Standing on the edge of the town square in Ardres, close to the Channel ports, the Clément is a convenient and friendly stopping-off point. François and his wife, Isabelle, speak English.

Situated 17km/10 miles south-east of

Cookery Breaks at Château de Montreuil

Cookery breaks at Montreuil are not at all like the normal courses run by specialist schools. Participants are asked to make up their own group of from four to eight people, for a course that runs from Tuesday to Friday during February and March, November and December. There is a definite 'holiday' aspect so that in addition to actual cookery sessions in the kitchen, wine tasting and shopping trips, guests are also offered canoe-kayaking on the River Canche or clay pigeon shooting at nearby Merlimont. There are tennis courts just opposite the Château de Montreuil and bicycles may be hired at the hotel.

Prices start at FF2,550 per person which includes 3 nights accommodation, 3 breakfasts and dinners, 1 lunch, cooking in the kitchen, a wine tasting and shopping trips.

For more information in English, contact Château de Montreuil (see left).

Calais and 35km/21 miles north-east of Boulogne. Nearest international airport: Paris at 276km/165 miles. Nearest national airport: Le Touquet at 65km/39 miles or Lille at 90km/54 miles. Nearest station: Calais.

Additional information:

Open all year except mid-January to mid-February. 17 bedrooms all with private showere or bath/WC; telephone; TV. Price FF220-FF320 single or double. Breakfast FF35. Lunch and dinner FF95-FF320 or à la carte (closed all day Monday and Tuesday lunch in low season). Parking. Amex, Diners, Eurocard and Visa. Colour brochure in French and English sent on request.

Château de Cocove
Recques-sur-Hem, 62890 Tournehem
Tel 21 82 68 29, Fax 21 82 72 59

Château-Hotel *** with restaurant

The splendid Château de Cocove is set in a magnificent *parc à l'Anglais* in quiet countryside between St-Omer and Calais, close to the A26 autoroute. Completely renovated in 1986, it provides comfortable and well-furnished accommodation plus a range of additional facilities – a gastronomic restaurant, golf practice, stables and riding, sauna and a fine wine cellar where French wines may be purchased at very competive prices. Many drivers rush through this area of France on their way to and from the Channel ports, but there is much of interest in the region. The hotel has full information on all local attractions, many of which are overlooked by travellers: St-Omer with its majestic cathedral and glass production (with factory shop) for one; the famous lace-making centres of Calais and Cambrai for another. Guests are made very welcome at Château de Cocove and English is spoken.

Situated 30km/18 miles south-east of Calais and 18km/11 miles north-west of St-Omer via N43 and D217, or exit autoroute A26 at Nordausques. Nearest international airport: Paris at 260km/156 miles. Nearest national airport: Lille at 70km/42 miles. Nearest station: St-Omer.

Additional information:

Open all year. 22 bedrooms all with private bath/WC; telephone; TV. Price FF320-FF625 double. Special gastronomic weekend FF690-FF1,240 single, FF925-FF1,680 double. Breakfast FF40. Lunch and dinner FF99-FF195 or à la carte. Golf practice. Sauna. All major credit cards accepted. Full colour brochure in French and English sent on request.

Golf Holidays with Bed & Breakfast Accommodation in Northern France

Sue and Alan Fields, an English couple and keen golfers, have devised a golf holiday formula with a difference. They offer extremely comfortable guest house accommodation in their family home plus access to the seven golf courses that are within easy driving distance of their home — Hardelot Pins (5,870 metres par 72), Hardelot Dunes (6,095 metres par 73), Wimereux (6,150 metres par 72), Le Touquet mer (6,082 metres par 72), Le Touquet Forêt (5,035 metres par 71, Aa St-Omer (6,400 metres par 72), Nampont St-Martin (5,855 metres par 71).

The Fields house lies in fact just a few minutes from the first tee of the Hardelot Dunes course, and a few kilometres from the older Hardelot Pins course. The others are all within 45 minutes' driving, offering quality and excellence for both the beginner and the experienced golfer. Mid-week fees are very competitive, but most courses charge a weekend supplement of FF50-FF200 per person. In addition there is tennis and riding nearby; plus at Le Touquet, 10 kilometres away,

fine sandy beaches with sand-yachting, speed sailing and wind-surfing. Sue Fields is an enthusiastic cook and houseguests are invited to dine en famille; she specializes in good home cooking using fresh produce from the vegetable garden.

For golfers coming from the United Kingdom, attractive cross-Channel ferry rates are available. The Fields also own a self-catering apartment for up to four people on the Hardelot Pins Golf course.

Additonal information:

Open all year. 4 bedrooms all with private shower or bath/WC. Price FF250 double including breakfast. Dinner FF60-FF100. Inclusive holiday rates also available Self-catering apartment with 2 bedrooms FF2,500 per week including electricity.Bed linen supplied at an extra charge.No credit cards accepted. For further information in English, please contact Alan and Sue Fields, Fields Fairway, 91 rue du chemin, 62152 Neufchâtel-Hardelot. Tel 21 33 85 23. Fax 21 33 85 24.

The First World War

Much of the most bitter fighting during the First World War took place in Picardy. The Battle of the Somme started on July 1, 1916, and war memorials to the French, British, Canadians, Americans, Australians and New Zealanders who lost their lives during that offensive are to be found along a signposted route (marked by a Picardy rose), beginning in the town of Albert (80) which was almost entirely destroyed during the First and Second World Wars. Memorials on the route include Beaumont-Hamel (80) between Arras and Amiens, with its bronze statue of a reindeer in memory of action involving the Newfoundland Regiment together with the British 29th Division; the New Zealanders memorial at Longueval (80), south of Arras; the British memorial at Thiepval (80) between Arras and Amiens, with the Belfast Tower as a memorial to Irish troops; Vimy Ridge (62) near Arras, where many Canadians lost their lives in 1917; Nôtre-Dame-de-Dames (02) near Soissons, which the French attempted to take with great loss of life, Château-Thierry (02) where 2,500 American soldiers died in 1918.

Bois de Bonance
Port-le-Grand, 80132 Abbeville
Tel 22 24 11 97 or 22 24 34 97

Chambres d'Hôtes/Bed & Breakfast

Set in lovely gardens, Bois de Bonance is a charming country house of mellow pink brick offering very comfortable and tastefully-furnished accommodation. Near to both Calais and Boulogne, it is an ideal nightstop for anyone driving to or from the Channel ports but with a swimming pool in the garden, golf nearby and within easy reach of the coastal resort of Le Touquet plus the fishing villages of the Somme Estuary, it is also suitable for a longer stay. Your hosts, Monsieur and Madame Maillard, are very welcoming and speak English.

Situated 84km/50 miles south of Boulogne and 11km/6 miles north-west of Abbeville via D40 towards the coast. Nearest international airport: Paris at 150km/90 miles. Nearest station: Abbeville.

Additional information:

Open all year except Christmas. 5 bedrooms all with private shower or bath/WC. Price FF280 single, FF320 double including breakfast. Swimming pool. No credit cards accepted. Brochure in French and English sent on request.

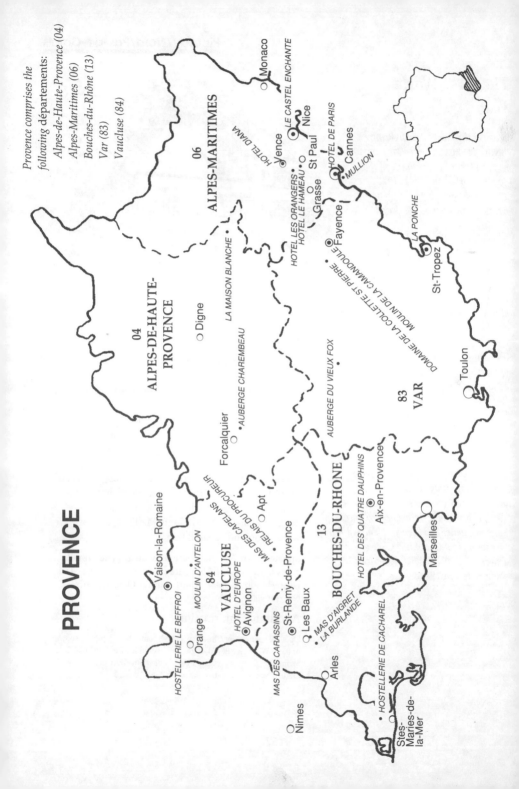

PROVENCE

Provence comprises the
following départements:
Alpes-de-Haute-Provence (04)
Alpes-Maritimes (06)
Bouches-du-Rhône (13)
Var (83)
Vaucluse (84)

ALPES-MARITIMES
06

Monaco

LE CASTEL ENCHANTE
Nice
Vence
HOTEL DIANA
St Paul
HOTEL LES ORANGERS
HOTEL LE HAMEAU
Grasse
HOTEL DE PARIS
Cannes
Fayence
MULLION
LA PONCHE

ALPES-DE-HAUTE-PROVENCE
04

LA MAISON BLANCHE
Digne

AUBERGE CHAREMBEAU
Forcalquier

DOMAINE DE LA COLETTE ST PIERRE
MOULIN DE LA CAMANDOULE

AUBERGE DU VIEUX FOX

St-Tropez

VAR
83

Toulon

RELAIS DU PROCUREUR
Apt

MAS DES CAPELANS

Vaison-la-Romaine
HOSTELLERIE LE BEFFROI
MOULIN D'ANTELON
VAUCLUSE
84
Orange
HOTEL D'EUROPE
Avignon
St-Remy-de-Provence
Les Baux
MAS D'AIGRET
LA BURLANDE

BOUCHES-DU-RHONE
13
HOTEL DES QUATRE DAUPHINS
Aix-en-Provence

Marseilles

MAS DES CARASSINS

Arles

Nimes

HOSTELLERIE DE CACHAREL

Stes-
Maries-de-
la-Mer

*F*OR TRAVELLERS THE WORLD OVER, *Provence is a magical region of France. The Romans called it Provincia – the most-favoured of all their colonies – and embellished it with outstanding buildings, monuments, viaducts and roads, many of which have survived to this day. After the fall of Rome, Provence was successively coveted and fought over by Vandals, Goths and Moorish Saracens from North Africa. Early Christianity had a firm hold here and the main pilgrim route from Rome to Santiago de Compostella traversed Provence. During the 14th century the church was so powerful that a papal hierarchy was established at Avignon rivalling the authority of the Pope in Rome. It was not until the end of the 15th century that Provence was annexed to the north and it took another 400 years before the County of Nice at the eastern extremity was absorbed into France.*

Little wonder then that sunny Mediterranean Provence seems to be not only 1,000 kilometres away from the chilly north, but in a different world. It is not surprising either that its very popularity seems – in some areas – almost to have obliterated the 'real Provence'. Almost ... but not quite, for Provence is a vast area of startling contrasts, from the exotic sophistication of the French Riviera to the unspoilt mediæval hilltop villages of the Nice hinterland; from the watery wastes of the Camargue, home of wild white horses, black bulls and migratory birds to the carefully-cultivated rolling vineyards of the Rhône Valley; from the sun-baked plains of the Var to the wild Alpine foothills of haute Provence. These are the landscapes that inspired some of the world's greatest painters and although much has changed in Provence during the last century, much remains as it ever was. The brilliant light, the vibrant colours, the heady perfumes, the exotic food, the so-very-drinkable wines, the leisurely life-style of Provence still have a wickedly seductive appeal.

Auberge Charembeau
Route de Niozelles,
04300 Forcalquier
Tel 92 75 05 69

Country hotel**

Set deep in the unspoilt countryside of Haute Provence yet only a few minutes' drive from the market town of Forcalquier, the *auberge* is an 18th century farm in the midst of

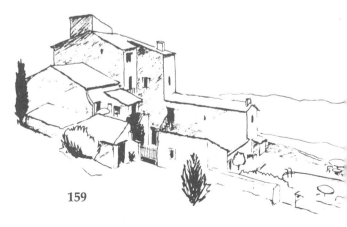

seven hectares/15 acres of farmland and woods. Furnishings are simple but tasteful. A swimming pool, tennis court and mountain bikes are available to guests and accompanied walks can be arranged. Although there is no restaurant, there is a good choice nearby and some rooms are equipped with a kitchenette. These rooms are for weekly lets only. The Charembeau is perfect for discovering a part of Provence that is often overlooked. M et Mme Berger speak English.

Situated 42km/25 miles north-east of Apt. Auberge Charembeau is 4 km/1.5 miles east of Forcalquier via D12 and then N100 to Niozelles. Nearest international airport: Marseilles at 80km/50 miles. Nearest station: Digne at 48 km/29 miles.

Additional information:

Open mid-February – mid-November. 12 bedrooms all with privatge shower or bath/WC; telephone; some with kitchenette. Price FF222-FF288 double. With kitchenette FF1200-FF1900 per week. Breakfast FF35. Swimming pool. Tennis court. Mountain bikes. Visa. Colour brochure inFrench sent on request.

La Maison Blanche
04320 Entrevaux
Tel 93 05 46 50, Fax 93 05 48 16

Self-catering cottage and studio

The historic village of Entrevaux straddles the River Var in the Alpine foothills behind Nice. A unique unspoilt mediæval 'city', it retains its original drawbridge and decorated gatehouse, narrow winding streets (no motorised traffic), and hilltop citadel approached by 20 fortified gates. At the entrance to the village, La Maison Blanche is a turn-of-the -century house with two pretty houses built in the old orchard;

each is traditionally Provençal in style with pastel-tinted walls, shutters and canal-tiled roof. The Cottage has two bedrooms and can accommodate up to five people; the Studio is for two. Both are very comfortable and are simply but prettily furnished. Set in the spectacular scenery of Haute Provence, Entrevaux makes an ideal base for discovering the hinterland of the French Riviera but is only a hour's drive from the famous coastal resorts. The owners of La Maison Blanche are the author of this book and her husband. They, of course, speak English.

Situated 70km/42 miles north-west of Nice and 75km/45 miles south-east of Digne. Nearest international airport: Nice. Nearest station: Entrevaux which is on the narrow gauge railway – Chemin de Fer de Provence – which runs between Nice and Digne.

Additional information:

Open all year. The Cottage has two bedrooms; shower/WC; living/dining/ kitchen; outside vine-covered dining terrace; garden. Price FF2,160-FF3,600 per week including electricity and bed linen. Studio has bed-sitting room with kitchenette; shower/WC; outside vine-covered dining terrace; garden. Price FF1,680-FF2,160 per week including electricity and bed linen. Daily rates also available on both properties. No credit cards accepted. Further information in English sent on request. Suitable for visitors without a car.

Hôtel Le Hameau
528 route de la Colle, 06570 Saint-Paul-de-Vence
Tel 93 32 80 24, Fax 93 32 55 75
*Hotel*** without restaurant*

Since the last century, Saint-Paul-de-Vence has attracted painters partly because of its unrivalled hilltop position with views over the Cote d'Azur to the Mediterranean Sea, but also for the architectural excellence of the village itself. Not surprisingly, it attracts great numbers of visitors. The narrow 16th century streets are full of souvenir shops and a large carpark caters for tourist cars and coaches. Even so, Saint-Paul is still a painter's village with numerous small galleries and craft shops; the Maeght Foundation is a museum containing many fine contemporary works. Perhaps the best way to enjoy Saint-Paul is to stay nearby, within walking distance, to arrive early or late and avoid the crowds. Hôtel le Hameau will allow you to do just that. At 1 km/.5 mile from the village, idyllically set in a terraced landscape of lemon trees and olive groves, the old white-washed house is grown over and around with vines and honeysuckle to form shady, sweet-smelling patios, cool under the Provençal sun. Bedrooms are furnished in local style with tiled floors and traditional furniture; many have superb views. In an area where hotel accommodation can be very expensive, the Hameau is reasonably priced and has great charm. Although Madame speaks only French, Monsieur Huvelin's English is good. No restaurant but a good choice in the village.

Situated 18km/11 miles west of Nice at 1 km/1/2 miles from Saint-Paul on D7 toward La Colle-sur-Loup. Nearest international airport and station at Nice. Bus connections to Saint-Paul.

Additional information:

Open mid-February – mid-November. 17 bedrooms all with private shower or bath/WC; telephone; mini-bar. Price FF295 single, FF320-FF580 double. Breakfast FF40. Swimming pool. Garage parking FF40 per night. Amex, Carte Bleue, Mastercard and Visa. Information in French and photos sent on request. Suitable for visitors without a car.

Walking holidays in Provence

Walking holidays in the département *Alpes de Haute Provence* are organised by an English company, *Somewhere in Time*. The accompanied walks are designed for two kinds of participants: Those who prefer a reasonably flat terrain and walks of a moderate duration (Level 1); and those who are comfortable with more demanding trails lasting more than five hours each day (Level 2).

Level 1 is based in the ancient village of Bauduen situation on a hillside beside Lac de Sainte-Croix. The six daily walks take full advantage of the spectacular scenery, each one lasting from three to five hours. One route follows part of Grande Randonné 99, one of the many marked trails that criss-cross France; another starts with a boat trip on the lake, then up a gently flowing river until the water becomes so shallow that walkers continue on foot deep into a canyon with sheer walls and lush vegetation; yet another includes a stroll through the famous lavender-growing area of Haute Provence.

Level 2 is based in the attractive pottery village of Moustiers-Sainte-Marie close to the western tip of Lac de Sainte-Croix. The six walks from here are designed to satisfy experienced walkers and include Martel's famous path that descends to the bottom of the Gorge du Verdon and follows the course of the river, then climbs again to Point Sublime where support vehicles wait to ferry walkers back to their hotel. Another day is spent on a section of Grande Randonné 4 along a path that rises to the crest of the Barbin mountain.

The hotels chosen at each base provide bedrooms with private bathrooms; the restaurants specialise in local food and wine. On arrival, guests are greeted by their English-speaking guides who explain the week's programme, discuss the walks and give information about restaurants, sailing, windsurfing and places of interest in the immediate vicinity.

The two centres are 30 km/17 miles apart; thus walkers who would like to change from one base to another for part of the week may do so.

Additional information:

Holidays are for one week Saturday-Saturday from mid-April to end of September.

Bauduen – Level 1

Price FF3800-FF4600 per person per week. The price includes accommodation in a lakeside hotel, breakfast, full picnic lunch, evening meal, six walks, guides, local transport.

Moustiers-Sainte-Marie – Level 2

Price FF2900-FF3900 per person per week. The prince includes accommodation in a hotel in the centre of the village, breakfast, full picnic lunch, six walks, guides, local transport. The hotel serves an excellent evening meal but this is optional and is not included in the price; thus guests can choose to eat in the hotel or at on of the excellent restaurants in the village.

Transfer from Nice to the hotel is available at FF300 per person (minimum two people sharing).

For further information and full colour brochure, please contact:
    Somewhere in Time,
    Tyn-y-Beili,
    Llanafan Fawr,
    Powys,
    Wales, United Kingdom.
    Tel (0) 5912 656, Fax (0) 5912 697.

Hôtel Les Orangers

Quartier Les Fumerates, 06570 Saint-Paul-de-Vence
Tel 93 32 80 95, Fax 93 32 00 32

Hotel***

Just a 10-minute walk from the centre of Saint-Paul, Les Orangers is an old farmhouse set amongst lovely gardens and orange groves, with superb views over the surrounding countryside. Bedrooms are very tastefully furnished in traditional Provençal style with tiled floors and authentic 18th century furniture. Guests have the use of a homely sitting room with log fire in winter or, during the long sunny summers or southern France, drinks are served on an attractive terrace overlooking the distant Mediterranean. No restaurant but there is an excellent choice in Saint-Paul. Les Orangers is under the personal supervision of the English owner, Thomas Franklin.

Situated 18km/11 miles west of Nice. Nearest international airport and station at Nice. Bus stops 20 metres/yards from the hotel.

Additional information:

Open all year. 8 bedrooms all with private bath/WC; telephone. Price FF460-FF620 single or double. Breakfast FF40. Eurocard, Mastercard and Visa. Colour brochure in French and English sent on request. Suitable for visitors without a car.

Hôtel de Paris

34 Boulevard d'Alsace, 06400 Cannes
Tel 93 38 30 89, Fax 93 39 04 61

Hotel*** with restaurant

Cannes is one of the brilliant stars of the Côte d'Azur with a wide choice of glamourous and luxurious accommodation. A hotel of great charm and character, Hotel de Paris offers comfort and elegance at a very reasonable price. The building is typical of the flamboyant *belle époque* architecture of the turn-of-the-century. It stands in lovely well-established gardens with a swimming pool surrounded by palm trees and cyprus. Within walking distance of the town centre and 300 metres/yards from a private beach and the famous Croisette, Hotel de Paris has all the evocative atmosphere of the French Riviera. Private parking for 18 cars. Most staff speak English.

Situated in the centre of Cannes. Nearest international airport: Nice at 30km/18 miles. Nearest station: Cannes at 300 metres/yards. Reduced rates are available for advance bookings of 3 days/2 nights and 8

days/7 nights. These include bed and breakfast, use of the hamman and Jacuzzi, and a trip to the nearby Lerin Islands. The half board package allows guests to choose between dining in the hotel or at any of 15 specially selected restaurants in Cannes..

Additional information:

Open all year except mid-November to mid-January. 48 bedrooms with private shower or bath/WC; telephone; TV; hair-dryer; safe. Price FF380-FF650 single, FF420-FF1800 double. Three-day B&B package FF480-FF680 per person, half board FF650-FF850 per person. Eight-day B&B package FF1225-FF2275 per person, half board FF1820-FF2870 per person. Breakfast FF50. Lift. Swimming pool and private beach. Private parking at FF80 per day. All major credit cards accepted. Full colour brochure in English sent on request. Suitable for guests without a car.

Le Castel Enchanté

61 Route de Saint-Pierre-de-Férie, 06000 Nice
Tel 93 97 02 08

Chambres d'Hôtes/Bed & Breakfast

Le Castel Enchanté enjoys a privileged position in the hills behind Nice yet is only five minutes' drive from the city centre. The house is in the typical turn-of-the-century Niçoise style with long shuttered French windows opening onto a magnificent garden. Flowers ramble over the walls and tall trees provide essential shade from the hot Mediterranean sun. Breakfast takes the form of a generous buffet which is served either in the dining room or outside on the terrace. Le Castel Enchanté makes an excellent base from which to discover the French Riviera and your hostess, Madame Jacqueline Olivier, speaks very good English.

Situated just north of central Nice off the *voie rapide* (expressway) via Place Saint-Philippe and Avenue Estienne d'Orves. Nearest international airport and station: Nice.

Additional information:

Open all year. 4 bedrooms all with private bath/WC. Price FF360 double including breakfast. Parking. No credit cards accepted. Further information in English sent on request. Suitable for visitors without a car.

Mullion

Berthed in an exclusive mooring at Cannes, adjacent to the Palais des Festivals and within easy reach of the Croisette, one of the most famous shoreline promenades in the world, Mullion is a luxury ocean-going cruiser. Sleeping accommodation is in three double air-conditioned cabins with en suite bathrooms and there is also an elegant saloon. A large upper sundeck is perfect for sun-bathing or pre-dinner cocktails. For at-sea leisure activities, Mullion has a Novamarine ski-boat and a windsurfer. For quieter moments a cassette/CD deck, video recorder and television are provided. The crew is Anglo-American and food on board is of Cordon Bleu standard. The boat is 22.4 metres/73 feet long and 6 metres/18 feet wide. Powered by quiet economical diesels, she has a cruising speed of 10 knots and a range of more than 6500 km/4000 miles. Mullion can therefore take her passengers wherever they may wish to go ... but she can equally serve as a most glamorous floating apartment; she need never leave her privileged marina mooring.

Mullion is available for charter all year round, by the day or for longer. Daily rates begin at FF13,500 for up to six passengers. for more information, please contact the owners.
Tel 94 76 96 79, Fax: 93 39 26 37

Hôtel Diana

avenue des Poilus, 06140 Vence
Tel 93 58 28 56, Fax 93 24 64 06

Hotel***

The Diana is one of the few modern hotels to be featured in this guide. It has, however, been chosen for a good reason – some of the rooms have a fully-equipped kitchenette which is such a good idea for those who may tire of eating out in restaurants for every meal. In addition, each room opens onto a sunny terrace for outside dining and the daily food market in the old town of Vence will be a happy hunting ground for ingredients. Vence itself is an ideal town base being placed just inland between Nice and Cannes. With many excellent restaurants, good shops, lots of craft shops and art galleries, it also has regular bus connections to all the major places of interest on the Cote d'Azur. Or for drivers, yet another bonus point for the Diana is its large underground carpark.

Situated 21 km/12 miles north-west of Nice and 30 km/18 miles north-east of Cannes. Nearest international airport: Nice. Nearest station: Nice or Cannes.

Additional information:

Open all year except the last two weeks in November. 25 bedrooms all with private bath/WC; telephone; terrace. 15 fitted with kitchenette. Price FF340-FF360 single or double, FF380 with kitchenette. Breakfast FF36. Lift. Garage FF15 per day. All major credit cards accepted. Colour brochure in French and English sent on request. Suitable for visitors without a car.

Mas des Carassins

1 chemin
Gaulois, 13210
Saint-Rémy-de-
Provence
Tel 90 92 15 48

Hotel ***

Admirers of the
painter Van Gogh are

practically guaranteed to fall in love with this small family-run hotel. Van Gogh lived and worked in Saint-Rémy-de-Provence in 1890-91 during which time he produced more than 100 paintings. For some of these his viewpoint was very close to the *mas*, which was built by the present owners' great-grandfather in 1849. Prints of these works are on show at the hotel and visitors are able to see (or even paint) a similar landscape. The family home was transformed into a hotel in 1980 and is very tastefully decorated with typical Provençal furnishings. Although within walking distance of the town centre, it is set in its own peaceful gardens. There are many recommended restaurants nearby but light meals and refreshments are available. M et Mme Ripert speak only a little English but guests can be sure of a warm welcome.

Situated 20 km/12 miles south of Avignon. Nearest international airport: Marseilles at 86 km/53 miles. Nearest national airport: Avignon. Nearest station: Avignon (TGV). From the town centre take Avenue Van Gogh due south; cross over the canal and turn immediately right into Avenue Joseph d'Arbaud; continue into Chemin Gaulois and Mas des Carassins is on the left.

Additional information:

Open mid-March – mid-November. 10 bedrooms all with private bath/WC; telephone. Price FF310-FF410 single, FF340-FF480 double. Breakfast FF25-FF42. Carte Bleue, Mastercard and Visa. Colour brochure in French and English sent on request. Suitable for visitors without a car.

Hostellerie de Cacherel

Route de Cacharel, 13460 Les Saintes-Maries de-la-Mer
Tel 90 97 95 44, Fax 90 97 87 97

Hotel***

Set deep in the marshlands of the Camargue, home of migratory flamingoes, wild white horses and black bulls destined for the bull-ring, this hotel is surrounded by 65 hectares/26 acres of private land and is on the borders of the Camargue Nature Reserve. From the hotel daily trips on horse-back are organised into the Camargue, accompanied by a *gardian* – the local cowboy. Short outings may last one or two hours but full-day rides (with a picnic) will appeal to experienced riders. The hotel itself is a traditional long, low-lying *mas* that has been nicely restored and decorated. There is no restaurant but *une assiette campagnarde* – a country platter – and a *pichet* of wine can be ordered at any time. Your friendly English-speaking host, Monsieur Colomb de Daunant, knows all the best restaurants around and will be very happy to make sure you do not go hungry. Follow his expert advice and you will probably discover establishments that other tourists never find.

Situated 130 km/80 miles west of Marseilles and 50 km/30 miles south of Nîmes and 4 km/1.5 miles north of Les Saintes-Maries-de-la-Mer on D85a called Route de Cacharel. Nearest international airport: marseilles or Montpellier at 40 km/24 miles. Nearest station: Arles at 38km/23 miles.

Additional information:

Open all year. 11 bedrooms all with private shower or bath/WC; telephone. Price FF526 single, FF572 double. Breakfast FF40. Swimming pool. Eurocard, Mastercard and Visa. Further information in English sent on request.

Mas d'Aigret

13520 Les Baux-de-Provence
Tel 90 54 33 54. Fax 90 54 41 37

Hotel*** with restaurant

A cluster of prestigious hotels has grown up in the shadow of the romantic perched village of Les Baux.

Les Baux-de-Provence

Clinging dramatically to a desolate outcrop of the craggy Alpilles range, Les Baux-de-Provence has an undeniable allure. Originally belonging to the Counts of Baux, the old citadel was the scene of one of the most brilliant troubadour courts of the Middle Ages. It later passed to the Counts of Provence, famous for their brutal lawlessness and passion for blood-thirsty pursuits. The imposing castle was eventually razed to the ground during the 17th century, leaving only the evocative skeletal remains that can be seen today. The village that grew up beneath the ill-fated castle has,however, survived and contains some remarkable examples of Renaissance architecture. These fine houses have been beautifully restored and bear testimony to the village's glorious – and

inglorious – past. Inevitably Les Baux, with its striking setting and romantic history, has become a popular tourist attraction but the hoards of curious sight-seers cannot completely destroy the magic. It is well worth a visit especially out of season or early in the morning before the coachloads arrive.

On Christmas Eve the traditional Provençal midnight mass in the form of a nativity play, is celebrated – as it has been for more than 400 years – in the Romanesque church on Place Vincent. The event draws a large congregation so plan to arrive early if you wish to attend.

Since Mas d'Aigret came under the direction of its Anglo-French owners in 1988, its reputation – especially for its restaurant – has been steadily growing. Enjoying a superb south-facing position with wonderful views over Les Baux and beyond, the *mas* and its swimming pool are set in lush perfumed gardens. Bedrooms are light, airy and flowery-pretty with long French windows opening onto a patio on the ground floor, or onto a balcony on the floor above. It is the restaurant, however, that steals the limelight. Built into a natural cave, it is as dramatic as any stage set. The lightest and brightest of furnishings ensure that there is no hint of subterranean gloom and in summer meals are served on the idyllic adjoining terrace. Mas d'Aigret is centrally placed for travelling around this area of Provence and will also be of interest to golfers. With two golf courses within a 10-minute drive and another dozen or so within a 90km radius, it offers considerable scope. During the low season months of November, December and March, the hotel can organise special golf packages with a tempting discount off the standard half-board tariff.

Situated 15km/9 miles north-east of Arles and 9km/5 miles south of Saint-Rémy-de-Provence. The hotel is clearly signposted. Nearest international airport: Marseilles at 60km/37 miles. Nearest national airport: Avignon or Nîmes at 30km/18 miles. Nearest station: Avignon (TGV).

Additional information:

Open all year except January and February. 15 rooms all with private bath and separate WC; telephone; TV; minibar. Price FF450-FF850 single or double. Half board FF795-FF935 single, FF1140-FF1540 double. Breakfast FF65. Lunch FF130. Dinner FF200-FF400 or á la carte. Swimming pool. All major credit cards accepted. Colour brochure in French and English sent on request.

La Burlande
13520 Le Paradou
Tel 90 54 32 32.

Chambres d'Hôtes/Bed & Breakfast

Just a few minutes from Les Baux and approached via a long gravel driveway that winds through olive groves and woodland, La Burlande is a sophisticated modern villa set in its own well-kept gardens with a swimming pool. The bedrooms are decorated in immaculate taste combining antique Provençal furniture and modern fitting. Most have full-length sliding windows that open onto the garden. Jenny Fajardo de Livry is an elegant and vivacious hostess who gives her guests a warm welcome although she speaks only a little English.

Situated 15km/9 miles north-east of Arles. Take D17 from Arles and then D78F towards Les Baux. La Burlande is signposted to the right at 1500 metres/1 miles. Nearest international airport: Marseilles at 60km/37 miles.Nearest national airport: Avignon or Nîmes at 30km/16 miles. Nearest station: Avignon (TGV)

Additional information:

Open all year. 5 bedrooms with private bath/WC. Price FF230-FF300 single, FF250-FF320 double. Breakfast FF45. Dinner FF125. Tray meal FF100. Swimming pool. Laundry room. No credit cards accepted. Further information sent on request.

Hôtel des Quatre Dauphins
54 rue Roux Alphéran, 13100 Aix-en-Provence
Tel 42 38 16 39. Fax 42 38 60 19.

Hotel** without restaurant

This really delightful small hotel is right in the centre of Aix, five minutes' walk from Cours Mirabeau and just off Place des Quatre Dauphins. The building, originally a *maison bourgoise*, was completely renovated and turned into a hotel in 1990. The bedrooms are adorable, decorated with traditional Provençal printed fabrics and painted furniture. One of the owners, Monsieur Juster, is an ex-teacher of English.

Nearest international airport: Marseilles at 30km/18 miles. nearest station: Aix-en-Provence.

Additional information:

Open all year. 12 bedrooms all with private bath/WC; telephone; TV; minibar. Price FF250-FF280 single, FF320-FF360 double. Breakfast FF30. parking nearby. Amex, Eurocard, Mastercard and Visa. Brochure in French and English sent on request. Suitable for visitors without a car.

Moulin de la Camandoule

Chemin Notre-Dame-des-Cyprés, 83440 Fayence
Tel 94 76 00 84.
Fax 94 76 10 40.

Hotel*** with restaurant

This old mill has a long history. Although the present building was substantially rebuilt in 1834, it probably dates back to the 15th century but it seems likely that there was a mill on the site well before that. Roman artifacts were discovered some years ago when excavations for the swimming pool were in

progress and the distinctive low-level aquaduct that traverses the property is also believed to be of the same period. Since the English owners, Shirley and Wolf Rilla, took over the hotel in 1986, the accommodation has been completely refurbished to provide comfortable prettily-furnished bedrooms, most of which open onto a ground floor terrace or a first floor balcony. Under the direction of its present owners, the hotel has acquired a reputation for fine food. The chef is a native of Nice and his creative cuisine is based on traditional Provençal dishes using the best of local ingredients. During the winter months it is Shirley – an accomplished cook – who prepares the meals. The dining room is an interesting blend of rustic sophistication with the original mill machinery forming an imposing centrepiece. In summer, the restaurant moves outside into the garden. The nearby village of Fayence is a noted European gliding venue. Enthusiasts will find Moulin de la Camandoule a very hospitable place to stay.

Situated 25km/17 miles west of Grasse, just outside the village of Fayence on D19 to Seillans. Nearest international airport: Nice at 57km/35 miles. Nearest station: Cannes at 25km/17 miles or Frejus at 30km/18 miles.

Additional information:

Open all year except November 1 to December 20 and January 1 to March 15. 11 bedrooms all with private bath/WC; telephone; TV. Price FF225-FF415 single, FF415-FF600 double. Half board FF400-FF615 per person. Breakfast FF45. Lunch and dinner FF180-FF280 or á la carte. Swimming pool. Eurocard, Carte Bleue and Visa. Brochure in English sent on request. Suitable for guests without a car.

Domaine de la Collette Saint-Pierre

Seillans, 83440 Fayence
Tel 94 76 96 79,
Fax 92 98 71 58.

Self-catering apartments

Placed well off the beaten
track yet only 2km/1 miles
from the village of Seillans and
less than an hour's drive from
Nice airport, La Collette Saint-
Pierre is a gracious old
farmhouse set in 105
hectares/260 acres of private
woods and parkland. The house belongs to a
bilingual Anglo-American couple, Brian and

Vikki Jackson-Pownall, and their family, who have spent 20 years
restoring it to its present high standard. In addition to the owners'
private quarters, the *domaine* offers five self-catering apartments for two to four people. The units
have independent entrances, private dining patios and easy access to the large communal
swimming pool. The apartments offer every comfort, quality furnishings and individual character.
Kitchens are well-equipped and effective central heating allows for year-round occupation.
Collette Saint-Pierre is convenient for exploring the Cote d'Azur and there is much of interest to
art lovers and gastronomes. The international gliding centre at Fayence is 6km/2miles away.

**Situated 31km/19 miles west of Grasse, 30km/18 miles east of Draguignan and 2km/1 miles east of Seillans.
Nearest international airport: Nice at 100km/62 miles. Nearest station: Cannes at 35km/22 miles.**

Additional information:

Open all year. 5 apartments: Cabanon – with living/bedroom, bath/shower, kitchenette; Garden – with bedroom, sitting
room, kitchenette, bathroom; Terrace – with bedroom, bathroom, kitchenette, dining room, cloakroom, optional extra sleeping
area; Tower – with bedroom, bathroom, sitting room, kitchen, cloakroom; Archway – with 2 bedrooms, 2 bathrooms, kitchen,
living/dining room. Price FF450-FF1250 per night (minimum two nights) including all heating, electricity and bed linen.
Swimming pool. Shared laundry facilities. No credit cards accepted but payment may be made by cheque in your own
currency. Full colour brochure in English available on request.

La Ponche

Place du Revelin, Port des Pêcheurs, 83990Saint-Tropez
Tel 94 97 02 53, Fax 94 97 78 61.

*Hotel*** with restaurant*

Expensive and chic, the fashionable old fishing village of Saint-Tropez is today a lively resort of
busy harbourside cafés, open-air restaurants, trendy boutiques and sophisticated nightclubs.
Despite its popularity a few fishing boats continue to operate out of the Port des Pêcheurs where

early-morning quayside stalls sell the day's catch. This is the picturesque setting for Hotel La Ponche. The original inn dates from 1885; adjoining fishermen's cottages have recently been incorporated to provide additional accommodation which combines antique furnishings with discreet modern comfort. Some of the rooms have delightful roof-top terraces. The restaurant serves local specialities and La Ponche is within walking distance of Saint-Tropez's many attractions. A car is not necessarily an advantage in the narrow crowded streets of Saint-Tropez but if you are driving … don't worry, the hotel has private parking. Reception and restaurant staff speak English and are very friendly.

Situated 120km/74 miles south-east of Aix-en-Provence and 48km/30 miles south of Draguignan. The hotel overlooks the Port des Pêcheurs in the old *quartier* of La Ponche. Nearest international airport: Nice at 100km/62 miles. Nearest national airport: Toulon at 45km/28 miles. Nearest station: St-Raphael at 35km/22 miles with regular bus connections to Saint-Tropez.

Additional information:

Open mid-March to mid-November. 20 rooms all with private shower or bath/WC; telephone; TV. Price FF375-FF750 single or double. Breakfast FF60. Lunch FF115. Dinner FF200 or à la carte. Amex, Carte Bleue, Mastercard and Visa. Colour brochure in French and English sent on request. Suitable for visitors without a car.

Auberge du Vieux Fox
Place de l'Eglise, 83670
Fox-Amphoux
Tel 94 80 71 69.

Village auberge ** with restaurant

The Vieux Fox is the kind of simple French country inn that one dreams of. Perched on a hilltop with stunning views over Provence and the foothills of the Alps, it nestles next to the 12th century church and faces onto a quaint village square. The building was originally an ancient priory and resting place of the Knights Templars. Today it retains many of the original

features – low ceilings, exposed beams and centuries-old tiled floors. The dining room is warm, welcoming and cosy with an open fireplace and lovely antique polished dresser. In summer meals are served on a tree-shaded outside terrace with those marvellous views. As one would expect, the cuisine is excellent country cooking using the best of fresh ingredients. Portions are generous and prices are reasonable. Bedrooms are comfortable and guests have use of a sitting room with grand piano, a stone-vaulted TV den and a (French) billiards room. The staff are friendly and *le patron*, Monsieur Martha, speaks English. Who would ask for more?

171

Situated 125km/77 miles north-west of Nice, 100km/62 miles north-east of Marseilles and 37km/22 miles west of Draguignan. Nearest international airports: Nice or Marseilles. Nearest station: Les Arcs at 40km/25 miles.

Additional information:

Open all year except mid-December to mid-January. 10 bedrooms all with private shower or bath/WC; telephone. Price FF115 single, FF225-FF320 double. Breakfast FF35. Lunch/dinner FF65-FF165 or á la carte. All major credit cards accepted. Colour brochure in French/English sent on request.

Hôtel d'Europe
12 Place Crillon, 84000 Avignon
Tel 90 82 66 92, Fax 90 85 43 66.

City hotel**** with restaurant

A splendid 16th century mansion located inside the city walls within a few minutes' walk of the Palais des Papes. The building retains its former splendour and character – marble floors, antique furnishings, paintings and carpets. The hotel restaurant, La Vieille Fontaine, has been awarded a Michelin rosette and in summer, meals are served outside in a delightful internal courtyard shaded by giant plane trees. Reception staff speak English and there is private garage parking … a great advantage in central Avignon.

Nearest international airport: Marseilles at95km/59 miles. Nearest national airport: Avignon. Nearest station: Avignon (TGV).

Additional information:

Open all year. 47 bedrooms all with private bath/WC; telephone; TV; some with minibars. Price FF550-FF1250 single or double. Breakfast FF85. Lunch or dinner FF250 or à la carte. Lift. Garage parking Ff50 per day. All major credit cards accepted. Full colour brochure in French and English sent on request. Suitable for visitors without a car.

Hostellerie Le Beffroi
rue de l'Evêche, 84110 Vaison-la-Romaine
Tel 90 36 04 71, Fax 90 36 24 78.

Hotel*** with restaurant

Vaison-la-Romaine is an attractive, bustling town clustered around a central market place, lined with open-air bars and restaurants. Of much earlier origins, excavations have revealed the layout

Cycling Holidays in Provence

Cycling holidays around western Provence and the Camargue use as their base a pretty village auberge in Le Barroux, 30km/18 miles north-east of Avignon. From this centre cyclists are offered a choice of itineraries which demand varying degrees of exertion depending upon the terrain. Tours may last for seven, nine, 10 or 14 days with routes that go northwards into the stunning scenery of Haute Provence; or wander through the countryside around Avignon then up into the hills of the Alpilles and Lubéron; or pass by the Roman sites at Arles and Nîmes before entering the Camargue National Park.From two to six nights will be spent in hotels other than the main base, many of which have swimming pools.

Holidays are available from mid-May to the end of September and prices start at approximately FF4,500 per person per week which includes half board at all the hotels on the itinerary and use of a specially manufactured six-speed bicycle. For further information please see page 101.

of a complete Roman town which, unlike the grandeur of other Roman remains in the area, such as Arles and Nîmes, reveals fascinating domestic architectural detail. Le Beffroi is in yet another *quartier* of this interesting town – the old mediæval hilltop township built on the site of a 12th century fortress. In the heart of the *haute ville*, divided between two ancient and imposing houses, Le Beffroi retains all its 16th century character and allure – beamed ceilings, majestic staircases, carved fireplaces and wax-polished antique furniture. The views are stunning and in summer meals are served on a delightful outside terrace. English is spoken.

Situated 47km/31 miles north-east of Avignon and 25km/15 miles east of Orange. Once in Vaison-la-Romaine the old town and Le Beffroi are clearly marked. Nearest international airport: Marseilles at 100km/62 miles. Nearest national airport: Avignon. Nearest station: Avignon (TGV).

Additional information:

Open mid-March to end-November. 20 bedrooms all with private shower or bath/WC; telephone; minibar. Price FF160-FF440 single, FF265-FF550 double. Breakfast FF40. Lunch and dinner FF98-FF215 or à la carte. Closed Monday in low season. Parking. All major credit cards accepted. Colour brochure in French and English sent on request. Suitable for visitors without a car if you do not mind walking up to the old town.

Relais du Procureur
rue Basse, 84710 Lacoste
Tel 90 75 82 28, Fax 90 75 86 94.

Chambres d'Hôtes/Bed & Breakfast

Deep in the Luberon – an area that Peter Mayle has made well-known – is the interesting old hilltop village of Lacoste. It lies beneath the menacing ruins of the castle belonging to the infamous Marquis de Sade, a sleepy village these days, basking in the hot Provençal sun. On the main street you will find a handsome 17th century house, Relais du Procureur, that has been expertly and imaginatively restored by its English-speaking owner, Antoine Court de Gebelin. Once inside the monumental front door, a grand staircase in white stone winds up three floors

giving access to the spacious bedrooms, all tastefully furnished with antiques and decorated in neutral shades. On the top floor a tiny courtyard swimming pool is tucked into a hillside terrace and has a little paved patio where summertime breakfast is served. No other meals are available but there is a choice of restaurants in the neighbouring villages.

Situated 23km/14 miles east of Avignon, 10km/6 miles west of Apt. Turn south off D22 at Lumières. Once in the village of Lacoste, the relais is clearly marked. Leave cars in the parking by the Post Office. Nearest international airport: Marseilles at 47km/29 miles or Nice at 200km/125 miles. nearest national airport: Avignon. Nearest station: Avignon (TGV).

Additional information:

Open all year. 5 bedrooms all with private bath/WC; TV; minibar. 2 additional studios in preparation. Price FF470 single, FF500-FF650 double including breakfast. Swimming pool. All major credit cards accepted. Information in English and photos sent on request.

Moulin d'Antelon
Crillon-le Brave, 84410 Bedoin
Tel and Fax 90 62 44 89.
Chambres d'Hôtes/Bed & Breakfast; Self-catering apartment

Moulin d'Antelon is a romantic old olive oil mill situated close to the ancient village of Crillon-le-Brave in the shadow of Mont Ventoux. Built of mellow creamy stone, it has been completely renovated by its present owners, Bernard and Marie-Luce Riquart to provide three spacious guest bedrooms. The mill stands in its own lawned gardens with a

rippling stream, pond and giant-sized swimming pool. Breakfast – with Marie-Luce's home-made preserves – is served in the family dining room or, in summer, on the vine-covered patio. Bernard, who speaks English, is very knowledgeable about his local area and is delighted to tell visitors the best places to explore. He acts as an official guide and every Wednesday from June to September takes a small group of walkers on a (gentle) six-hour hike to the lower slopes (up to 600 metres) of Mont Ventoux. Guests at the Moulin are, of course, welcome to join the expedition.

The Riquarts also have an independent apartment with kitchen, living/dining room, double bedroom and bathroom. It is simply but comfortably furnished and has an attractive private paved patio which is shaded by a giant linden tree. Guests have use of the swimming pool.

Situated 13km/8 miles north-east of Carpentras on D974. The driveway is on the left just after the turn to Crillon-le-Brave and 3km/1 1/2 miles before Bedoin. Nearest international airport: Marseilles at 95km/57 miles. Nearest national airport: Avignon at 35km/21 miles. Nearest station: Avignon (TGV).

Additional information:

Chambres d'Hôtes: Open all year. 3 bedrooms all with private bath/WC. Telephone and TV on request. Price FF200-FF250 including breakfast. Swimming pool. No credit cards accepted. Information in English and photo sent on request.

Apartment: Open all year. Sleeps 2/4. Price Ff1500-FF2800 per week (Saturday to Saturday) depending on season. Price includes heating, gas and electricity. Bed linen and towels available on request. Telephone and TV also on request.

Mas des Capelans
84580 Oppède-le-Vieux
Tel 90 76 99 04,
Fax 90 76 90 29.

Chambres d'Hôtes/Bed & Breakfast

Although this old *magnanerie* (farm for silk worm breeding) has been thoroughly modernised, it retains all of its rustic charm. Set in a typical Provençal landscape of extensive vineyards and sun-baked villages, it has been cleverly and competently re-designed to give very comfortable bedrooms and suites that are tastefully decorated and full of character. Outside the pool and shady patio are perfect for long lazy summer days. Every evening as the sun sets, Monsieur Poiri invites his guests to sip a complimentary cocktail before enjoying one of Madame's superb dinners which are romantically served beneath an enormous mulberry tree. For cooler weather a large, convivial family living/dining room is available. The *mas* is a pleasant and civilised base for exploring Avignon, the historic villages of this corner of Provence and the wild unspoilt Parc de Luberon. The Poiris receive an international selection of visitors to their delightful home and speak a little English.

Situated 20km/12 miles east of Avignon and 13km/8 miles west of Apt on D22. Nearest international airport Marseilles at 70km/43 miles. Nearest national airport: Avignon. Nearest station: Avignon (TGV).

Additional information:

Open all year except February. 8 bedrooms all with private bath; telephone; TV; minibar. Price FF560-FF700 double. Breakfast FF50. Swimming pool. Dinner FF155 (except Wednesday and Sunday evenings). Amex, Mastercard and Visa. Colour brochure in French/English sent on request. Suitable for guests without a car.

VALLÉE DU RHONE
RHONE VALLEY

Vallée du Rhône/Rhône Valley comprises the following départements:
Ain (01)
Ardéche (07)
Drôme (26)
Loire (42)
Rhône (69)

*S*INCE TIME IMMEMORIAL, *the River Rhône has been one of Europe's foremost waterways and its valley a major overland route from north to south. This is the gateway to the Mediterranean lands and the most southerly département of Drôme borders onto Provence. It is understandable then that for many visitors the Rhône Valley is no more than a region to speed through rather than to stop and explore ... which is a pity for it has many attractions. Above all the banks of the Rhône are excellent wine-producing areas, from the famous Beaujolais vineyards north of Lyon, to the Côtes de Rhône villages further south. It is an invariable rule in France that areas that make fine wines also breed excellent cooks; the Rhône Valley certainly has its fair share of gastronomic restaurants. For nature lovers, the Pilat National Park is a superb area of mountain woodland with fine walks, in the département of Loire around St-Etienne; the spectacular canyons of the Ardèche Gorges are accessible by road, offering exceptional views and good conditions for kayaking and canoeing; while in the east, the lovely stretches of the Jura mountains reach down almost to Lake Geneva and to the frontier with Switzerland.*

Claude Lutz
17 rue de Lyon, 01800 Meximieux
Tel 74 61 06 78, Fax 74 34 75 25

Restaurant with rooms

Chef Claude Lutz's cooking has won him a Michelin rosette but happily this is not a hotel/restaurant that has become too grand as a consequence. Prices for both accommodation and meals are still unexpectedly reasonable ... but the cuisine is very good indeed. This is the place to try some of the regional specialities at their refined best ... *poulet de Bresse à la crème*, for example, the classic dish of locally-raised Bresse chicken in a cream sauce. There is a warm and cosy ambiance in the oak-beamed restaurant, with comfortable tapestry-covered chairs, but on warm days meals are served outside on a pretty terrace. Chez-Lutz is conviently placed in the village of Meximieux just 20 minutes from Lyon and close to autoroute A42 from Lyon to Geneva. It is also handy for the airport at Lyon and has easy access from the A43 to the ski slopes of Savoie and the A7 to southern France. English is spoken.

Situated 36km/21 miles north-east of Lyon via A42. Nearest international airport: Lyon at 36km/21 miles. Nearest station: Lyon.

Additional information:

Open all year except 2 weeks mid-February, 1 week mid-July and mid-October to mid-November. 15 bedrooms all with private shower or bath/WC. Price FF160-FF300 single or double. Breakfast FF30. Lunch and dinner FF135-FF310 (restaurant closed Sunday evening and all day Monday). Amex, Carte Bleue and Visa. Colour brochure in French and English sent on request.

Les Hospitaliers

Le Vieux Village, 26160 Le Poët-Laval
Tel 75 46 22 32, Fax 75 46 49 99

Hotel *** with restaurant

Poët-Laval is a delightful hilltop village — an ancient knights' fortress dominated by a ruined castle — with magnificent panoramic views. Abandoned until recently, the village is now being carefully restored and the hotel occupies some of the renovated houses. The reception rooms are full of mediæval character and there is a splendid mosaic-lined swimming pool. The hotel's restaurant has been awarded a Michelin rosette and summer meals are served on a spacious terrace with those great views. A unique hotel with courteous service, where English is spoken.

Situated 27km/16 miles east of Montélimar via D540 and 5km/3 miles west of Dieulefit. Nearest international airport: Lyon at 170km/100 miles. Nearest national airport: Valence at 70km/42 miles. Nearest station: Montélimar (TGV).

Additional information:

Open March to mid-November. 24 bedrooms all with private shower or bath/WC; telephone; TV; minibar. Price FF520-FF940 double. Breakfast FF70. Lunch and dinner FF200-FF420. Swimming pool. Amex, Diners, Mastercard and Visa. Colour brochure in French and English sent on request.

Hostellerie du Bois-Prieur

Domaine de Grandjean-Galafray,
42360 Cottance
Tel 77 28 06 69, Fax 77 28 00 55

Private country house hotel with restaurant

Set deep in lush undulating countryside and surrounded by 15 hectares/38 acres of private parkland and woods, this old farmhouse has

Route de Beaujolais

The wine road that passes through the famous Beaujolais vineyards is well signposted, starting in the village of Crêches, in the département of Saône-et-Loire (71), and roughly following N6 southwards on the western side. It includes villages with such evocative names as Juliènas, Chénas, Fleurie, Morgon and Brouilly before arriving at Villefranche-sur-Saône (69) — the main marketing centre for Beaujolais wines. All along the route there are coopératives and private caveaux for tasting and buying.

been sympathetically restored by its friendly French owners, Hélène and Jean-Louis Bonard. The country-style bedrooms are all different and very prettily furnished; some have a lounge area with log fire. Guests have the use of a cosy sitting room and candle-lit dinners are served in the homely dining room or in the flower-filled courtyard. The emphasis is on traditional French home cooking. Bois-Prieur has its own swimming pool and tennis court; golf and water sport facilities are nearby. Hélène and Jean-Louis keep their own horses on the properpty and these are available to experienced riders. Bois-Prieur is a delightful overnight stop or for a longer stay. As an extra bonus Hélène, who lived for some years in England, speaks perfect English.

Situated 65km/40 miles west of Lyon, 50km/36 miles north of St-Etienne and 10km/6 miles from the small town of Feurs. Nearest international airport: Lyon at 80km/50 miles. Nearest national airport: St-Etienne. Nearest station: Feurs.

Additional information:

Open mid-April to mid-October. 5 bedrooms all with private shower/WC. Price FF320-FF590 double. half board FF300-FF435 per person. 7-day holiday special at an inclusive price of FF3,900-FF5,800 double per week including bed, breakfast, dinner, welcome drink, swimming pool with loungers and parasol, tennis, horse-riding, mountain bikes, table tennis and boules. Breakfast FF35. Dinner FF105. Swimming pool. Tennis court. Visa and Eurocard. Full colour brochure in French and English sent on request.

Château de la Motte
42640 Noailly
Tel 77 66 64 60,
Fax 77 66 64 38
Château-hotel with restaurant

Set in 10 hectares/23 acres of wooded parkland, Château de la Motte is an elegant fairytale castle dating from the 17th and 18th centuries. This was the family home of the grandmother of the present owner, Sylvie Fayolle, and as a child, Sylvie spent many holidays here. After extensive renovation, the château now offers very beautiful and luxurious accommodation that will appeal to the most discriminating of houseguests. The château has its own riding stables and guests are able to enjoy accompanied rides within the park and countryside. Very comprehensive information is available on all local places of interest, plus wine-tastings in nearby vineyards, recommended restaurants and river cruises. A combined holiday of one week at La Motte and a week on a luxury cabin cruiser can also be arranged by Sylvie, who speaks perfect English.

Situated 15km/9 miles north-west of Roanne via N7 to St-Germain-Lespinasse and then D4. Nearest international airport: Lyon at 100km/60 miles. Nearest national airport: Roanne. Nearest station: Roanne (TGV).

Additional information:

Open all yea. 8 bedrooms all with private bath/WC; telephone; TV; some with open fireplace.Price FF500-FF850 double depending on season. Half board FF715-FF1,110 double. Breakfast FF40.

Residential French language courses at Château de Matel

What better place to learn French ... or to improve your French ... than in France? René Dorel and his Australian wife, Margaret O'Loan, direct Ecole des Trois Points, a residential French language centre, from Château de Matel in Roanne. Guest/students live, study and have all meals at the château which is surrounded by 13 hectares/30 acres of private grounds with a swimming pool. There is tennis and golf nearby, and bicycles can be hired at the château. Mornings are devoted to classes and afternoons are free for private study, sport, sight-seeing etc. Evening sessions are more informal with the emphasis on French conversation

One, two, three or four-week courses are available for students at beginner, intermediate and advanced levels. Classes have a maximum of seven students who are taught by professional native French instructors. Optional private courses can be arranged and the school also offers a specially designed intensive Business French course.

At certain times of the year, a French Cookery Course is run, plus a Ceramics Tour for serious or professional potters. During the summer a separate French course for university students is available, with accommodation at the University of Roanne.

Additional information:

Courses operate from April to November. Price FF4,000 for a one-week course which includes 7 days accommodation, 3 excursions, 3 hours of morning tuition per day for 5 days, 2 hours of evening classes twice a week. Two-week course: FF7,600. Four-week course: FF14,600. Intensive Business French: FF9,400 per week with groups limited to two people. Cooking course: FF4,400 per week.

For further information in English please contact Margaret O'Loan, Ecole des Trois Points, Château de Matel, 42300 Roanne. Tel: 77 71 53 00, Fax: 77 70 80 01.

*T*HE TWO PROVINCES OF ALSACE AND LORRAINE *are split by the impressive Vosges mountain range that runs from north to south. Lorraine, to the west, borders onto Champagne; Alsace, in the east, is divided from Germany by the mighty River Rhine. For centuries, this corridor has been the scene of continual European conflict and devastating war damage. It is therefore no accident that the French city of Strasbourg, on the banks of the River Rhine facing Germany, is now the seat of the European Parliament and the European Court of Human Rights. Despite its turbulent past, this is a serene and pleasant country. The wooded mountains and glittering lakes of the Vosges are popular leisure resorts in both summer and winter; the wine villages of Alsace are among the prettiest in the whole of France and produce some of France's most distinctive wines; the major towns of Strasbourg and Colmars are steeped in history and have a popular appeal.*

Auberge La Meunière

30 rue Sainte-Anne, 68590 Thannenkirch
Tel 89 73 10 47, Fax 89 73 12 31

*Hotel ** with restaurant*

In the heart of Alsace wine country, this pretty-as-a-picture auberge is on the main street of the tiny village of Thannenkirch. The wood-pannelled facade has flowers tumbling from every window and there are superb views from the spacious dining terrace. Bedrooms are comfortably furnished and each carries a girl's name ... Angélique ... Sophie ... Joséphine. English is spoken.

Situated 80km/48 miles south-west of Strasbourg and 15km/9 miles south-west of Sélestat. Nearest international airport: Strasbourg. Nearest station: Sélestat.

Additional information:

Open mid-March to mid-November. 15 bedrooms all with private shower or bath/WC; telephone; some with TV. Price FF260-FF300 single and double. Half board FF220-FF250 per person. Breakfast FF25. Lunch and dinner FF95-FF180 or à la carte. Sauna. Jacuzzi. Amex, Carte Bleue and Visa. Colour brochure in French and English sent on request.

Vosges/Alsace-Lorraine
comprises the following
départements:
  Meurther-et-Moselle (54)
  Meuse (55)
  Moselle (57)
  Bas Rhin (67)
  Haut Rhin (68)
  Vosges (88)

55
MEUSE

Verdun ○

CHÂTEAU DE LA
BESSIERE ●

Metz ○

57
MOSELLE

67
BAS-RHIN

Bar-le-Duc ○

Sarrebourg ○

AUBERGE DU
KIBOKI ●

Strasbourg ○

Molsheimo ○

● HOSTELLERIE DES
   CHÂTEAUX

Nancy ○

WINSTUB
GILG ●

54
MEURTHE-ET-MOSELLE

Domrémy ○

Sélesta ○

88
VOSGES

Épinal ○

Gérardmer ○

AUBERGE LA MEUNIÈRE ○

HOSTELLERIE ●
DES BAS-RUPTS

Colmar ○

68
HAUT-RHIN

Mulhouse ○

○ Basel

VOSGES / ALSACE / LORRAINE

Auberge du Kiboki

Route de Donon, 57560 Turquestein
Tel 87 08 60 65, Fax 87 08 65 26

*Country hotel ** with restaurant*

In the depths of the Forest of Turquestein, in
the Valley of Turquestein, enclosed by tall
pine trees, the Kiboki is a traditional
Vosgian inn set in a grassy meadow. The
internal decor is charmingly rustic and the
pretty country-style restaurant with gay red
check table cloths, is furnished with antique
dressers to display old china plates. Outside
is a swimming pool, tennis court, table
tennis and a *boules* pitch. Your friendly
hosts, Monsieur and Madame Schmitt,
speak English and have details of all nearby
places of interest.

Situated 70km/42 miles south-west of Strasbourg and 25km/15 miles south of Sarrebourg. The Kiboki is in
deep forest on D993 which runs from Blâmont (23km/13 miles south-west of Sarrebourg) to Schirmeck
(48km/29 miles south-west of Strasbourg). Nearest international airport: Strasbourg. Nearest station:
Sarresbourg.

Additional information:

Open all year except February. 15 bedrooms all with private shower or bath/WC; telephone; TV. Price FF280-FF450 single and
double. Half board FF300-FF350 per person. Breakfast FF35. Lunch and dinner FF180-FF280 or à la carte (restaurant closed
Tuesday). Swimming pool. Tennis court. Carte Bleue, Eurocard, Mastercard and Visa. Colour brochure in French and further
information in English sent on request.

Winstub Gilg

67140 Mittelbergheim
Tel 88 08 91 37

Winstub (wine bar/restaurant) with rooms

Mittelbergheim — on the Alsace wine route — is one of
the prettiest villages in France. In the centre of the village
is Winstub Gilg, a typical Alsation wine bar/restaurant
serving local wines with regional cooking. Monsieur
Gilg's cuisine is a blend of traditional dishes with some
more up-to-date adaptations. His restaurant is nicely
rustic with fancy carved-back chairs and sparkling white
table cloths. Bedrooms are comfortable; prices are
reasonable; service is friendly ... and English is spoken.

183

Situated 37km/22 miles south-west of Strasbourg and 2km/1.2 miles south of Barr. Nearest international airport: Strasbourg. Nearest station: Sélestat.

Additional information:

Open all year except January, the last week of June and the first week of July. 10 bedrooms all with private shower or bath/WC; telephone. Price FF200 single, FF210-FF330 double. Breakfast FF25. Lunch and dinner FF125-FF325 or à la carte (restaurant closed Tuesday dinner and all day Wednesday). Amex, Carte Bleue, Diners and Eurocard. Colour brochure in French and English sent on request.

Hostellerie des Bas-Rupts
88400 Gérardmer
Tel 29 63 09 25, Fax 29 63 00 40
*Hotel *** with restaurant*

Gérardmer is a popular all-year resort splendidly sited on the shores of Lake Gérardmer in the southern Vosges mountains. Although the old town was almost destroyed during the Second World War, it has since been rebuilt with a casino, ice rink, smart discotheques and boutiques plus skiing during the winter months. Located just outside the main town, Bas-Rupts is contained within two adjoining buildings. In the main hotel block are some of the bedrooms, reception rooms and a first-class gastronomic restaurant which, under the direction of chef/owner Michen Phillipe, has been awarded a Michelin rosette. His inventive cuisine features personal interpretations of classic Alsation dishes; his desserts too have won wide acclaim. The nicest bedrooms are next door in the Chalet Fleuri, a typical mountain chalet with colourful flower-decked balconies. The accommodation is luxurious and the decor features very attractive hand-painted Alsation furniture. With a swimming pool, tennis courts, lakeside walks, boating in summer and winter sports for the rest of the year, Bas-Rupts makes a very civilized base from which to discover the region. English is spoken.

Situated 55km/33 miles west of Colmars and 4km/2.4 miles south-west of Gérardmer via D486. Nearest international airport: Basel/Mulhouse at 60km/48 miles or Strasbourg at 100km/60 miles. Nearest station: Colmar.

Additional information:

Open all year. 32 bedrooms (14 in Chalet Fleuri) all with private shower or bath; telephone; some with TV and minibar. Price FF330-FF380 (FF600 in Chalet Fleuri) double. Half board FF380-FF560 per person. Breakfast FF55. Lunch and dinner FF140-FF420 or à la carte. Swimming pool. Tennis. Amex, Carte Bleue and Visa. Colour brochure in French and English sent on request.

Hostellerie des Châteaux

11 rue des Châteaux, 67530 Ottrott-le-Haut
Tel 88 95 81 54, Fax 88 95 95 20

Hotel *** with restaurant

One of the villages on the picturesque Alsace wine route, Ottrott is particularly well-known for producing what is generally acknowledged to be the best red wine in Alsace, which is traditionally a white wine region. This pretty rose-tinted hotel is an attractive old village house that has been substantially enlarged, offering very comfortable bedrooms and sophisticated cuisine. With an indoor swimming pool and sauna, Hostellerie des Châteaux makes an ideal base in the celebrated vineyards of Alsace. English is spoken.

Situated 35km/21 miles south-west of Strasbourg and 4km/2.4 miles west of Obernai. Nearest international airport: Strasbourg. Nearest station: Molsheim at 15km/9 miles.

Route des Crêtes

The southern stretches of the Vosges mountains are distinctive. In times past, glaciers wore away much of the pink sandstone rock that is so typical in the northern Vosges, leaving grey granite peaks and ridges. Above the tree-line, there are great dome-shaped high pastures (called ballons*) together with deeply-etched valleys and pretty glacial lakes. The Route des Crêtes (D431) is a stunning 75km/45 mile road connecting peaks, running along the ridge at the very top of the Vosges mountains. It has breath-taking views and links many of the highest summits including the Grand Ballon. The route begins at Cernay (17km/10 miles west of Mulhouse) and winds its way northwards to Col du Bonhomme.*

Additional information:

Open all year except February. 65 bedrooms all with private shower or bath/WC; telephone; TV. Price FF210-FF350 single, FF370-FF660 double. Half board FF350-FF650 per person (3 days minimum). Breakfast FF50. Lunch and dinner FF160-FF360 (restaurant closed Sunday evening and all day Monday in low season). Indoor swimming pool. Sauna. Amex, Diners and Eurocard. Colour brochure in French and English sent on request.

185

Château de la Bessière

rue du Four, 55320 Ancemont
Tel 29 85 70 21, Fax 29 87 61 60

Château-Chambres d'Hôtes/Bed & Breakfast

Guests can expect a warm welcome in this 18th century château situated between Alsace and Champagne. Bedrooms are spacious and very prettily furnished in period style. There is a salon for the use of houseguests and home-cooked meals are served in the attractive dining room. The house has been restored and decorated with flair and taste by the owners, René and Marie-José Eichenauer, who speak English and have full information on nearby places of interest including the First World War battlefields around Verdun. Your hosts can also arrange fishing, riding and golf.

Situated 10km/6 miles south of Verdun via D34. Nearest international airport: Paris at 270km/160 miles. Nearest national airport: Metz at 70km/42 miles. Nearest station: Verdun.

Additional information:

Open all year. 4 bedrooms, two with private shower/WC and two with shared shower/WC. Price FF250 double including breakfast. Dinner FF100. No credit cards accepted. Further information in English and photographs sent on request.

Joan of Arc

In 1412, Joan of Arc was born in the tiny village of Domrémy-la-Pucelle, on the banks of the River Meuse in the extreme west of the Vosges département. The house in which she was born is still standing and there is a small museum next door. Just outside the village a small chapel marks the spot where she received the divine message urging her to fight for France and expel the English.

Domrémy-la-Pucelle is situated 58km/35 miles south-west of Nancy and 11km/7 miles north of Neufchâteau.

Index

Please note that accommodation addresses beginning with 'hôtel' have been listed under the actual name of the hotel.

187

Index

Readers' comments are always appreciated. Please let us know about any accommodation that you particularly enjoyed. Suggestions for new entries, too, are very welcome. Write to Meg Jump, La Maison Blanche, 04320 Entrevaux, France.

Acknowledgments

Meg Jump wishes to thank the following people for their generous help with the preparation of this book: Chantal Webster, Rémy Maurin, Alan Hill, John Wilkinson, Rex Barr, Norman Smith, Pam and Grahaem Murray.

Special thanks to Chuck Grieve for his invaluable assistance with the design and production; and to Gordon Jump for his unfailing support, in addition to drawing all the maps and illustrations with the exception of those that were supplied by owners.